FION/

Fiona's varied career design, retail and film. Sne originally trained as a solicitor, and practised law for several years, before pursuing a number of different interests. During all of that time she continued to write, and when she turned to film making and screenwriting she found that her true passion was in fact creating life from ink on the page. Fiona lives in Sussex, England with Jazz, her beloved Jack Russell terrier. Visit her website at www.fionahjoyce.com for news and interviews. You can also read the first chapter of her second novel at the back of this book. Oh yes, and she did actually own a bookshop once upon a time...

By Fiona H. Joyce

Dirty Weekend in Brighton

Bonfire Hearts (a screenplay)

Dirty Weekend in Brighton

Fiona H. Joyce

Brighton Rock Press

Published by Brighton Rock Press 2016

First published in Great Britain in 2016 by Brighton Rock Press

A CIP catalogue record for this book is available from the British Library.

ISBN 978-1-5262-0402-8

www.brightonrockpress.com

For
Mum & Dad. Of course.

Thus they stood,
"Long tears upon their faces, waxen white
With extreme sad delight."

Thomas Hardy, *The Woodlanders.*

ONE

Undertakers are full of bullshit. That's a little-known fact. And since the average funeral currently tops out at a shade under four grand – with no shortage of willing punters – they have no incentive not to be. What other profession dealing with corpses uses the phrase "At Rest"?

The doctor certifying the death doesn't announce, "I'm very sorry Mrs So and So but your husband is now resting."

If it's a road traffic accident, the police don't turn up to your door and say, "Mrs So and So? We are sorry to inform you that Mr So and So is now at rest."

And when you visit the register office, the registrar doesn't ask what caused Mr So and So to be "at rest".

No. They all refer to the dearly departed as "the deceased". Full stop. "At Rest" my foot. The only time the old bat was at rest was when she was consuming large quantities of Mr Kipling's cakes. Even then the peace and quiet didn't last long, ending with the inevitable row over the last Battenberg slice, and how all the sugar sent her glucose levels through the roof – all under my bloody roof as it happened, but that was another matter. And I'd bet that she isn't resting up above, or maybe down there, even now. And as for the notion of being "dearly departed". Departed yes, dearly was debatable.

The Indians had the right idea, putting them on a floating funeral pyre, or was that just the Hindus? Well anyway. The idea of sending her off down the Ganges in flames would have been very appealing. And not just now that she was dead.

Dana's eyes flicked briefly to the casket sitting on the passenger seat beside her, and then back at the wet road and driving rain, that obscured further the steamy windows of her genteel, but decidedly clapped out, Volvo estate.

Pissing rain. She gritted her teeth and seethed with resentment at Hugo for asking her to go and collect his mother's ashes from the absurdly named Hope and Sons Funeral Directors. Her mother-in-law had been dead for four years for God's sake, why the rush to collect them now? They'll only sit in the sodding shed with her equally dead father-in-law, until finally disposed of when either Hugo or she were "At Rest" themselves. Didn't pay the sodding bill, that's why I had to go and fetch them. Even had a debt collector's letter about it a couple of years ago. Still, no questions had been asked when she picked up the casket. Just a knowing look from the receptionist.

"Hope and Sons". What hope might there be once you were chalked up in the right-hand column of *The Telegraph's* Births, Marriages and Deaths? Dana decided that the "Hope" element related to the next-of-kin, therefore the heirs, and therefore the beneficiaries of the Will.

But not in this instance. Any proceeds from the Will having long since been disposed of.

She turned on the radio.

*...it was a game of two 'aves. Cracking start, United on the attack from the get-go, one in the net straight off but somehow they just lost the pace in the second 'af...*Talk Sport. On the AM waveband.

"For God's sake!" she said.

That really pissed her off as well. On two counts – first of all she only allowed Radio 4 in her car, and secondly the signal was too bad on AM to hear what was being said properly. And she hated football. Well, that was three counts. Sodding Hugo using her car. Still, the old bat had hated sport even more than Dana so perhaps she might just leave the station on.

That thought brought a smile to her lips.

The traffic inched forward. At this rate she would be late fetching Cressida from basketball practice. Basketball. More nonsense. In my day it was hockey or netball. Bloody school – for the money they charged you'd expect lacrosse or tennis. Wasn't basketball American? She turned the radio dial.

*...with a fantastic range of designer kitchens from only four-nine-nine-nine to choose from and nothing to pay for twelve months you can't afford not to visit Only Kitchens dot com today, but hurry offer must end...*local radio.

They can fuck off too. Utter nonsense anyway. Why the reluctance to say the word "thousand"? What's this "four-nine-nine-nine" rubbish? Does not saying the price properly somehow make it sound cheaper? Idiots. Maybe the undertakers could pitch their services in the same way. But they didn't need to, they softened the unsavoury subject of death by pretending that the corpse was just resting. Mind you, if they combined the two approaches, nine-nine-nine-nine and the resting element, they could market themselves as a bargain basement Jesus, one step removed from performing miracle resurrections: the body was pronounced dead, went to the undertakers and was then transformed into "resting".

Idiots.

Dana flicked the wipers on and off in the rear window. Nothing. Still broken. Still waiting for Hugo to take a look. Six months later. She'd look it up on YouTube and have a go herself.

Dana realised that she had been shaking her head from side to side, and talking to herself with animation, when she glanced to her right, and saw the bloke who had pulled up alongside in the plumbers van smiling at her. She involuntarily flicked her long hair back. She wasn't at her best today, and her blonde roots needed touching up, but still, she didn't look too bad. Mind you, not that Hugo would ever notice. Last time she had come home from the hairdresser with a new colour and stood smiling in front of him, he'd asked her if she had been to the dentist.

The plumber bloke winked before he pulled away. "Bloke", Dana pondered. Funny how he is a "bloke" in a plumber's van but would be a "man" in a Range Rover or BMW. If he drove a Bentley would he be a "gentleman"? Interesting. And what about a motorbike? Would he be a bloke or a man? No, he'd be a "guy", she decided. Yes, a "guy on a motorbike".

Hugo was a "man". Definitely. He probably thought that he was a "gentleman" – his father certainly would have held that opinion.

A Ferrari pulled up alongside her. Red. The driver revved his engine. Unnecessarily. What is he? Dana wondered – bloke, man, gentleman, guy? He continued to rev his engine without looking over at her.

"Wanker," she said, as she herself pulled away in the traffic.

Her phone vibrated on her lap. A message. She wasn't in the mood for conversations and couldn't call or text back. Not while driving. A red light ahead. Dana stopped short of the car in front and picked up her phone. If it's him he can sod off too. Always calling when it is convenient to him. She tapped in her password – Scarlett – and looked at her phone in spite of herself.

It wasn't him.

"Where r u. waiting in rain outside sports hall." Cressida. Text message.

No, "Hello Mum." No affection. Not even proper grammar. What were they paying these school fees for? Even if the payments weren't up to date, they still had the right to know exactly how their children were being taught, and what they were getting for their money. Bloody school. All that formality: expensive uniforms, business suits in sixth form, all that kit and equipment, all the options extras, all the House Dinners, chapel, prize giving, "prep" for homework. And the kids still sent missives like "where r u".

She touched the brakes just as she turned into the road beside the school. Dana could see her friend's new black Audi a little way ahead. She didn't fancy running into Camilla just now. Camilla would get out, in her suspiciously clean riding boots, and make a big show of standing in the rain beside Dana's window, very much in a I'm-a-hearty-outdoor-type-what's-a-bit-of-rain attitude. Camilla would peer at her and ask her how she was "getting on" – whatever that euphemism was supposed to mean – and oh, what's that beside you dear? As Camilla would look gleefully at the casket of ashes in the passenger seat. But who's died darling? Camilla would ask. And how could Dana explain that it was only now, four years later, that she was picking up Hugo's mother's ashes? No. I'll wait here and pretend to be on the phone while Camilla whisks her spoilt brat Lucas off to his extra maths lessons.

While Dana pretended to take a call, her phone did actually beep, making her jump. Incoming call. In her surprise she hit the home button by mistake and answered it.

"Oh, hi," she said. "It's a bit awkward now, just picking up Cressida, can I call you later?"

Dana glanced up at the window and saw Camilla and Cressida standing there. Camilla gave a cheery wave and made a motion for Dana to wind the window down. Bugger. Dana forced a smile and pointed to her phone, while Cressida went around and opened the passenger door. She stood there in a sulk, staring at the casket on the seat.

Dana wound the window down and Camilla stuck her head in. She, too, looked at the casket.

"Hi Dana, is that Hugo?" she asked, gesturing to the phone.

"No, it isn't," Dana replied.

"How's the book coming along? Do give him my love," Camilla called towards the phone.

She was eternally oblivious and never listened to what anyone said.

Camilla continued peering at the passenger seat. She had rather a soft spot for Hugo, misplaced in Dana's opinion. Actually, soft spot wasn't quite accurate – more of a flirty crush. Which Hugo of course revelled in. He dismissed even the mere idea of it when mentioned. But the truth was, like most men, he was flattered by Camilla's attention. There had been a couple of incidents. Harmless. But amusing from Dana's perspective. A dance during the school end-of-year ball last June. Camilla had dragged Hugo up to do the tango. Or was it the rumba? Dana wasn't sure. It might as well have been an impersonation of Rudolf Nureyev's solo in *Swan Lake*, for all the justice Hugo did it. He had two left feet, and hands that hung limply by his sides whenever he stepped onto the dance floor. Camilla, by comparison, could have carried off the trophy on *Strictly Come Dancing*. And she "rumbaed" every week. Or was it salsa? Anyway the effect was the same.

And then there was that occasion one Christmas at a school quiz. Hugo had partnered Camilla, at her insistence, thinking that he would get all the sport questions correct. In fact, it turned out to be all chess and checkers, and neither of them had had a clue. Ended up getting very squiffy and giggly over a bottle of Merlot.

Hugo was terribly impressed with Camilla's husband too. "Awfully well connected in the City," Hugo would say.

"In what way?" Dana would ask.

"Well, you know, he's a name and all that."

"What? Tristram?" Dana would say, being sarcastic.

"No, not his actual name. A, you know, a Lloyds name. Awfully well connected in the City," Hugo responded.

Truth was Hugo didn't have a clue. Tristram guffawed and snorted into his drink every time they met, and Camilla droned on about how "awfully jet lagged" Tristram was from all that travel, and then staying up all night to keep pace with "the markets" – whatever that meant. It could have been Billingsgate for all they really knew. Still, one way or another, where there's muck there's brass. Camilla wanted for nothing and their home, cars and children rivalled the glossiest photos from *Hello* magazine. And so Tristram by a process of logical reasoning, whether he traded in the metal markets on the stock exchange, or scrap metal off the back of a lorry, was doing something right, since Camilla had never worked a day in her life.

None of it impressed Dana. But all of it apparently impressed Hugo. And none more than Miss Riding Boots herself. Be bloody glad when we are shot of this school. And the socials, Dana had decided some time ago.

"Can't really talk now," Dana tried to whisper into the phone. "Call you back."

She cut the connection as she dropped the phone into her lap, grabbed the casket and slung it in the back, and said with a loud, "Sorry Camilla, desperately late for Alex, he's been waiting forty minutes in the rain." Dana wound the window up, and was pulling away from the kerb, before Cressida had even closed the door.

"Sugar Honey Iced Tea Mum! I haven't even got my seat belt done up. Are you having another one of your hot flushes?" Cressida asked from the passenger seat.

"No, I am not having 'another one of my hot flushes' thank you very much, and either swear properly or not at all. Nonsensical snotty language."

"Okay then. S H I T. Is that better?"

Dana glared at her daughter, stick thin, pale, but beautiful, beside her.

The traffic was heavy as they inched along. Range Rovers inexpertly driven by oblivious mothers, Audis, a few Mercedes convertibles and other, much later model Volvos, all competed with each other in the dash home in the rain. A jungle green BMW four-by-four cut her up, the driver chatting animatedly to the inch-high passenger beside her. Stupid cow.

"Stupid cow," Dana said aloud. "If she'd actually earned the money to buy that car she wouldn't drive it like that."

"Well you didn't earn the money to buy this one – Dad gave it to you, so you can't talk," Cressida said, as she swiped at her phone, multi-tasking.

"Ha! Aren't I the lucky one? So fortunate to be in their league, all with cars we didn't earn, only difference between mine and theirs is fifteen years. Anyway, don't be so cheeky."

"Well don't be so sexist," Cressida said.

God, times have changed. How politically correct a 16-year-old can be. No sense trying to tell her that I am right though. Camilla et al proves the point: Tristram had given her the new black Audi. And Hugo had indeed "given" Dana the clapped out Volvo. But only because they'd had to sell her new Golf to balance the books.

"Have you cooked?" Cressida continued to swipe at her phone.

"I have prepared a family meal if that is what you are asking, yes. Butternut squash, avocado and parmesan pasta. One hundred per cent vegetarian before you ask."

9

Dana smiled in triumph.

"Well I can't eat that, can I?"

"Why the bloody hell not?"

"Hello. Earth to Mum. I'm a vegan."

Fuck a duck. There was just no pleasing them all. Alex wouldn't eat anything that didn't have meat in it, Hugo liked "proper food", which meant three courses with wine, and the entire family had been forced into vegetarian exile since Cressida announced that she no longer ate anything that she was not prepared to kill herself.

"Since when?" Dana said.

"Since I told you."

"Well that's too bad because it's cooked."

"Fine. I won't eat. I'll just starve."

"Fine you do that then."

Dana drove the next few minutes in simmering silence. She was, however, concerned about Cressida's wan appearance. And her weight. She would have to discuss it with Hugo later.

Cressida prodded her phone in silence and then her face lit up.

"Can you drop me at Emma's tomorrow after school? She's invited me over to stay and then we are going shopping on Saturday."

"No, don't you remember? This is my birthday and our family weekend away together," Dana replied.

"Our what?"

"Dad's booked a hotel for us for the weekend. Bit posh I think – cocktail bar, health club, dinner, all that. Just the four of us?" Dana turned her head to Cressida.

"No! No one told me! This is the first I heard of it. Well

I can't go, I've got other plans."

Cressida finally looked up, stricken, from her phone.

"Sorry madam, but you are coming with us, it's all booked, everyone is looking forward to it." Dana forced herself to remain calm.

"Well I'm not. You must be joking. It's your birthday so you go."

"No joke. Just a fact, you'll love it."

"I won't and I don't care where it is but I can't come," Cressida said.

"It's in Brighton and you can, and are, coming."

Dana slowed the car as she pulled up outside the house.

"Brighton? Now you really are joking. It's full of old people, no way, not going."

Cressida jumped out and slammed the door behind her.

"That's Eastbourne. That's full of old people. Brighton is full of young people and you bloody well are coming," Dana shouted at the slammed door, as Cressida ran up the drive towards the house.

A man walking his dog shifted his route slightly to the right, and away from the car, as Dana banged the window and shouted silently inside.

TWO

Hugo heard the front door slam. For Christ's sake, how often did he have to tell them? They didn't need to slam the door, just turn the brass handle anti-clockwise. He'd spent hours planing the wood down when it swelled in the wet weather, under-coating it, painting it Farrow and Ball's Heritage Blue top coat. Infernal regulations, that was the curse of living in a grade-two listed house, lovely as it was, the outside had to conform to type, no doing what his dear mother had called a "naily up job". Everything had to be done properly, correctly. Using the correct tools. His father had been a stickler for that. Take your time, do your research, carry out the job with the requisite skill and competence, don't cut corners. Yes, that's the way to get on in life.

Hugo's thoughts drifted to his childhood, watching his father painstakingly renovate The Old Rectory – parquet flooring, elliptical arches, sash-cord windows, quarry-tiled floors. All done by hand, the old-fashioned way. Taken years to complete. And then, some minor financial misfortune. Well, major actually. And a bit of a scandal, hushed up, an irregularity at the bank. Father had been a bank manager, the old-fashioned kind. The house had had to be sold. Nearly broke his dear mother's heart. Had to go and live in Weymouth in a flat, bestowed on them by some dragon aunt.

Still, his father had taught him the importance of doing everything correctly and properly. The front door was another matter though. Over 200 years old, truth be told it needed replacing, had done for years but it would have to last a while yet. I'll see about taking it off the hinges in the spring, he thought, see if I can't sort it out once and for all.

He heard Oscar, their medium-legged Jack Russell, barking in the kitchen. Don't suppose anyone will bother to walk him now. Something else down to me.

"Shut up short arse," Hugo said under his breath.

Even though Dana insisted Oscar was the medium-legged breed and not short-legged, Hugo still insisted on calling him short arse – he was, after all, just over ten inches high. Hugo had measured him once to prove a point.

The barking continued. Every time anyone came or went, knocked on, or banged, a door, Oscar made his presence known, not infrequently accompanied by evidence of his now weakening bladder.

Hugo was about to go back to his laptop – he was googling "strength training for teenagers", and had another window open on "first cold press of olive oil" – when he heard stomping up the stairs and another door bang on the landing. God's sake, I never get any peace and quiet to work here, this bloody book won't write itself. Reluctantly, he got up from his handsome Chippendale chair – a relic of The Old Rectory days, now somewhat rickety and with an Ikea cushion for comfort – and muttering under his breath, climbed the stairs to Cressida's bedroom. Oscar was still yapping, and even though he had probably peed in the kitchen, Hugo would have to leave him for now.

"Priorities," he said.

The door was shut and Cressida's cat-shaped, pink, fluffy, Do Not Disturb sign was on the handle. Actually it was always on the door handle, wasn't that what teenagers wanted? Never to be disturbed, at least not by their parents in their own domains. And that suited Hugo fine. He rarely knew what to say to them these days, it was great up until the age of about fourteen, but now at sixteen and nearly eighteen, he might just as well be living with Amazonian tribesmen, for all the conversation and understanding he had with Alex, and to a lesser extent, with Cressida. At certain times, mostly when she wanted something or was feeling frightened or worried, she became Daddy's Girl again. He knocked tentatively on her door, hoping that this was one of those times.

"Everything all right Cress? You okay?"

Nothing. No answer. Maybe boy trouble, Hugo thought. God, I hope not. Can't cope with that on top of everything else. Bloody school. Thought paying all those fees meant they kept them away from all that and focussed on study and A-star results. Not that there had been too many of the latter.

Hugo winced when he thought about the school fees. There had been a letter this morning. From the Bursar. Addressed to them both. Hugo had got to the post first. Dana didn't know. Hugo hadn't had the courage to read it all. Still, no sense in worrying about that this weekend. This weekend was about Dana's birthday and relaxing as a family.

"Sweetheart. It's Dad, what's up? Can I help?"

He ventured another soft knock on the door.

Some banging about from within. Sounded like drawers opening and closing. Then silence. At least she wasn't playing that ghastly music that Alex did – all that electrical noise and screaming. Made no sense to him at all. Infernal racket his father would have said. Hugo didn't go quite so far, mainly for fear of alienating Alex even more, but it was a noise that still made him recoil.

"I know it's you Dad, who else would it be, Jihadi John?"

Hugo took a step back. Christ, they were well up these days, weren't they? Jihadi John? What does she know about all that ISIS stuff? Most teenagers couldn't name the prime minister. The internet. Probably. YouTube certainly. God knows what they got up to locked in their rooms with their MacBooks and iPads. We sit and wag our heads and click our tongues when we watch the news about those kids going off to Syria. Where were the parents? Why did they allow it? But look at my own kids. Christ, they could be getting up to all sorts in there and what am I doing about it?

Hugo knocked more firmly.

"Can I come in Cressida please?"

"No. I'm busy."

"Doing what?"

"I have a headache."

"That's not an activity. That's an affliction."

He was irritated now, but impotent nevertheless.

"Whatever. You still can't come in." Sulking.

"Cress, look I only want to make sure you are all right." A softer approach.

"I'm fine. I just want to be alone."

"Well you can be darling, after I've come in for a chat."

"I don't want to chat. Tried that with Mum. She was really horrible to me."

"Oh dear, was she? Want to talk about it, Cress?"

"No. And I'm not eating dinner either. I'm busy and I've got things to do."

"What things? And why are you not eating again?" Hugo's patience would only last so long.

"Girl things. And it's not 'again'. I ate at school."

More noise from drawers being opened and closed.

"Okay. Well I hope all that noise in there means that you are packing for our weekend away. We're leaving tomorrow afternoon after school. Okay?" he said.

Silence. No noise. No drawers opening or closing.

"Cress? Did you hear me? We're going to Brighton, I've booked the Metropole Hotel, just the four of us and birthday dinner on Saturday night. We can shop for Mum's present in the Lanes. Okay?"

The door opened a crack. Hugo went to put a foot in it but thought better of it. He saw one tear-stained eye peering out at him. Reminded him of the *War Horse* poster. That had been a fiasco too – Dana thought it would make a nice pre-Christmas treat for everyone to go and see the play at the National in Covent Garden. Big mistake, that one. Alex loitered in the foyer throughout and even tried to buy a drink in the bar. Cressida had tapped into her phone after the first act, and Hugo had spent the entire performance apologising to people beside him for disturbing them every time Dana sent him out to check on Alex.

"I'm not going. I already told Mum."

Ah. Trouble ahead then, Hugo thought.

"Why not?" he asked.

"Because I already made plans to visit Emma for the weekend and we are going shopping on Saturday and then to Yo Sushi for dinner, so that's that."

"But Cress, it's Mum's birthday and you know how she likes us all to spend a bit of time together. Plus you'll love Brighton, you really will, there's all that – stuff to do there."

Hugo the understanding parent.

"It's full of old people. Mum said so."

"No, no darling. It's not, it's really not. Brighton is fun, it's happening. It's full of bars, and clubs that stay open all night, it's got a vibrant culture, they have that Fringe Festival there, and then there's the shopping. It's got designer shops, and loads of well – makeup shops and all that girl stuff…" Hugo was running out of steam.

Cressida sniffed.

"And of course, if it's shopping you want, then I can help out there. Give you some money to buy something nice. Maybe find one of those French Connection shops you like?"

Hugo instantly regretted this. Money. But it was said now.

The door opened a little further.

"What about Yo Sushi? They do vegan food and I am a vegan," Cressida said.

A crack.

"Absolutely darling - yes, they have sushi in Brighton!

Of course they do!"

"Not sushi, that's not vegan, not even vegetarian. I mean the restaurant Yo Sushi." Cressida waited expectantly.

Hugo stood nodding, his hands clasped in front of him.

"Yes, yes of course that's what I meant. Lunch in Yo Sushi on Saturday in Brighton. Okay?"

A beat. Another sniff. Door opened further.

"Okay, I suppose. As it is her birthday. But I'm not sharing a room with Alex. He smells. And he looks at stuff on his phone all night. Nasty stuff."

Cressida came out of her room, pecked Hugo on the cheek then withdrew and closed the door, locking it again.

Hugo stood motionless for a few minutes. Processing.

Then Cressida shouted through the locked door, "And it's not French Connection, that's for old people. Mum likes that. I shop at H & M."

Hugo remained outside the door. Alex? Phone? "Nasty stuff"? Christ, what was this about? And how much did a shopping spree at H & M cost? More than French Connection? He had no idea. And Yo Sushi? Was it fish? Cressida was vegan so probably not, but it sounded like fish to Hugo. Alex would never eat that "muck." God! How much would the lunch set him back? There was the birthday dinner to pay for yet, and he'd already held his breath when he gave his credit card details to the receptionist – Veronique as she'd told him – when he made the booking with the hotel.

And then there was the letter from the Bursar, lurking, hidden in his manuscript pile. Christ. Was the sun over the yard-arm yet? Wonder how much is left in that bottle of Highland Park? Hugo thought, as he now stomped down the stairs back to his study.

THREE

Dana pushed her key into the lock. Turned it. Nothing. She took the key out, reinserted it. Jiggled it around a bit. The key turned but the door stayed shut. God damn door. Why can't Hugo just sort it out? Dana banged the frame, rattled the handle and turned the key again.

"Come on Mum. I'm soaking wet. And freezing. And starving to death standing here!" Alex protested behind her.

"Well if your father had fixed it then I wouldn't have to be rugby-tackling it open, would I?"

"Give it here."

Alex pushed in front of her and kicked the door with his football boot. It swung open. Leaving the imprint of his boot studs on its lower half.

"Oops. Better not let Dad see that," he said.

Alex touched the damage to the door with the toe of his other boot, then walked through, dumped his kit bag on the large oak ottoman in the hall, while simultaneously answering his phone, before striding up the stairs, two at at time, saying, "Yeah. You all right mate?" And disappearing into his room.

Hugo appeared from the dark recesses of the house, Oscar bounding after him.

"Hi. What's all that racket? I've just had Cressida banging doors upstairs and making a fuss about the weekend and now this."

He eyed the front door suspiciously and gave Dana a peck on the cheek.

"Anyway, how was your day?" he asked her.

"Wet. Boring. Funeral like." Dana held up The Casket.

"Ah, dear old Mum, yes, sorry about that darling." He took The Casket and patted the lid. "Back home at last, where she belongs."

Dana rolled her eyes while Hugo set it on the oak ottoman next to the wet kit bag.

"I'm not sure she envisaged ending up at the bottom of the garden in the potting shed, but it's none of my business what you do with your dead parents."

Dana knelt on the floor cuddling and kissing Oscar.

"Come on Dana, let's not start that. I was only waiting for them to be reunited so that I could scatter them together, over the loch in Scotland."

"And how might you achieve that? Via Royal Mail? We're not exactly flush at the moment for 1,600 mile round trips."

"No of course, I realise that but things will look up soon enough. Now, I put your supper dish in the oven, so why don't you go and have a nice bubbly bath while it heats through? I'll bring you a drink up," he said.

Hugo picked up the casket and went towards the kitchen. What's he being so jolly and nice about? Dana wondered. But, as she was feeling cold and damp, the idea of a bath seemed very cheering.

"Has Cressida calmed down?" Dana asked his retreating back.

"Yes, yes I've sorted that all out. No longer any problem there. Except she says she's not eating again."

Dana slumped slightly as she climbed the stairs and thought that Cressida couldn't get any thinner, that's for sure. Maybe they could tackle the issue over the weekend.

"Come on Oscar – you fancy a bath?"

At that suggestion Oscar retreated, tail between his legs, back into the safety of the kitchen.

Steam, frothy bubbles, hot water and flickering, freesia-scented candle. Lovely. Dana sank back into the deep enamel, claw-footed Edwardian bath. Well, reproduction bath. Hugo's dad had helped fit it. Done a very nice job too, and on the walk-in shower. Gorgeous sandstone tiles. Expertly cut and laid by her father-in-law. It was just the luxurious bathroom Dana had always wanted. Unfortunate that he had died before finishing the plastering to the other walls, or refitting the cords to the large sash window, which now operated like a guillotine: ready to fall at any moment on the unwitting if they were foolish enough to lean out of the window to gaze upon the garden below.

Hugo knocked tentatively at the door, came in with two glasses of wine, and handed one to Dana. She sank back into the water again as she sipped it.

Thank God for Sauvignon Blanc. Thank God even more for Carrefour selling it at £1.79 a bottle. Stocks were running low though after their last French trip. Probably wouldn't be going again for quite a while.

"That lock on the front door needs changing. I couldn't open it again today, and Mum can never get in when she calls round, it's too stiff," Dana said, keeping her eyes closed.

"I've fixed it several times but I'll try another lock, although I don't think that's the problem. There's one in the shed from the Old Rectory, it's Georgian I think, worth a bob or two and built to last," he said.

Hugo sipped his own wine and didn't sound in the least convincing about sorting out the door, Dana thought. After all tomorrow is another day. Isn't that what Vivien Leigh had said? Should be Hugo's motto too.

"Oh and there's something wrong with the battery on my car. Didn't start first thing and then again when I picked up Alex," she said.

"Just needs charging or maybe the water needs topping up. I'll have a look in the morning."

"Okay, thanks. God, I'm looking forward to a bit of luxury this weekend. And some peace and quiet," Dana said, sinking even further under the bubbles.

"Yes, be nice to have a rest for a change," Hugo responded.

Dana opened one eye and peeked at him with a raised eyebrow. He didn't notice. Swilling his wine around in his glass.

"And a bit of, well, you know," he suggested.

Dana sat up slightly. Looked at him.

"Don't suppose there's any room in there for me now?" Hugo gestured at the bath.

She slid under the bubbles again and said, "Dinner will be ready in a moment and Alex is starving. Now, what about Cressida? First healthy eating, then calorie-counting, then vegetarian, now vegan. What's next? Only eating fruit that falls from the tree?"

Hugo shrugged his shoulders, his gaze still lingering on the bath and Dana in it.

"She'll get over it. It's just a phase."

"No Hugo, it is not *just a phase*. She's been tricky about food for over a year now and it's getting worse. She weighs no more than seven stone, stick thin, pale and insipid looking. How she has the energy for basketball, let alone getting out of bed I don't know. We have to do something."

"What do you suggest?" He finished his wine.

"Go and see someone about it."

"Like who?"

"For goodness sake! A doctor, a nutritionist, an expert," Dana said, half out of the water.

"It's not that bad. We can just talk to her. Try and help her see it's not doing her any good." He tipped the empty wine glass to his head, savouring the last few drops.

"I've tried talking to her. It is counter-productive. She just thinks I am disapproving and interfering and it makes her dig her heels in even more," Dana said.

"Look, let's see how we get on this weekend. Maybe away from the house, relaxed, she might eat better and talk to us about it."

Again, he didn't sound convincing.

Dana got up out of the bath, causing a mini-tsunami, and pulled her bathrobe on roughly. Bloody typical Hugo: talk, manyana. Useless.

"You are blind. She needs help. Not ours. An experts. Before it escalates. Otherwise your daughter, my darling, will develop an eating disorder. Called anorexia."

Dana pulled the plug, pulled the light cord and swept out of the bathroom, leaving Hugo sitting in the dark.

"What's this Mum?" Alex prodded the contents of his plate with his fork.

"Dinner," Dana said, as she refilled her wine glass from the half-empty bottle on the kitchen table.

"Is it experimental again?" Alex cut a bit up and examined it.

"All cooking in this house is experimental. An experiment to see how many of the inhabitants will eat it."

She took a long pull on her drink. At least she wouldn't have to cook, and therefore try and please them all, over the weekend. Well she wouldn't have to cook at any rate.

"It's very tasty and very nutritious. So eat," Hugo commanded.

Alex ignored him.

"Is this chicken?" he asked, as he skewered a piece of something yellowish and held it up to Dana.

"Could be. How was football? Does Mr Stonewall think you will make the seven-eleven this term?" she said.

"But it's got no − substance. It's just, well, mushy. I don't think it's chicken."

Alex put his fork down and peered at the rest of his plate.

"Everything on that plate was prepared by your mother who goes to a great deal of trouble to ensure that we eat well as a family, so stop complaining. Dana can you top me up?" Hugo asked, holding up his glass and motioning to the bottle at Dana's left arm.

Alex continued to ignore him.

"It's all a bit bland. Like baby food, all one colour. Definitely not chicken," Alex continued.

Dana slammed her own knife and fork down on the well scrubbed, oak table.

"Does it bloody matter whether it is sodding chicken or not?" she shouted.

"Yes actually it does Mum. I'm a growing lad and I need protein, not baby food. I know you went to tons of trouble and stuff, and I'm sure Cress loves it and that, but – can I make a sandwich?"

He grinned at her, his winning grin. Always worked, her Alex. Annoyed though she was, Dana relented, shook her head and nodded.

"But put your plate on top of the Aga, Dad might finish yours later."

Hugo said nothing as Alex got up from the table and proceeded to make an almighty clatter, and mess, with all manner of spreads, cheeses, salamis and pitta breads from the fridge.

"We got any olives?" he asked over his shoulder.

"Yes, in the cupboard in front of you, top shelf, unopened, green pitted with pimento. The kind you like," Dana instructed him.

"Thought you were making a sandwich, not running a deli," Hugo commented from the other side of the kitchen table.

Alex did not respond. He found the olives, threw in a handful to the open pitta bread, several chunks of feta cheese, three slices of Milano salami and a dollop of cheese spread and left the kitchen chewing a mouthful as he went.

"Thanks Mum. And yes I did make the team, the *First*

Eleven by the way, the Seven Eleven is a shop," he said over his shoulder on his way out.

His heavy, but springy, tread resounded through the kitchen as he bounced up the stairs. Oscar, ever vigilant and on the lookout for scraps, trotted like a show-pony after him.

"You could have asked him about the football Hugo, you really should have."

Dana got up and started to clear the table.

"He was clearly more interested in insulting your cooking than talking to his father, though God knows what I've done to incur his silence, never used to be like this."

Hugo peered into the recesses of his glass.

And he was right. Alex and he used to be the best of pals. Went everywhere together. Hugo would spend hours cleaning Alex's football boots, driving all over the county – and often further afield – to away games, cheering him on, arguing with the referees, running on at half-time with refreshments for him. Alex used to be a mini Hugo too. Copied his father. It was always "Daddy this" or "Daddy that", even made Dana feel excluded. And then it all disappeared, seemingly overnight. No more take me to football Dad, no more where's my boots, is my kit ready, where's the game next Saturday? No more. What had happened, how had it happened?

Alex had become an adolescent, and then suddenly he was on the verge of his eighteenth birthday. Very much his own lad, or maybe man, now. And he and Hugo had grown apart, and Hugo, being Hugo, had not handled it well.

"That's because you don't say the right things to him,

you need to engage on his level now," Dana said.

She scraped the remnants of their plates into the blue Le Creuset enamel casserole dish, chipped now and showing its age, and took it all over to the sink to wash up. No dishwasher. Hugo said they didn't need one, waste of money. She ran the water, tepid, not hot. The boiler was being temperamental again.

"I engage very well with young people thank you Dana. I am, after all, an athletics coach and part of what I do is responding to and understanding the needs of young athletes on the field."

He continued to sit, swirling his wine.

Dana looked up at the ceiling and pursed her lips. Yes, athletics coach. Three afternoons a week at primary schools, and two evenings at the local club, the latter unpaid.

"That's not the same thing. Alex is your son, not a project. When you talk to him you should perhaps be a little more understanding. It's no longer any good to just tell him to do this or do that, like when he was nine or ten. Now you need to discuss things, and see his point of view."

"I am very much up for discussion with Alex, when a discussion is warranted, and it was not in the case of dinner, which I might add you had gone to a lot of trouble to make," Hugo replied.

"Well anyway, whatever. Can you go and make sure that they pack up their things for the weekend, I'm not going to run around in the morning like a blue-arsed fly doing it all. Oh, and ask Cressida if she wants a sandwich as she didn't eat dinner, although I'm not sure there's any hummus in date…"

Dana opened the double door, American-style, fridge and peered inside. After the ravages of Alex's sandwich making there was not a lot going on in there, she'd have to do some serious grocery shopping on Monday. She closed the door and then gave it a shove with her backside – the seal not being quite tight anymore.

"There's a bit of tzatziki I can put on some pitta for her, oh no, wait, that's got yoghurt in it. Oh sod it, tell her I can toast some pitta for her, that'll have to do."

Hugo went into his study and sat at his desk. Stared at his MacBook screen for a few minutes and his new chapter heading entitled, "Body Mass Index – Fact or Fiction?". It was, at this stage, neither. He had managed about sixty words today. Still, it was substance that counted. And it was early days with his research.

He closed a window on his computer and saved ten others to "favourites", they'll all come in handy, he told himself, particularly the one about olive oil. Hugo had ideas – as opposed to actual strategy – about importing olive oil from Provence. His research, based mainly on trips to the supermarket and a week on a campsite near St Tropez, had revealed that almost none of the olive oil produced in the South of France was exported. Everything bought here in the UK was from Italy, or Greece, or somewhere. Not France. There's a market there for sure. Why was no one else doing it? Dana had pointed out that there may well be a good reason for that, but Hugo wasn't convinced. No – it was a sound business idea. One of many he had.

He took out a micro-fibre cloth and carefully cleaned his computer screen. Picked up his document in-tray, full to the brim, and emptied everything out, before carefully aligning the top edge of each page of each document and putting them all back in again. He took an "urgent" sticker from his desk drawer and slapped it on top of the in-tray.

Then he shook his document "out-tray", containing one half-finished query letter to a literary agent, so that the document sat in the centre of the tray. He lifted up his old school trophy cup – bronze and crested with a long dead Latin motto at the bottom – and tipped it upside down spilling pens, pencils, erasers, paper clips, scissors, staples and bits of blu-tack on the green leather top of his dear father's mahogany desk. Hugo cleaned the shaft of each pen and pencil with the micro-fibre cloth and carefully reinserted them back into the trophy cup. He was about to sit back when he noticed that the edge of his ink-well was not quite perpendicular to the desk edge, he sprung forward and corrected it.

Then Hugo nodded in satisfaction, smiled and spread his hands over the gilt-edged leather top in a sweeping motion. Can't work in chaos, he told himself. A tidy desk is an ordered and productive mind.

In doing so he caught the edge of his manuscript pile – in actuality research notes – and the whole lot fell to the floor. The Bursar's letter sailed down last and landed on top. Hugo *tut-tutted* and cast his eyes at the floor. And spotted the letter. Then he bolted up from the desk, ran to the door and locked it.

Christ. Was there never any relaxation after a day's work? He picked up the notes, put the letter into the middle of the sheaf, and stuffed it all into his briefcase. Then he sat back again in his chair.

A knock at the door made Hugo jump. The handle turned and rattled.

"Hugo?" Dana's voice.

"Yes darling?"

"What are you doing in there? Why's the door locked?"

"Oh, just, you know…"

You know what? His mind whirled. What explanation could there possibly be? But stop, he was being paranoid. There was no way Dana could be privy to what he had just concealed.

"No, I don't know." Her tone was frosty.

"Writing of course."

"Well it can't be the athletics book, unless it's now for MI6 operatives, and you've signed the Official Secrets Act."

"Don't be silly darling. I was just seeing how the locking mechanism on this door functioned, so that it might help me work out how to fix the one on the front door and then I started some more writing."

Hugo was thinking on his feet. Damn good at it too, he decided. Should have been a barrister.

"Right. Well now that you've achieved that might you open the door?" she asked.

Dana didn't sound convinced, and wild thoughts flashed through Hugo's mind: not least the obvious one that when a man is locked in his study on his own with a computer, a wife might legitimately suspect that he was availing himself of some pornographic entertainment online. Christ. Mind you better that, bad as it was, than the truth.

Hugo jumped up again and unlocked the door, but not before he had hastily typed a few more lines of text under

"Body Mass Index – Fact or Fiction?".

The door then open, Hugo sauntered back to his desk. Dana stood on the threshold.

"Have you sorted them out upstairs?" she asked him.

"What?"

"Packing? Cressida? Sandwich?" Dana responded. The frost had now become irritation.

"Oh right, yes of course. Just on it now – wanted to get some important things down before I lost my train of thought."

Hugo gestured to his computer.

Dana walked over to his desk and stood behind him, peering at the screen.

"Perhaps you'd better bring it with you over the weekend. You might want to redraft what you've written there."

Dana patted him on the shoulder and walked out.

Hugo looked at the page on his Mac, the last two lines of text read: "In essence and in summary, in actuality and reality the factuality and accuracy of the factualness of the matter are in reality based on validity and authenticity of the facts of the matter."

Dana opened a wardrobe door and surveyed the contents. What to pack. Something lovely, but not sexy. Definitely not sexy. Don't want to give Hugo any ideas or encouragement. She went through the rails, pulling out that dress and this top and those trousers. Put them all back in. Opened another wardrobe door and took out a silk dress. Red. Short. No good – sexy. She put it back in. Glanced at her mobile phone. No new messages. The word *sexy*, always made her think of him. Dana sighed.

She pulled out a black slip-dress edged in lace with little straps from Zara. Short, and maybe sexy, but definitely not in a come-on way. She put it on the bed.

What else to take? Swimwear for the pool and spa. Underwear, comfortable and no more – that was an even more dangerous area. And nightwear – off the scale in terms of hazard. Dana opened a drawer and took out fleecy pyjamas. Warm and sensible, and they sent the right signal. Probably need a windproof and waterproof coat too. Brighton in winter was not the Bahamas. In fact, with miles of exposed coastline and a seafront that bore the brunt of a year-round unrelenting sea breeze, Brighton, even in summer, was often more Stornaway than St Tropez.

She put everything into her weekend hold-all, and then took her black leather Gucci handbag, with the discreet chrome logo, carefully out of its dust bag. She'd paid a fortune for it several years ago in Selfridges. Now it was scuffed at the corners and had a scratch on one side. But some black polish hid it well. Those were the days – sweeping into the plush Gucci concession just inside the entrance of Selfridges. Handing over a small fortune to some slick-haired, snotty assistant. And if she'd stuck with being a full-time solicitor she would probably have graduated to a Hermès bag by now, leather though, not crocodile: even if she'd made it to partner in the firm, her earnings wouldn't have stretched to those celebrity shopping heights.

The thoughts of her profession, one that she convinced herself was not her destiny and was certainly only short-term, felt like a bucket of cold water poured on her from a great height. Although she only worked three days a week in the law firm now, the work of a conveyancing solicitor depressed her beyond words. But they needed the money. And someone had to bring it in. But. She would not worry about that this weekend.

Sometimes Dana felt like a small animal trapped in a confined space. Or a patient upon a bed, paralysed or comatose. Seeing, but unable to speak, hearing, but unable to move. She would wake sometimes in the dead of the quiet night, in a blind panic. She worried that her anxiety about her life and the disappointments in it were not normal. That her reaction was extreme. And that in turn caused her further panic.

On a particularly bad occasion – and they were fairly few in number – Dana would wake suddenly in the black stillness, and she would know it was two or three in the morning just by the desolate feel of the hour, without needing to look at her watch. And she would think about Hugo, and how he would cope without her. About her mother, and her inevitably failing health, and about how she couldn't live forever.

And then about her children. She felt she had failed them. In every way: materially by failing to provide them with a secure financial environment, by not having the money to give them cars for their seventeenth birthdays, or having the deposit for their first homes, by the fact that they would have to work their way through university when they got there. And failed them emotionally by not being able to put her own needs to one side, and just get on with their father. And then about her husband. She had failed him. She wasn't a good wife, not like Camilla. Dana had failed to just turn the other cheek and accept Hugo's – what was it? Lack of ambition, inertia, whatever. But she was a failure as a wife, not least because she yearned for more. Surely there must be more? Sometimes she felt guilty even thinking this. Other times she defended it passionately.

But most of all, Dana had failed herself. And this is what caused terror to strike her on occasion. She had failed to become what she knew she had the capacity to become – a happy, fulfilled, successful person. She had failed to be at peace with herself. And this caused her to become in turn like the paralysed person on the hospital bed, or the small animal trapped in fright.

She knew that she could not remain terrorised for ever. Because even the small animal, trapped and cornered, would either die of fright. Or fight back.

But for now, the dog needed watering and popping outside on the front step before bed, the kids needed organising, and she had to make sure her mother still remembered that she was supposed to be coming over tomorrow to look after Oscar.

She took one last, sneaky look at her phone. No message.

Hugo bounded up the stairs and rapped on Cressida's door. To his surprise he got a "Come in".

"Mum wants to know if you'd like a pitta bread thingy and have you packed up a hold-all for tomorrow?"

Hugo pushed at the door but there was some resistance from the other side, he gave it a shove, and something pink and nylon rolled up underneath the door, like a giant tentacle, which he stumbled over before looking up.

"Bloody hell Cress – what's happened in here?"

Hugo was met with a veritable armageddon. Cressida's

room was strewn with well, girl stuff. Every inch was covered – the entire bed was covered in clothes, dresses, skirts, blouses, jog bottoms, leggings, coats, jackets, scarves, hats, gloves. And the floor – this was covered in bags: handbags, clutch bags, hold-alls, with a mini mountain of shoes, trainers and boots in the middle. The dressing table was a blur of cosmetics, creams, makeup bags, hair brushes, hair straighteners, hair bands.

"What are you doing?"

"Packing?" Cressida said.

She was wriggling around on top of something on the other side of the bed.

"But it looks like – I don't know a botched robbery or a nightmare jumble sale."

"Thanks Dad! These are my clothes if you don't mind and I had to sort out what to bring, didn't I? And you did tell me to pack."

Cressida got up, and pulled something after her round the bed. She presented Hugo with an enormous, hard-shell suitcase.

"What's that?" he asked, his eyes wide.

"My weekend bag?"

Cressida excelled in up-talk: every sentence was a question.

"That's a fortnight's holiday's worth! No more – it's a leaving home, away to university trunk, that's what that is! You can't take all that!"

Cressida regarded him for a moment.

"You and Mum said it was posh. So what did you expect? A carrier bag? I've got lunches, breakfasts, dinners, clubs – you said – shopping, spas, cocktails. I can't do all that with one change of clothes can I?"

"But!" Hugo was speechless.

Mother job. This was a mother job. He was out of his depth.

Still, perhaps it was better to just take the suitcase than incur Dana's wrath by beginning The Packing operation all over again.

"Well, you'd better clear up the rest of this stuff before your mother comes in, although I cannot imagine for the life of me how you manage to have any more clothes left when this suitcase feels the weight of your entire wardrobe."

Hugo took the suitcase and bumped it down the stairs, while Cressida smiled in triumph.

Cressida shut her bedroom door behind her father. Fuss, fuss, fuss. Parents were always so extreme. Always sweating the small stuff. Jesus. The earth wouldn't stop spinning on its axis just because she had a few clothes laid out. And why did it matter that she brought a couple of changes of clothes in her bag? I mean really. Come on.

Jesus. The weekend would be no fun if they kept stressing all the time.

Cressida picked up the two top ends of her purple bed-cover and shook it, so that all the clothes fell off the bed onto one side of the floor.

"See. That's sorted isn't it?" she said.

She went over to her big wicker basket full of soft toy kittens. She had all shapes and sizes. She had been collecting them since she had been a little girl and her beloved cat, a tabby called Fluffy, had been killed in front of her on the road outside. She had cried for weeks but had vowed never to have another cat again if the nasty road killed it. She rearranged the basket and picked out a tiny little fluffy kitten on a key-ring. She always took this one with her when she went away anywhere. Silly really. But she was still a little girl at heart, well a bit of her was and always would be. She put the kitten key-ring on her bedside table, ready to put in her bag in the morning.

Cressida pulled up the top of her computer, Skyped her friend Emma, and a pretty blonde-haired, blue-eyed girl appeared on screen.

"Hi Cress."

"Hi Em, how's it going?"

"Yeah, okay. Been blogging on my fashion channel for a bit, that's all. Shit! Look at your room! It's insane! Ha!" Emma laughed.

"Yeah, it is! My dad just got all stressy about it."

"Your dad? Jeeze I don't even answer my bedroom door to my dad, deffo wouldn't let him into my bedroom." Emma shook her head.

"Yeah well, I had to. He was hassling me about my suitcase for tomorrow, so you know."

"Oh yeah, got your text. Sorry about that babe. It sucks. But I got Abi to come over instead so…but wish you were coming as well."

"Me too. It'll be crap in Brighton, but it's Mum's birthday so have to go. On the plus side, Dad is giving me a ton of money to spend in H & M, so that's okay, and I'm also going to wangle some new MAC makeup and stuff. Plus he's says I can go to bars and clubs and all that, so might not be totally crap in the end, you know?"

"Cool. My dad wouldn't even let me drink at Christmas, so you've got it made. He'd have a cardiac if he found our vodka under the bed! Wish I was coming with you now!" Emma pouted and pretended to cry.

"Not with my family you wouldn't. I have to share a room with my disgusting brother. And you know what he does on his own!"

"Gross. Same as my brother, only now he does it with his girlfriend which is totally sick." Emma put her fingers down her throat.

"Yeah sick. Think I'll become a lesbian that way I won't have to do any of that." Cressida laughed.

"No you won't. What about Piers? You know you like him."

"Maybe. He's okay. His sister's nicer!"

"Cress! Now you are being gross! Stop it!"

"Yeah well, at least it would piss off my parents if I became a lesbian."

Both girls broke into hysterical laughter.

"Cressida – did you want that sandwich or not?" Dana's voice, raised, from the bottom of the stairs.

"Shit, they're on my back again. Call you tomorrow." Cressida went to cut the connection.

"I want a full report," Emma said, as her face vanished from the screen.

"Has Alex done the same?" Dana asked Hugo.

He was humping Cressida's suitcase over the last step of the stairs.

"I sincerely hope not darling. Otherwise you and I will be walking to Brighton, as there won't be room in my car for all of us and all of their luggage."

Hugo parked the suitcase just behind the ottoman in the hall.

"Well you'd better go and check that he has put

something together for the trip. And we're going in my car — I'm not sitting with pucks and bundles all around me on the motorway. My car's one virtue is space," said Dana.

She put Oscar's lead on and took him towards the front door, in an effort to get him to relieve himself in the garden before bed.

Hugo was just making the return journey up the stairs when Dana called him back.

"I shouldn't leave that suitcase there behind the ottoman — it's bound to be forgotten in the morning," she said.

He didn't look back.

"If it's left in front someone — *me* in all likelihood — will fall over it. And it will hardly be forgotten, all the fuss that has gone into filling it," he said, before disappearing upstairs.

The floorboards on the landing vibrated as Hugo stepped onto them. It felt like at least 7.5 on the Richter scale. The bass tone of the music reverberated up his legs and the entire length of his spine. He thought that his vertebrae might shatter. This was then followed by a scream so high pitched that Hugo wondered if he had gained Oscar's sense of hearing. It was in fact Alex's music, or what passed for music in this part of the house. Hugo immediately recoiled from the task at hand and hovered outside Alex's room for a minute or two. He couldn't bear the noise, and was also certain that any messages he feebly relayed from Dana would be studiously ignored.

A particularly piercing scream made him straighten his back and stiffen his lip. Nonsense. It's my house. When they start paying the bills, then they can call the tune so to speak. Hugo went to knock on the door, but instead made a large fist and pounded on it in competition with the music.

Nothing. No response. He couldn't even be certain that his banging could be heard.

Hugo tried the handle. Locked. He pounded again. Then again. Then with both fists.

Still nothing. Still no response. This is nonsensical, he decided.

"Alex!" Hugo shouted.

Then he banged and shouted.

Nothing. The music thundered on, the floorboards continued to vibrate.

Then Hugo kicked the door savagely with the toe of his walking boot. He hadn't actually done any walking today. He had meant to walk Oscar several miles, but he had been too busy with his writing. And research.

Still no response. And, truth be told, the kicking had hurt his big toe. Sod it, he thought.

Right. I'm not having this. He went downstairs to his study, picked up the land line, and dialled Alex's mobile phone, making sure that he withheld his own number first.

It was instantly answered. Christ! Just goes to show, doesn't it? What their priorities are.

"Yeah?" was the greeting from Alex.

"This is your father speaking. No, do not hang up if you please. I have just spent the better part of fifteen minutes attempting to gain access to your bedroom. I have knocked, banged and kicked your bedroom door. I have called and shouted, all to no avail due to the decibels being emitted from your hi-fi. I have done all that for the purposes of conveying a message from your mother which is the following – have you packed for the weekend?"

Hugo was red with anger, and now quite out of puff, with both his exertions and delivering his message all in one breath.

"Yeah," came the response. And then the line went dead.

"Well, I – look here, I…" Hugo's intended fury came out spluttering instead.

He pulled the phone away from his ear and stared at it.

"Oh sod it. I give up. He can wear his underpants for the entire weekend for all I care."

He went over to his drinks cabinet, grabbed a glass – dear old Dad's Edinburgh Crystal tumbler, and poured himself a good two-fingers worth of Highland Park. It was the last of the bottle.

Alex lay sprawled across his bed. His iPhone connected to his bluetooth speakers. Present from Grandma for his last birthday. She was great. Grandma Bella. She often sat with him in his room. Quite liked his music, at least she didn't complain about it. Mum said that was because she was deaf as a post but nah, I don't reckon that's why she sits here with me sometimes while I'm playing my stuff. Grandma knows where I'm coming from. Always buys me gig tickets and never tells them. Let me take her into Maplins and pick out the most powerful speakers. Brilliant. Alex loved his grandma very much.

His room often bewildered first-time visitors. Violent posters for obscure Japanese films – depicting all manner of horrible and untimely demise – and posters of death metal adorned with inverted crosses and satanic Latin mottos, stood cheek by jowl with pictures of him as a boy in football kit at matches. Black candles in skull holders, and long sticks of incense completed the look.

He was also building a collection of empty beer bottles, which his old man objected to, and which had caused an almighty row when Hugo had broken into his room one day and taken the lot away in a black bin liner. They were empty for fuck's sake! How is that "harming your development" as his father had said? Anyway. Whatever. He had had no problem replenishing his stocks. Truth be told, there were several full bottles under his bed. But Alex was careful to construct the illusion of chaos, clutter and downright filth in his room, so that any would-be snoopers were deterred by the dual offences of a highly unpleasant odour, and a mountain of detritus upon opening the door.

That soon drove them back.

Alex had certain items that he would not wish anyone to find in his room.

He stretched, yawned and switched off his music. It was after eleven and he was tired. Full day tomorrow and football training first thing. Oh shit, he thought, and the weekend away.

His phone rang.

"All right mate?" Alex answered.

He laughed at something said to him on the other end of the phone.

"Yeah, Brighton with the folks." He laughed again. "Nah, it's Mum's birthday, so gotta go. But then I'll be hitting the pubs and that. I'll just get wasted for the weekend. So could be wicked. Yeah, you too mate, have a good one. Cheers."

Alex slung his phone down, switched off the light, and was sleeping the sleep of the dead in two minutes flat.

Surrounded by the remnants of her unpacked wardrobe, Cressida counted not sheep, but the latest catwalk designs on the rails at H & M, and drifted off into a smiling slumber.

Dana lingered in the limbo between sleep and consciousness, with visions of red silk dresses and a handsome man caressing her lips with his.

Hugo tossed, turned and seethed into the small hours, as the music continued to play in his head.

The dog – nestled between him and Dana on the queen, not king, size sleigh bed – bit him savagely, twice, on the ankle, when he rolled over disturbing it.

FOUR

The traffic was hopping, even at six o'clock, on the road outside. Still dark, but more like rush hour at night than first thing on a Friday morning. The curse of living on a main road. The engine noises were accompanied by the *pitter-patter* of rain falling on the clay tiles of the roof. It was the latter noise that woke Dana, and not the alarm that she had asked Hugo to set before going to sleep and which had mysteriously failed to go off. She lay for a minute or two running through the to-do's of the coming day, trying to summon some positive thoughts to get out of bed on. A few hours in the office this morning, Friday was not usually her day to work but one of her clients had an urgent completion on a property purchase and she had to be there to oversee it. It was tricky, as was the client from abroad, and it involved a lot of money, as London transactions usually did. Then she had to dash back home, make sure her mother was safely installed with the dog, pick up her things, pick up Hugo, and then fetch the kids before setting off.

After all that she might start to relax.

A mammoth engine noise laboured outside. Then the sound of a smaller engine breaking sharply. A horn being pounded. A raised voice. An obscenity uttered. Both vehicles then drove on. How unforgiving and unyielding us humans are, Dana thought, as she stepped onto the cold, mahogany-stained floorboards, and then into her slippers.

Her phone pinged. She didn't wonder who it might be at this hour.

"You free for lunch?" a text message asked.

She frowned. And then smiled in spite of herself.

Dana glanced at Hugo, now sleeping like an infant: swaddled in his big tartan rug, breathing softly in contentment. She sighed, put on her dressing gown and went downstairs, Oscar following at her heels.

As Dana sat on the loo, she tapped in a reply, "Probably not. Tricky completion this morning and then have to dash as off to Brighton for a few days."

"Okay. Keep in touch. Enjoy your dirty weekend xxx," said the reply.

Dana got up and flushed the toilet. She was about to tap in a sharp retort but resisted the temptation. Instead, she squirted some Toilet Duck disinfectant around the rim. Let him think that, suits me fine, she thought.

In the kitchen, Dana savoured a few moments of peace and tranquility sipping her Earl Grey tea and soya milk as Oscar watched her every move from his basket. Dana had given up cow's milk in preference for soya as she had read somewhere that soya was high in oestrogen. Mind you, that was before she had succumbed to the HRT she now relied upon to keep the worst of the menopause symptoms at bay. *Premature* menopause, she corrected herself. At least, it had been at forty-two, now, at forty-nine she supposed it was just normal. Nothing special about her now in that regard. Her mother still insisted that it was just a "glitch", and delighted in telling her how she and all her side of the family had been fertile well into their fifties, and even Aunty Ag – who only had one child – had managed to do so at fifty-two.

Yes, well. Modern life was stressful and having the entire responsibility of the family on her shoulders had probably caused Dana's ovaries to fail early.

Fail.

There was that word again. It seemed to crop up when she least expected it. It was the word the gynaecologist had used when he diagnosed her premature menopause. Her ovaries had *failed* he'd told her as she sat there anxiously watching him look at her scan report. She blamed herself of course. Even though the gynie, a lovely man with an engaging smile and calm voice – he could afford to be calm at £250 a visit – assured her that it was just unfortunate, the luck of the draw. Her luck, Dana decided. Always seems to be me.

Not that anyone would have guessed it of course. Dana looked much younger than she was and beautifully feminine. She thought back to her first panicked visit to the gynaecologist's clinic, prompted by a sudden onrush of symptoms – feeling exhausted getting out of bed, sleepless nights, restless legs, constant urge to rush off to relieve her bladder, panic attacks, no periods – she had felt a bit of a fraud sitting there. She'd never had a hot flush. They didn't figure in her repertoire of ailments. At first she had suspected, with alarm, that she might be pregnant. But after the menopause diagnosis she was distraught. Even though she had been horrified at the thought of a third pregnancy, now the knowledge that she would be permanently denied another child, had filled her with remorse. And she blamed herself again.

And then when the lovely gynaecologist had filled out her prescription for the pills, she had sat there, disbelieving. The idea that she now had to rely upon hormones to keep her going. She'd made jokes in the consulting room as the chaperone nurse stood guard by the door.

"Goodness, will I now get a deep voice, put on two stone and sprout a hairy chin, like my old maiden aunt?" she'd asked.

Half in jest, half in anticipating horror.

"Like all those sad, menopausal, 'women of a certain age' one sees at evening classes!" she continued.

The lovely gynaecologist had laughed, said nonsense of course you won't, and patted her hand.

Dana had glanced over at the nurse. She wasn't smiling. She was overweight and had a five o'clock shadow.

Anyway, that was some time ago now. Thank God for medical science. And of course soya milk.

Radio 4 twittered in the background, and Dana caught snatches of the conversation as she made a list for her mother while sipping a second mug of Earl Grey. Cressida then sailed into the kitchen, turned off the radio, slapped on MTV at full volume, sat in the middle of the floor, and stretched her hands towards the ceiling.

"I was listening to that. What in God's name are you doing?" Dana asked with her mug half way to her lips.

"Yoga?"

"At six thirty in the morning?"

"Of course. Morning is the optimum time to exercise Mum. You know that, you go running."

Cressida closed her eyes and clasped her hands together, as if in prayer.

Dana closed her own eyes in despair.

"Please tell me this is nothing to do with losing weight?" Dana said.

Cressida remained focussed and shook her head.

"Mother if you don't mind I cannot concentrate and clear my mind of extraneous matter if you keep talking. It's all about discipline. Of the mind. And the body."

Dana put her mug on the beechwood worktop, still waiting to be sealed and oiled.

"Well in that case, perhaps you could ask your father to join you. Group session, group therapy. I'm going for a shower, please let the dog out when you've finished the Lotus position," Dana said.

Cressida opened one eye and Dana caught her about to stick out her tongue at her retreating back, but the dog, now well attuned to the family dynamics and never failing to miss an opportunity, jumped up and licked her, knocking the Lotus attempt over.

Thank God for Zara, Dana thought as she slipped her slim-fitting jacket on over her well-above-the-knee, black jersey dress. If she squinted she could almost see Yves Saint Laurent in the mirror instead of the high street. Her long, high-heeled black boots though, were Prada. Thank God for eBay as well.

Nice. Quite nice, she thought. Shame she wasn't meeting you-know-who for lunch after all. She took a deep breath. Now, are they all up, fed and watered? Dana wondered as she walked onto the landing.

"Alex," she bellowed at full volume.

Nothing less worked "in the middle of the night", as Alex termed seven in the morning.

"Yes Mum," came his soft response from behind her.

He stood on the landing, dripping wet, with a large towel draped over his lower half.

"Oh! You did make me jump," she said.

"How's that? You are the one shouting."

"Well yes, but I didn't expect you to actually be out of bed, let alone showered."

Goodness, he was a good looking boy, she thought, muscular for his age, good head of hair, albeit now growing very long as befitting a heavy metal fan. Takes after my dad. He was a handsome man, a true gentleman too.

"Yeah, I went asleep early – have to limber up for our weekend away," he explained.

"Oh. Great. Okay, well, have you packed?" Dana asked.

"Yeah, I'll sling a T-shirt in a rucksack in a bit."

Alex walked towards his bedroom.

"Do please bring a collared shirt, I think hotels have policies about that sort of thing for dinner, and especially if you are hoping to persuade Dad to buy you a shandy in the cocktail bar," she said.

"Yeah, okay, I'll sort it," he said as he disappeared.

Dana looked at her watch, and then rushed down the stairs, she wanted to beat the traffic into the office.

"I'll see you later," she called up to Hugo. "Don't forget to look at my battery – I'm taking your car to work, and don't forget Mum, she's calling over around eleven. Susie's picking up the kids in a moment and dropping them at school so you can get some work done."

No response. She looked at her watch again and ran out the door.

Hugo could still hear the music. He turned over and covered his ears with his hands. But this time it was different. Instead of a constant beat and vibration, now it was intermittent. And accompanied by shaking. And then as though someone were beating something with a stick. And rattling. Bang, shake, rattle. Hugo took his hands away and opened his eyes.

Broad daylight streamed in through the window. He sat up slightly. His head was fuzzy. He looked at the bedside table. The digital clock read 11:12 a.m.

"Christ Almighty!" he said, as he leapt out of bed, then bent double and nursed his back. "I'm too old for this."

He inched along towards the end of the bed and gingerly stood upright.

Meanwhile, the music continued. Wait a minute, that's not music. Fuck. Dana's mother. Front door. Can't get in. Oh fuck.

Hugo stumbled about in a fog in the bedroom: located his dressing gown, threw it on, dashed into the bathroom, flung some water at his face, grabbed a hand towel and was pulling it around his neck as he hopped down the stairs, his back killing him. He was dimly aware of Oscar reducing the closed kitchen door to splinters in an effort to get out.

He managed to pull the front door open just as another sequence of blows were about to be rained down upon it.

"Sorry Bella, I didn't hear you. I just finished a run and was in the shower."

Hugo had prepared that one as he had descended the stairs.

A stout, but perfectly coiffured and immaculately dressed, woman of advancing years stood on the doorstep. She held in her hand a thick walking stick, the tip of which appeared to have been daubed in white paint. Bella stood for some seconds regarding Hugo and summing up the situation.

"Fun?" was her eventual response.

"What? No, run," he said and laughed.

It sounded hollow even to him.

"Really?" She looked him up and down.

Hugo stood aside and waved Bella into the house. She carried an old-fashioned case, small but jam-packed. He took it from her. Oscar's scratching continued.

"Has the dog been out?" she asked.

"That was next on my list," Hugo explained, mustering a cheery manner. "And the front door, dreadful nuisance – sticking a little after all this rain."

Bella raised an eyebrow.

"It never opens. Which is why I had to prod it with this," she said.

Bella held up her walking stick.

"Ah yes, well never mind, all sorted in a hour or so."

And then, to divert attention from the door, he changed the subject.

"The walking stick is new. Are you feeling a little unsteady?" Hugo asked.

He uttered the latter words with a certain measure of glee, it had to be said.

"Of course not. Steady as a rock. It's my eyes. I'm practically blind and the incompetent hospital would not supply me with a white stick, so I bought a walking stick and painted it," Bella told him.

Bella moved towards the kitchen.

"Your cataract. Yes, can make things tricky. Still they'll be lasering it off in a jiffy won't they? And it's only one eye," said Hugo.

For someone practically blind, Bella studied him intently.

"One eye at the moment but these things have a tendency to spread. Just you wait until you are my age. You'll know what pain and suffering really is."

She wagged the stick at him.

"Hmm. Well how about a cup of coffee? I was just about to make one," he said.

Hugo gestured towards the kitchen.

Bella swept her eyes over him again.

"I rather think you had better finish whatever it was you were doing, while I go and let Oscar out."

She took her suitcase from Hugo, and advanced towards the kitchen door, leaving a clear view through to the large gilt mirror that hung in the hallway.

Hugo glanced in it as he passed. Then froze in horror.

He was wearing Dana's silk, leopard-print dressing gown, and had tucked a pink, fluffy hand-towel into the collar. Several possibilities raced through his mind. One, his mother-in-law now believed him to be a cross-dresser. Two, he was in fact gay – or maybe that was the same thing, he didn't know. And three: he was bone lazy idle, had slept in late while his wife toiled away in the office, abandoning the dog in the kitchen in an act of abject cruelty to suffer starvation and wallow in its own filth. Instead of fixing the door, prepping the car for the road trip and cleaning the house. And had grabbed the first item of clothing that had come to hand, as he stumbled out of bed in a post-alcoholic haze.

Hugo was still weighing up the preferred possibility as he nursed his back ascending the stairs.

Standing with a can of WD40 at the open front door, Hugo breathed a sigh of relief as the postman passed by without a delivery for them. He carried a fat wad of brown envelopes for next door. Hugo allowed himself a small smile of conceitedness. Then stabbed at the nozzle of the spray can and aimed it at the recalcitrant lock on the door. A crunch of gravel on the drive wiped the expression off his face and made him turn around again. Perhaps he had smiled too soon, but no, it was Dana, in his car back from work.

Was it that time already? Hugo looked at his watch. Nearly three o'clock. Crikey, how time flies.

Dana laboured up the steps with some shopping bags as Hugo hopped down to take them.

"How was the completion?" he asked.

"Completed. Finally. Contentious to the last minute. The client wanted money off for a defective balcony repair, but the seller wouldn't budge. In the end he paid the full price. Cash is king as they say, if you have it. Is Mum here?"

"She's in the kitchen. Walked the dog, settled in," Hugo said.

He chose his words carefully as he put the shopping bags down and squirted some more lubricant at the lock.

"Good. I thought you were going to take him into the fields today?" Dana said.

Long experience, Hugo acknowledged, had taught his wife to never take anything at face value.

"I was anxious to fix this, and your mother insisted on taking him out. She's now got a stick by the way."

Hugo polished the lock with a flourish.

"Stick?"

"Yes, a walking stick that she has painted white, because she says she is 'blind'." He took his tools from the step, put them under his arm and then picked up the shopping bags again. "She may be deaf but she's by no means blind, hasn't missed a trick since she's been here."

Dana groaned and walked towards the house.

"Are you ready to go? I'll just get changed," she asked, as she went through the door.

"Yes, yes, all ready. Everything's packed up in your car, I put your bag in as well, and your running shoes."

"Thanks, I'd forgotten those."

"Well you see – I do think of everything," Hugo muttered, with a small measure of triumph.

Dana went up to her bedroom and changed into a pair of black jeans, and a crisp white shirt. She put the Prada boots back on after a second of hesitation. Casual, but stylish. Possibly what Victoria Beckham would wear for the weekend, albeit her own label, if not from Rodeo Drive. Although, she was more likely to be weekending in the Hamptons than Brighton, but the analogy was the same.

The Brighton hotel's a luxury one, not their usual Travelodge budget choice. Trackie bottoms and fleecy top might work in the latter, but not for this weekend. And anyway Dana needed to feel good about herself. Wearing stretch clothing made her feel sloppy, and as she was approaching a decade that scared her, she wanted to steer clear of anything associated with slip-on, stretch, elasticated, comfortable, or even wide-fitting. Otherwise, before she knew it, she would be buying "discreet" pantyliners, American Tan support tights with tummy control and denture fixident.

It was the same with her hair. Dana's was very long. And that worried her too. Should it be long at forty-nine still? Was it decent? Or more to the point, did it look ridiculous? She'd canvassed opinion from her friends, and they all agreed that she looked gorgeous with long hair. And she knew she didn't look forty-nine, so why worry? Well she did. She doubted herself. She doubted others. So she kept her hair long, even though she wanted it a bit shorter now to revive the style. But she was equally terrified of cutting it in case she ended up looking like her mother – all shampoo and set. And that thought brought her back to the moment.

She breathed a sigh of relief. All good so far: Mother installed, front door repaired, dog walked. Now just the kids to collect, and they could be on their way.

Her phone pinged again. Text message. "Missed you at lunch. How about next week? Or dinner? Behave yourself in Brighton…"

Dana smiled. Dinner maybe. Lunch probably.

Dana hugged her mother when she went into the kitchen. She should have gone straight in before she got changed, but sometimes Dana needed a moment to brace herself.

She loved her mother and was very close to her. She didn't know how she would ever cope without her, on many levels. Dana had relied heavily upon her mother emotionally and physically when the children were younger, less so now as Bella got older. And more argumentative. And a little more feisty. Their relationship was sometimes love-hate, particularly now that Bella spent more time with them, and the question of her moving in loomed large. The angst was more the result of the clash between her mother and husband, than any disagreement between Dana and Bella. The latter was no fool and usually had the measure of a man within a few minutes of meeting him.

Bella had not been over the moon when Dana had married Hugo. All mothers think that their daughters can do better, and in Dana's case perhaps she had been right.

Bella had changed too, since Dana's father had died. It had been difficult for them both. Bella and her husband had been inseparable. They had married a little later in life, against family wishes, but had defied the critics and the odds, and had been blissfully happy. Bella had adored her husband, and he in turn had adored Bella. They had lived in total harmony with great love and little kindnesses: if Bella went out, even for a few hours shopping, she would leave notes in the kitchen cupboard telling him she loved him, which he found when he went to make his lunch. They exchanged Valentines cards into their seventies with all the fervour of 16-year-olds.

And then suddenly, one dark dreary night, Dana's father had died. Just like that. One moment sitting on the sofa watching *Antiques Roadshow*, the next moment Bella was clutching the arm of a paramedic pleading with him to do something, as Dana's father sat with his head flung back and his mouth hanging open. Cold and dead. The effects of death seeping into the sofa. The *Antiques Roadshow* flickering in the background.

It had been a massive stroke. He wouldn't have felt a thing they said.

But Dana and Bella had felt it.

Dana had been in London on a rare night out with the girls from work. At a West End show. She didn't know anything about it until Hugo had walked into her office the next morning and looked at her. Without speaking. Then she had known.

No one had told her at the time it had actually happened. They didn't want her to be alone with the knowledge in her hotel room, and it was too late to drive up. So it was left until first thing in the morning. All evening she had enjoyed herself, eating, drinking, at the theatre. Oblivious.

Dana could never watch *Mamma Mia* again.

She felt guilty. She blamed herself.

Her father had been a wonderful man. Kind, gentle, generous, loving. Quiet and even-tempered. Once, when he had been required by Bella to chastise her sister for breaking an ornament and calling her mother a cow, Dana remembered him taking her sister into the sitting room and smacking her. They had heard it loudly through the door. When Dana followed her sister up the stairs afterwards, her sister was smiling. He'd clapped his hands together and slapped his own leg to mimic the chastisement, rather than hurt a hair on his daughter's head.

He was honest though. The odd little white lie, like the

slapping incident, but otherwise Dana's father had been honest, steadfast, truthful. Not in a stiff-upper-lip, honourable gentleman, type of way like Hugo's father – who in truth was no gentleman at all – but in an honest-to-goodness, down-to-earth type of way. A real gentleman.

Bella did not have fond memories, or indeed kind words to say, of Hugo's dearly departed parents. On the surface the two sets of in-laws had got on well together, spending the requisite Christmas holidays and children's birthday events together. But there was resentment there, for the way Hugo's parents had behaved, particularly to Dana, and Bella had never forgotten that Hugo's parents had failed to make the journey from Scotland for her husband's funeral. Hugo had said his mother wasn't up to it, too far to go on such a sad occasion.

Dana's father had died in the September. Hugo's parents had travelled to Madeira for a fortnight's holiday the following November.

And since he had died, Bella had been lost. She put up a good front but it was a defence mechanism, she felt that she had no one to look after her now, so she made up for it by having voracious opinions which she voiced loudly and dogmatically. And she had an opinion on pretty much everything. She also believed that men and women had a particular place in life, not necessarily that women should be in the home – she was more Emmeline Pankhurst than Mrs Beeton – but Bella did believe in men being men, and women being women, in certain respects. She also had a quaint notion that ultimately men should look after women. Which meant Hugo came under microscopic scrutiny in his own house.

Bella was installed at the kitchen table with one of her giant jigsaw puzzles. It amazed Dana how anyone could ever complete them – tiny, intricate pieces, all that detail, all those bits. But Bella was a master at them. Oscar sat happily at her feet, having been pampered and indulged.

"Remember not to give him any extras Mum, okay? He's only supposed to have his own food. The vet said he can't digest anything else properly, and he gets a very bad tummy if he's given scraps, and makes a terrible mess afterwards."

"I do know Dana dear, I have had dogs myself."

Bella pushed another tiny puzzle-piece into position.

Dana frowned as she saw the edge of a packet of biscuits on Bella's lap, and some crumbs around the floor beside Oscar's basket.

Hugo came into the kitchen with his briefcase and plonked it on the table, perilously close to The Jigsaw Puzzle. Oh God, please don't let it disturb the new masterpiece, Dana thought, or worse, please don't let Mother comment on Hugo's work.

"What's in there?" Bella asked without looking up.

"Just my work," Hugo replied.

Oh God.

"Work?"

Oh no.

"Yes, my book actually."

"You still writing that?" Bella asked.

She snapped a sharp-edged piece of the puzzle into place.

"Still?" Hugo said. "It's a relatively new writing project and it's coming along nicely actually Bella. Thank you for asking."

Hugo was handling it well.

"When will it be published then?"

Oh please. Dana looked at Hugo.

"In the fullness of time, one can't rush these things," he replied, smiling at Dana.

"God forbid anyone should try and rush you Hugo, I'm sure you'll take all the time you need."

Bella looked up at him and grinned.

"And so, there we are." Dana clapped her hands together. "All ready to go darling?"

She went to take the briefcase off the table.

Hugo stepped forward and picked it up.

"It's okay Dana I've got hold of the bag," Hugo said.

He swung it in front of him and walked towards the door. Oscar whined in preparation for a display of what the vet called "separation anxiety".

"I heard that," Bella remarked, with a puzzle-piece in mid-air.

"Heard what?" Hugo said.

"Old hag," she said without taking her eyes off the table. "I hear well enough."

"Bella you really do need to look at that brochure we got you. Those devices are almost invisible nowadays," Hugo responded, shaking his head.

"And we are off, bye Mum. I'll give you a ring tonight, remember what we agreed about Oscar."

Dana kissed her mother on the forehead and ushered Hugo out the door.

FIVE

In Dana's car, on the road, safely away. Hugo at the wheel, fiddling with the radio dial.

"Where's Talk Sport?" he asked as he fiddled.

Dana ignored the question.

"You really shouldn't wind her up like that you know. It's not fair. She's old and helpless," Dana said.

"Hardly helpless. And I didn't 'wind her up' as you term it. She's deaf as a post and needs to get a hearing aid. It's no good ignoring the ageing process and pretending it isn't happening. It just means the rest of us suffer. It will happen to all of us, and when it does I for one won't hesitate to get myself kitted out – dentures, hearing aids, walking sticks, scooter thingy if needed." He continued to fiddle with the radio.

Dana stared ahead.

"Mum's been very good to us and I would be grateful if you would remember that. She's helped us out on numerous occasions as you well know."

Hugo winced. Dana could see that he knew it was true. Bella had saved the financial bacon several times.

"She's afraid of being old. And alone. So what if she doesn't want to get a hearing aid? What's the big deal? She just misses a few words now and again, that's all. Ageing is not fun, and it's frightening at eighty-five. I don't blame her. She's right to stick up for herself. No one else does."

Hugo didn't respond.

The radio crackled, but not like in the Chris Rea song, with the soft piano keys in the background. This sounded scratchy and grating.

Eventually Hugo found Talk Sport, but had the good sense to keep the volume low.

Dana peered out of the window at the cars speeding past. A few drops of rain smeared the glass. A steely grey day. Cold. Depressing. She thought about her mother putting up a brave front, and all the jibes that Hugo made. She probably was frightened as she got older, and of losing control of her life. And of being all alone now. Dana felt a pang of guilt for not always taking her side, for often treading a fine line to keep the peace at home. That was wrong. She should stand up for her mother more, make her feel more valued. After all, how much longer would she be here?

Nothing should be taken for granted.

Despite her strong relationship with her mother, and the polar difference between Hugo's late parents and hers, Dana very occasionally felt distant from her. She caught Bella looking at her sometimes, and she just wondered. Wondered whether Bella wouldn't rather be gone too, with her husband, or that – wicked as the thought was – he was here instead of Dana. But of course it was just a wild idea. Her mother may have been thinking nothing of the sort. Might very well have been counting her blessings in having Dana as such a loving daughter, her sister being long since estranged from the family. But a daughter is no substitute for a husband – hadn't Norman Bates said that in *Psycho*, "A mother is a poor substitute for a lover"? The analogy was the same.

And Bella never let it be forgotten how Dana had acquired her name. Just after Dana's birth her father had been forced to rush off overseas when his own mother, Dana's grandmother, had died. Bella was left with a screaming toddler and a new baby, Dana. She was missing her husband desperately – they had never been apart since their wedding day – and so when she went to the Town Hall to register Dana's birth she had been distracted.

Bella had forgotten the *i* in her daughter's name, and so instead of "Diana", her daughter had become "Dana", in the swish of a registrar's pen.

After that the name grew on them, and then it was too late to change it, but Dana always remembered that her father had wanted her named Diana, after the Goddess of War.

As it turned out that was what Dana had become, in a mild domestic way.

Just then Hugo slapped her thigh and turned off the radio, making Dana jump.

"Chin up darling! It's the weekend! Brighton!" he cheered, as he drove on, smiling through the rain.

"Stop it! Mum? Can you tell him to stop shoving his big, fat feet onto my seat?"

Cressida smacked at Alex's muddy trainers as they

inched perilously close to her denim mini skirt and black lacy tights, in the back seat of the car.

"I have to stretch my legs out. I've got a hamstring injury and Mr Stonewall said to keep my legs straight," Alex said in protest.

He was leaning against the car door, as the motorway sped underneath them.

"Don't lean on that door Alex, it's not safe," Hugo commanded from the front.

Alex ignored him.

"Darling do sit up a bit, the door is locked but it's not secure and you could fall out," Dana said, turning around. "And do keep your feet in front of you, we'll be there soon and you can have a swim and stretch a bit in the hotel sauna, that should help your hamstring."

Alex sat back in his seat, away from the door, moved his feet off Cressida, and stretched them out full in front of him, kneeing Hugo in the back as he did so.

When the Welcome to the City of Brighton and Hove sign poked out of the sodden dusk, there was a general sigh of relief in the car. Hugo tapped at the satellite navigation. Christmas present from Dana. Seven years ago.

"Ruddy thing, doesn't give directions to the hotel itself," Hugo said.

He proceeded to fiddle with it until the screen went blank.

"Bugger," he muttered under his breath.

"It doesn't matter, it can't be that difficult to find. It's on the seafront, big hotel, white windows, just along from the Brighton Centre," Dana explained.

"How do you know?" Hugo asked.

"I had lunch there I seem to remember, when the firm came for the Law Society conference last April, at least I think that's the hotel."

"You didn't say you had been there before, it was supposed to be a bit of a surprise," Hugo said.

"I didn't stay there did I? Just had lunch, if it was even at that hotel. You know what these conferences are like, they all blur into one." Dana looked out at the passing buildings.

"I don't know actually, never having been to one, not being a *solicitor*."

He over pronounced the latter word, still a little miffed.

"That's it! There!" Cressida said.

She pointed to an imposing Victorian red stone building. It appeared to run the entire length of one block on the seafront, albeit with the busy road in between it and the grey sea, which seemed to move like lead in the winter weather and dying light. The incessant rain had given way to a fine spray, which in some ways was more of an irritant than the previous deluge. But the Metropole Hotel seemed to be brightly lit within, and a large white conservatory-style canopy projected out onto the pavement to welcome its guests.

Hugo pulled up outside.

"Right, Dana darling, you and Cress get out here, while Alex and I go and park the car and bring the luggage up. No sense in us all getting wet."

"Okay, I think the car park is underground, just around the corner, NCP, if I remember. We'll wait inside. Come on Cressida, quick, the traffic is piling up behind," Dana said.

She grabbed her handbag and got out of the car.

Cressida flapped about in the back, picking up iPods, ear phones, handbag, coat, magazines, drinks bottle, rucksack.

"Come on Cress. I'll get a parking ticket in a minute if you take any longer," Hugo cautioned from the front.

"I'm going as quick as I can Dad, don't fluster me or I'll forget something!"

Cressida finally opened the door of the car and stepped out.

Alex unfolded his legs from under the back of Hugo's seat, knocking him forward onto the steering wheel in the process, and jumped into the now unoccupied passenger seat.

"I'll give the directions to the car park, don't want to get lost," he advised his mother through the open window.

Hugo glared at him, before he manoeuvred the car back into the traffic, to the sound of several horns in protest.

Dana and Cressida hurried up the stairs to the revolving doors of the hotel as the wind freshened behind them.

Ah, this is nice, Dana decided, as they whirled inside to a blur of crystal chandeliers, plush red carpets, marble floors and polished mahogany staircases. A not disagreeable hum of noises met them – *clickety-click* of heels on the marble, chinking of glasses from the adjoining bar, murmur of conversations, laughter, mellow jazz from somewhere wafting through. Very nice. Lots of people milling about: a couple consulting the concierge with a map spread out in front of them, an elegant lady coming down the stairs wearing a full-length, blue velvet coat for an evening out, a woman with a baby in a very smart, very expensive pram – hope she's not next to our room though, an elderly couple on sticks – Dana prayed Cressida hadn't spotted them, and a young couple holding hands. A few people standing at the reception desk. Not overly busy for mid-February, which was probably why Hugo had been able to book it for the price.

"When can we go up to our rooms Mum?" Cressida asked.

She had taken a seat, and was flicking through the music on her iPod again.

"We have to check in first, and Dad has all the details, plus we need our bags, so as soon as they park up and come in."

The doors started to revolve again and Dana, who had also sat down, now stood up. A businessman in a damp suit came in flapping a black umbrella, like a large bat. She sat down again. A couple of minutes passed by. Traffic is jam-packed, Dana thought. Friday after all.

A pretty young woman with long, dark hair glanced at her from behind the reception desk. Dana smiled.

The side door opened slightly and the concierge rushed forward to open it further, Dana stood up again. A large woman and a small child bustled in – also wet. Dana stayed standing.

Another couple came in and went up to the reception desk. Checked in. Walked off with their keys.

"What's taking them so long?" Cressida asked unplugging her earphones.

"Oh you know, it's rush hour and wet. Road is busy, they're probably having trouble finding a parking space."

"I know Dad you mean."

A waiter came over to them and asked if they needed anything. Dana was tempted to ask for a G & T, but resisted. She thanked him and explained they were waiting to check in. The waiter pointed to the reception desk, and the dark-haired receptionist looked up. Dana thanked him again and said she was waiting for her husband to park the car.

The waiter bustled off. A few more people came down the stairs for evenings out. The music seemed to get a little louder. Cressida shifted position in her chair. The revolving doors circled again but no one came through them.

Cressida put her earphones back in.

Dana looked at her watch.

The woman behind the reception desk looked over at them again.

No sign of Hugo. Or the bags. Or Alex.

Dana relaxed her shoulders. Rotated her neck. Stretched her arms. It's only been twenty or twenty-five minutes. Not long in this weather. I am not going to get stressed or upset. She closed her eyes for a moment. Let the sounds wash over her, the ambience. She opened them again. Allowed herself to take in the luxurious surroundings. The detailed cornicing on the ceiling, the elaborate plasterwork motifs on the walls above the wood panelling. The mirror-like shine on the floor. The magnificent floral arrangement of white lilies and lush green vegetation on the central table in the entrance. The smart commissionaire uniform of the concierge, the bright buttons. The blue tailored suits of the receptionists.

The dark-haired girl caught her eye again. She was

slim and very well endowed. Her suit jacket was just a tad too tight and her skirt probably an inch too short if Dana was honest, or bitchy, or both. Whatever.

Sod it! Where was Hugo? Lost on the one way system no doubt.

A gust of wind swept through reception as the revolving doors whirled around, and someone carrying an enormous bunch of flowers emerged. Dana looked away. Where the fuck is Hugo?

The person with the flowers advanced towards her and, surprise! Hugo was revealed behind a forest of peonies, carnations, lilies, ferns, gypsophila, roses, tulips and miniature cabbages.

"Sorry darling, but we ran around like mad things after parking the car looking for a florist to surprise you. Hope we weren't too long."

Hugo gave her a peck on the cheek, and Dana was shocked, not so much at the size of the bouquet, but at the fact that Hugo's late arrival was not due to him mucking up the parking or getting lost.

Alex brought up the rear and nodded in affirmation.

"I told Dad to go for the big bunch, splurge, it's Mum's birthday," Alex said.

Hugo glared at him.

Then Dana overheard him say to Cressida, "Found a couple of wicked looking bars, literally round the corner, while the old man was paying for the flowers, think I'll check them out in a bit."

Cressida rolled her eyes at the bar comment, and her mother frowned, hoping it was a joke.

Dana smelled the flowers and smiled in spite of herself, the thought was very nice, and she now felt guilty as hell for thinking the worst.

"They're gorgeous, thank you darling," she said to Hugo. And then to Alex, "Thanks sweetheart, that's very thoughtful of you."

Mind you, she could imagine Hugo searching out the smallest bunch, or maybe a little posy in a fancy bag, or even haggling for a discount at the end of the day's trading. Alex though, always stepped up to the mark, only the best for his mum. So like her own father. She sighed.

"Right, well we'd better get checked in now or I'll be arrested for casing the place. Where are the other bags?" Dana asked Hugo

"Just outside the door, I wanted to make an entrance with those." He gestured to the flowers.

"You hold them for a minute," Dana said, handing the bouquet to Cressida. And then turning to Alex, "Can you get the other bags darling, while Dad and I check in?"

Hugo and Dana approached the reception desk and the pretty, dark-haired receptionist looked up from her computer.

"We'd like to check in please," Hugo said, presenting his email confirmation and booking reference.

The receptionist smiled at Dana.

"Of course, welcome back to The Metropole Hotel," she said, swishing her hair over her shoulder.

Dana froze. Her mind went blank and then little white lights flashed through her head. She tried desperately to process her thoughts.

Hugo looked at her, the receptionist continued to smile. Dana thought. No, wait a minute. We only had lunch here, nothing else. It was just lunch. She can't possibly remember me.

"Actually this is our first time staying in this hotel," Dana replied.

She tried to sound in command, but the words wobbled a bit.

The receptionist smiled again.

"*Oui* of course, but I see you standing there with your so pretty daughter for so long, and so I think you gets to know ze hotel so well by now!" the receptionist gushed forth in a frothy lather of foreign twangs and mispronounced syllables, and swished her mane of black hair over her shoulder again as she did so.

So sweet of her to point out how pretty Cressida was and to make the daughter point, Dana thought. An older woman, or more likely man, would have attempted a joke about a sister instead of a daughter. Oh, and of course the comment about waiting a long time was totally lost on Hugo, since its implication seemed to be that Dana was loitering, rather than waiting for someone who was late.

Dana forced a smile in reply while the receptionist took Hugo's booking reference.

"Ah! Ze Mister Hugo! Ze writer!" Another frothy lather of high pitched twangs.

"Veronique!" Hugo gushed from the other side of the desk.

What the fuck? What's going on here? Dana stood with a side-long glance and her head tilted, looking from one to the other of them, as Hugo and Veronique exchanged greetings, smiles and gushes. Dana waited for an explanation. Only the fact that other people were standing in the queue, and common decency, forced Dana to adopt a half-smile of delight and surprise. She felt only one of those emotions.

When Hugo was done shaking Veronique's hand and botching a greeting in a foreign language, he turned to Dana.

"Darling, this is Veronique! Who kindly took my booking when I called to reserve the rooms. Veronique is from France, from Provence to be precise."

Veronique beamed brightly at this.

"And we have had long discussions about ze olive oil industry there and ze Marseille soap business and all sorts," she twanged.

Hugo beamed back at her.

Dana still stood rooted to the spot, but was forced to utter an, "Ah, I see, really?" in response.

"*Oui*. And ze Mr Hugo tells me about his book, and about his importation plans for ze oil and ze soap."

Veronique now beamed at Dana, but not quite as brightly.

"Early days yet, though early days. Still researching the project," he said, laughing.

Hugo looked nervously at Dana.

Project? Dana thought. So now it's a Project. Right. Fine. This is all lovely, but can we get checked in? Dana was almost grinding her teeth.

"That's wonderful and fascinating," Dana said as she turned to face Hugo. "Darling, Alex and Cress are getting restless and probably hungry."

Hugo smiled again and looked back at Veronique.

"We will talk at length about all the possibilities for your wonderful natural resources later. For now the children are a little tired and hungry," he explained.

Children? Dana queried silently. Alex is practically a man and Cressida looks about twenty-five dressed like that. Then the realisation dawned. *Children* made Hugo look younger.

"But of course, you have ze credit card?" Veronique beamed.

Veronique was all efficiency as she tapped away at her computer, completing the check in process.

Hugo opened his wallet and briefly looked at Dana, who averted her eyes at once. Don't look at me darling, this was your idea. You deal with it. He handed over his credit card with an almost imperceptible tremor. Veronique nipped it from him and swished it into her machine, and handed it back to Hugo with a flourish. Hugo, Dana noticed, let out a little breath through pursed lips.

"How many keys for ze rooms?" Veronique asked.

"Just two each. *Merci beaucoup!*" Hugo said.

He was in jovial mood now that the payment had gone through.

"Actually we will have two keys for our room, but three for the *children's* room please," Dana said, countermanding.

She placed the emphasis upon the word "children" for Hugo's benefit.

Veronique tapped away again.

"It really is sensible to be able to get into that room if we need to," Dana explained to Hugo, who was still beaming at Veronique.

The latter handed over the keys and wished them a pleasant stay.

"*Adieu* and *bonsoir!*" Hugo said, as he shook her hand for the second time.

Dana grabbed the keys and walked towards the kids –

Alex had procured a large luggage trolley, with a gold domed top, upon which he had piled the bags, rucksacks, coats, running kit and himself.

"I thought you were about to leap over the reception desk and kiss her on both cheeks at one point," Dana told him.

"Now darling, no need for jealousy, she's just doing her job." Hugo patted Dana's arm.

Dana suppressed a laugh.

Jealous?

Hardly.

Irritated?

Highly.

SIX

Gosh, that's jolly nice, Hugo thought, when he opened the door to their room, 422, and walked inside. More of a mini-suite than a mere room. Cosy little sitting room with a plush sofa decorated in muted tones, through to a huge bedroom with a super king-size bed and elaborate padded headboard, walnut wardrobes, and two full-length casement windows overlooking the seafront. Now dark of course, but would look lovely in the morning with the sunlight streaming through.

He checked out the bathroom, all grey marble and curved edges. He made careful note of the bathtub – more than enough room for two. And his and hers sinks. Excellent.

Back in the sitting area Hugo made a reconnaissance of the mini-bar.

"Bravo. Any single malts?" he asked, as he fiddled about with the miniature bottles.

"Excellent again," he confirmed when he located an Old Poultney bottle.

Still congratulating himself on the relative splendour of

the hotel accommodation – Dana will be pleased with him he thought – he took up a glass tumbler, tossed in a few rocks of ice from the silver-plated bucket on the shelf, and was just unscrewing the cap of the whisky bottle when he heard an almighty scream from the adjoining room, 421.

Cressida.

He dropped the bottle and ran out, glass still in hand.

Alex was lying across one of the two double beds in the adjoining room looking at his phone, while Cressida sat in floods of tears on the sofa being consoled by Dana, who had both her arms wrapped around her.

"What the bloody hell is wrong now? Sounded like you had discovered a body in here. I sincerely hope it's none of that spider nonsense again, all you have to do is *shoo* them away with a paper or magazine or whatever. I was just about to relax with a drink." Hugo stood on the threshold of the doorway.

All eyes turned on him. For a moment or two he was puzzled, and as all eyes continued to bore into him he began to feel like a leper who had left the colony and wandered into the town.

"What?" he asked.

Dana pointed to the luggage trolley. Cressida continued to be wracked with sobs. Alex tapped away at his phone.

"What's up?" he said again.

Dana shook her head and clicked her fingers at the trolley.

"Has Alex run over her foot or something?" Hugo asked in irritation. "Alex? What have you done now?"

A trip to A & E would be highly inconvenient, Hugo

thought as he glanced at his empty glass.

Alex ignored him and stretched out on the bed.

"There!" Dana said and pointed again to the trolley.

"The trolley?" Hugo asked her.

Cressida wailed on the sofa.

"The luggage!" Dana shouted.

Hugo's irritation was growing.

"What about it? I cannot for the life of me understand what all this fuss is about, or, more to the point, what it has to do with me. Can't a man have a quiet drink in peace? I was just about to pour—"

And then the penny dropped. Hugo closed his mouth mid-sentence. Pursed his lips. Braced himself. He didn't think he had, but it was just conceivable. Just. But let's make certain, he thought.

"How could you Hugo?" Dana accused while stroking Cressida's hair.

"Well, look, let's not jump to any conclusions here, okay? It is probably in the car still, I'll go and have a look." And buy some thinking time, Hugo decided.

"Nah, it's not. We brought all the stuff up. Car was empty, I checked under the seats and the boot," Alex muttered from the bed.

Hugo glared at him.

"So what exactly is she going to wear Hugo?" Dana asked him.

Hugo spread his hands, then wrung them. Cressida started a fresh round of wailing.

"Well not the stuff in the suitcase that Dad left hidden behind the ottoman in the hall at home, that's for sure," Alex muttered again from the bed.

"Yes thank you for that overwhelmingly helpful

contribution to the discussion Alex," Hugo said.

Judas Iscariot himself could not have felt, at that moment, less worthy than Hugo.

Dana stood up. She took Alex's rucksack off the luggage trolley and threw it on his bed beside him. She then pushed the trolley towards Hugo.

"Oh there's no discussion Hugo, I can assure you. Only action, which goes as follows – you take our luggage to our room, pick up your wallet and meet Cressida and I downstairs in the hotel boutique where the essentials for this evening will be bought including, but not limited to, nightwear, underwear, swimwear, a dress and toiletries." Dana's voice was firm and resolute.

"Essentials? Sounds more like what was actually packed in that suitcase!" Hugo protested.

"Yes. To tide her over," his wife continued.

Cressida looked up from the sofa. Tear-stained and ruffled.

"*Tide her over?*" Hugo queried, but he felt himself fading.

"Indeed. Tide her over in the sense that tomorrow morning you will rectify the catastrophe by taking her shopping to replace everything that was left behind."

Dana swept out of the room.

Cressida straightened her hair a little, sniffed and stood up.

"Bloody hell! It's like that film with Julia Roberts where she goes shopping in Beverly Hills at all those fancy shops with Richard Gere's credit card!" Alex whooped from the bed and then fell about in hysterics.

Cressida smiled.

Hugo made straight for the mini-bar, and the unopened miniature bottle of whisky.

* * *

To his credit, Hugo had not uttered another word of protest in the hotel boutique, Dana reflected, as she floated in the enormous marble bath of their hotel mini-suite. Instead, he had stood there stoically, while Dana coaxed Cressida into trying on several outfits in the hope that one of them might meet her strict teenage code of suitability, for this evening at least. All but one item was rejected. They were all either too short, or too long, or too "gigantic" – even at a size eight – or too plain, or too frilly, or too old, or too young. Eventually, a plain, black strappy vest-top had meet Cressida's exacting standards, some forty-five minutes after they had entered the little shop.

And of course it had been the first one tried on, and not the latter five, that she had reluctantly agreed to wear. In the end the financial damage hadn't been too bad: a pair of knickers, some black tights, the little top and a speedo swimsuit – the last item deemed suitable only because Cressida had said it would be entirely covered by a towel in the spa in any case.

Hugo had handed over his credit card without a word, although Dana had detected a waft of distillery fumes as he did so.

She almost, but not quite, felt sorry for him.

Cressida meanwhile had rallied remarkably, aided very nicely by the fact that Hugo had also bought her a pretty, sparkly, kitten-pendant necklace that she had spotted in one of the display cabinets near reception.

Damage limitation, some bridges built, nerves soothed, major family fiasco averted.

Oh dear God, why can't it all be different? Dana wrung the soft white flannel out in the warm water, folded it into an oblong sausage and laid it over her eyes, as she sank back into the water. Why can't we be like other people?

She thought about a family she had observed during her vigil in the foyer earlier. A tall, handsome, dark-haired man, in a perfectly tailored suit, had clicked his fingers at the concierge to hold open the door for his wife, while he carried their child in his arms. He had guided his wife to a comfortable seat and placed the child in her lap, then he masterfully strode up to the reception desk and dealt with the formalities. Then clicked his fingers again and the concierge had sprung forward with the luggage and escorted them all to the lift.

Dana stretched her big toe towards the tap, it didn't quite reach. I bet he had champagne on ice in the bedroom too, and a baby sitter organised. She probably floated down to the spa for a facial and a massage, floated back up and slipped into a sexy dress. And then they'd gone to dinner, where he'd picked out an expensive bottle of wine, and only let the sommelier leave the table when he'd tasted it, smelled the cork, and checked that the temperature was correct. Hugo always waved away the suggestion that he should taste the wine first, probably because it usually cost £9.95 a bottle.

Dana ran the hot tap again. Turned it off. Sank back down into the now diminishing bubbles. And then after the tall, handsome, dark-haired man had paid the bill with a roll of notes and a large tip, and they had finished their digestivos in the lounge, the man would have taken her hand, kissed it and with his own hand just brushing her lower back, guided her towards the lifts. And once back in their room, with the sheer lace curtains fluttering gently on the midnight breeze through the open window, the man would have undressed her and she would have yielded to him as he gently, but very firmly, pressed himself into her while she groaned in ecstasy.

Dana could almost feel the slightly rough, but very sexy, stubble of the handsome man's chin on her face, and feel the soft sweet breath that came from his parted lips, as she lay back with her eyes closed. She parted her own lips in anticipation.

A sharp rap at the bathroom door startled her as she coughed up the frothy bubbles she had swallowed, and splashed water over the top of the bath in her rush to sit up.

"Dana? Darling?" a voice called from the other side of the door.

Hugo. Hesitant, apologetic but with an underlying, feeling-sorry-for-myself air. A bit like Oscar when he'd cocked a leg against the kitchen dresser and been told off.

At least he knows better than to try the door handle.

"Yes?" she replied.

"The restaurant downstairs confirmed the table for eight thirty, so if you like we can have a drink in the bar first?"

"Yes, fine."

"The kids are ready when you are," he ventured.

Dana sat back in the bath again. Looked at her watch.

"Fine. I'll be out in a bit."

"Okay. Shall we meet you down there?"

"Yes. Whatever. That's fine."

She heard Hugo's retreating footsteps. She shivered. The bath had gone a little cool. Outside the rain still smeared the windows, pitch black now and the wind had risen.

Dana tried to conjure up the image of the dark-haired, handsome, commanding, masterful man again. But he'd gone, faded back into the mists of her desperate imagination. The actual man she had seen down in reception had probably not been that good looking in reality, very likely had a bit of a paunch when he was stripped down to his underpants, and he was probably bickering with his wife in their own room now. Most of what we imagine other people have is often just a fantasy. The grass is not really greener, just a different variety.

Dana sighed at the thought of having to get out of the bath, get dried, slap on body lotion, put on makeup, get dressed, all that effort. She was tired, it had been a long day.

She needed the toilet though, so would have to get out now.

Oh sod it, she thought. It's my bath and I'll pee in it if I want to.

She waited thirty seconds more while she did just that.

Wearing the black, lace-edged Zara dress, and just as she was spraying a cascade of Chanel No 5 over the ensemble, Dana's phone pinged. I really must set it to silent for the weekend, she decided. She slipped on her Karen Millen chrome-heeled, sling-backs, and checked her appearance in the full-length mirror by the door, before looking at her new text message.

"Hey, hi gorgeous. How's sexy Brighton?" the message asked.

Dana smiled and looked again in the mirror. If she

squinted hard enough she could just imagine that tall, dark man behind her, maybe with an arm about to encircle her waist.

She tapped in a reply, "Hardly sexy with two moody teenagers in tow."

Straight away a reply came back, "But the romantic hotel, the sea breeze, the candle-lit dinners..."

Dana considered a response, but just then there was another sharp rap at the door.

"Jesus will you give me a minute? I said I would see you in the bloody bar!" she shouted, as she yanked the door open.

A squat, grey-haired woman in a white apron, holding a stack of towels, confronted her in wide-eyed surprise.

"Oh gosh. I'm ever so sorry. I thought you were my husband."

Dana tried to sound apologetic, but there was no getting away from the fact that she had sworn and shouted. What kind of wife must she appear to be? Talking like that.

"Would you like your room turned down for the night?" the woman asked with temerity, and then added, perhaps wisely, "I can come back later if that's better?"

"No, no. That's absolutely fine, thank you so much, I was just going out. Sorry again for my mistake."

Dana smiled very sweetly, held the door open for the woman, and then made her way down the corridor, silently cursing the sender of the text message for always distracting her. And causing her to say and do things that she didn't mean.

SEVEN

Cressida felt fat. No – not *felt* fat – she *was* fat. And ugly. I should be sitting here with a bin bag over my head, she thought as she looked around the posh cocktail bar. I'm the only girl in here who looks terrible. She eyed a small, strawberry blonde-haired woman sitting on a bar stool next to a tall man. The woman was wearing a short silver sequin skirt and a silk blouse with a pussy-cat bow. Her hair was freshly blow-dried. She made Cressida feel like Mrs Wrexham at school. Her housemistress was very old, at least forty – Cressida couldn't even understand how people were allowed to continue to work into such senility. And she matched her age year-for-stone in weight, with salt and pepper grey hair cut like a monk and a huge mole on her inner thigh, to which they were subjected in the sports hall where she insisted upon wearing very snug shorts.

And now here she sat, in this horrible sack-like, black top that Mum had made her buy, and her denim mini skirt, which had only been meant for shopping and arriving in, and not her black skater dress from River

Island that she was going to wear with her Kurt Geiger platform sandals. And to make it all a thousand times worse, Mum didn't even have any hair straighteners with her! How could she function on any meaningful level without hair straighteners? Cressida had tried to put her hair in the trouser press in the room, but found she couldn't close the metal lever with her head in the way. Then she had considered requesting an iron and ironing board from reception, but then it was too late because Dad was stressing and hassling them at the door.

At least she had her green lipstick on. And silver eyeliner. That helped to mitigate the disaster a little bit. But she still looked fat. And ugly. Tomorrow she would have to spend most of the day shopping to try and sort the mess out, but for tonight she would definitely not be eating. Jesus no. And what? Wake up even fatter? Be no point in shopping for anything then.

Cressida surveyed her surroundings. They were sitting on cold, uncomfortable, knackered sofas in a window bay, with some bloke playing a big piano nearby. Alex had immediately taken a seat at the bar when they had come in, but Dad had grabbed his arm and pushed him over to the sofas. There had been a hard stare between them, Cressida had noted.

Alex – thinks he's such a cool dude. They wouldn't serve him anyway without ID. Says he has some he borrowed from his mate, but Cressida thought that was BS.

Yes, Cressida decided, everyone in there was beautiful and thin. Except, of course, her. She sighed. She watched in amusement as an old man of at least fifty tried to chat up a woman in hot pants at a nearby table. He had leaned over from his own table and was explaining all the different cocktails. The woman in hot pants wasn't even pretending to be polite but he still didn't get it. Hope she whacks him one in a minute. That'll teach him.

Alex was pretending to take an interest in the non-alcoholic cocktails that their father was reading out from the menu, but Cressida wasn't fooled. That's only so he can try and wangle a beer by being uber polite, she decided. But it gave her an idea.

"Daddy?" Cressida said.

Cressida only ever used that word when she wanted something she thought it highly unlikely she would get.

Hugo smiled. He was on his second large malt from the bar. Cressida had also noted this fact.

"Yes sweetheart?"

"Daddy, do you think I could have a small glass of wine?"

Alex smirked at her and shook his head.

Hugo took a sip of his malt and smacked his lips while considering.

"Perhaps with dinner darling, but for now why not choose one of the sophisticated non-alcoholic cocktails from the list? You are a little too young to be drinking wine in a cocktail bar."

Alex laughed.

"She drinks vodka at Emma's so I wouldn't worry about wine," he informed Hugo.

Cressida scowled at him.

Hugo shook his head.

"I doubt that very much. Emma's parents wouldn't hear of it and Emma is such a sensible girl," Hugo said, smiling.

Alex and Cressida exchanged a look. Shut up Alex, Cressida thought, and then her look conveyed another message – we both know what tales I could tell too.

"Dad?" Now it was Alex's turn to try.

"Yes son?"

Ha! Cressida thought, Dad's tone says it all. He's called him "son", so he's already wise to what he's going to say next.

"Could I have a beer please?" Alex was obviously mustering all the respect he could summon.

Hugo shifted in his chair. "You can have a shandy. For now."

Hugo caught the waiter's eye. The latter came over to their table.

"Yes sir?"

The waiter stood with his tray poised in one hand.

"We would like a lager shandy—"

"Ale shandy," Alex cut in.

Hugo gave him a look.

"An ale shandy," Hugo continued, "a Pussyfoot non-alcoholic cocktail, and another Highland Park please."

"Certainly sir, shall I put it on your tab?" the waiter asked.

"Yes, yes on the tab. Thanks." Hugo waved a casual arm.

Pussyfoot! How embarrassing. Sophisticated? For children maybe. Cressida sat and sulked. Alex, she noted, smirked. Why? What's he up to?

While they waited for their drinks to come, Alex got his phone out and Hugo told him to put it away because it was rude, and anyway they should be talking while waiting for Mum, and not "playing with those infernal contraptions" as Dad had said.

"So what shall we do first thing tomor—" Hugo was in mid-sentence, when he suddenly jumped up as some young woman with dark hair touched him on the arm.

"Ze Mister Hugo!" the woman said in a foreign accent.

"Ah *bonsoir* Veronique!" Hugo replied.

Cressida sat and watched with her mouth open as Hugo proceeded to kiss this woman on both cheeks.

Alex looked at Cressida.

"What the fuck?" he mouthed.

Shit! Cressida thought. Who's this? She watched as Hugo chatted animatedly to the woman who, Cressida observed, couldn't have been much older than herself.

Hugo took a sip of his whisky during their convivial exchange of mispronounced French words by Hugo, and "ze this" and "ze that" by her. Cressida also observed that her father was probably encouraged in all this by virtue of the number of whiskies he had consumed.

Where's Mum? Cressida thought and looked around in a panic.

Alex was by now finding the exchange hysterical, the more so the longer it went on. Cressida, by comparison, was getting more and more embarrassed.

As Alex fought hard to subdue his laughter, Cressida kicked him under the table.

"Stop it!" she mouthed to him.

At some point – it seemed like hours to Cressida but was probably just minutes – her father appeared to realise that he hadn't introduced what Alex had already termed in a whisper, "totty", to Cressida, and he now turned to them.

"Children, this is Veronique, she is French and she

comes from Provence which is where I may be doing some business shortly."

Hugo stood smiling benignly at them.

Cressida knew she was French because Cressida was the best in her class at that language, and the entire family deferred to her during their holidays, especially when they got lost on French roads – her father having thrown the Sat Nav out of the car window in one particularly vicious exchange with her mother about which way to go to the campsite. It had been Cressida who had pointed out that *sur la droite* meant "on the right", and *à gauche* "on the left", and not vice versa.

Alex and she muttered a "hello" and a "hi", and then the waiter arrived with their drinks, and Veronique said her goodbyes. Fortunately Dad didn't kiss her again. That would have been one foreign exchange too many.

"Are you having an affair Dad?" Alex asked innocently.

Only it wasn't innocent as he and Cressida very well knew.

Hugo reddened visibly and took a long pull on his drink before answering.

"Don't be preposterous! That young lady works here and your mother and I exchanged a few words earlier about where she lives. You really do say the most absurd things Alex."

Alex in turn took a long pull on his own drink and grimaced. Not enough booze in it, Cressida suspected.

"Sorry," he said.

He's not in the least sorry, Cressida thought.

"Only you did look – well, very *friendly*," Alex continued.

"The French are a demonstrative race. It is customary

to exchange greetings in such a way. You should know that, we have been there often enough," Hugo said. Still red.

Cressida removed the little paper umbrella from her cocktail and took a sip. She now grimaced. Definitely be better with vodka in it.

"Yeah I know that. But we're not in France are we? We're in Brighton," Alex said, as he smirked behind the frothy head of his shandy.

Dana felt very sophisticated and, if she was honest, more than a little attractive as she *click-clicked* in her high heels through the foyer towards the bar. It was hard work, but all that running − even in the bleak, insipid winter months and the damp, cold weather − kept her slim, toned and frankly looking ten years younger than she was. Yes, definitely worth it, she thought as she looked down at her firm thighs and sculpted calves. The latter, in Dana's opinion, being very important. Most women had legs like pencils from the back − no definition to the calf, just straight up and down. And calves, as someone told her recently in a text message, were very sexy.

In fact, quite a few people admired Dana's legs. She had been shocked, and secretly flattered, once when a work colleague had said to her at the Christmas do, "I just wanted to tell you that you have absolutely gorgeous legs and they are the sexiest I have ever seen." The colleague was a woman, she was not gay and she was not drunk. It took Dana a while to figure it out.

Exercise was, though, important to her on a much deeper level. Yes, it was a form of therapy if people wanted to put it like that, and exercise helped promote positivity: lift the mood, released endorphins that could help keep depression at bay and so on. But for Dana, apart from the obvious physical benefits, it was a form of control. This was something she could do entirely on her own terms. If it was pissing rain, or howling wind or sleet and ice or even a blisteringly hot summer's day – Dana chose to step out in it in her running shoes and to put her body through a kind of torture. It was her choice. It was something within her control, that had nothing to do with keeping anyone happy, or fulfilling any duties or obligations. Other than to herself. And that control, in turn, led to another form of control over her physical body and her emotions. It made her feel good in every respect.

It was about having control of her own life. It was about feeling free.

People never understood that. Her mother told her to have a lie-in, or make a cup of tea, instead of going running, if Dana was feeling stressed or tired. But her mother just didn't understand that running was better than eight hours in bed or any amount of tea. Hugo thought it was all about "maintaining her curves" as he put it, and always suggested Dana should join a pilates or aerobics class – who still used that latter term after the 80s? – rather than go out running in the rain.

Camilla thought it was bonkers, all that huffing and puffing and sweating, and had offered Dana a hack through her woodlands on one of her horses. Superficially the latter suggestion might have been the most comical, but ironically Camilla was actually closer to the mark than one might have thought. Riding – although of no interest to Dana – was probably another form of control and escape to Camilla. And Dana could well understand any wife wanting to get as far into the woods as possible on her own when she had a husband like Toffee Nosed Tristram.

So, Dana decided, tomorrow would be a running day just like any other, in fact even more important on a birthday. To prove I still have it, she confirmed.

Now, let's try and relax, enjoy and have a nice drink. Maybe a Martini. With an olive. Very James Bond. And that immediately set her train of thought on the dark, handsome stranger of her earlier day-dreams.

A soothing melody of mellow piano music drifted towards her as Dana spotted her family sitting on deep, comfortable, leather Chesterfields near the window. She raised her hand in greeting. Hugo grinned and waved back a cheery reply. Alex was smiling with a beer in hand, and Cressida was sipping something that had fruit on the top, so that was a dent in the food issue made. They all looked happy. Thank God.

"So what fun and games have I been missing then?" Dana pecked Alex, then Cressida, and lastly Hugo on the cheek and sat down.

"Nothing really darling, just been planning what to do tomorrow and in what order," Hugo said, as he handed her the cocktail drinks menu.

Dana took the menu, but without looking said, "I think I will have a vodka Martini, shaken not stirred! Ha!" She laughed. "Isn't that what James Bond says?"

"Spot on," Hugo agreed and waved the waiter back over.

"So you got a beer then?" Dana asked Alex while smiling at Hugo.

"Shandy," Alex said. Sulking.

"Ah," Dana replied and smiled in sympathy.

"We don't want to get into bad habits, now do we?" Hugo remarked.

"But wine with dinner though!" Dana patted Alex's hand.

"Dad's been entertaining his new best friend, haven't you Dad?" Alex said, looking at Cressida who smiled back at him.

Dana shook her head, and looked at Hugo in anticipation of an explanation.

"Don't be silly, she's not my 'new best friend'." Hugo turned to Dana. "Alex is referring to Veronique whom we both met earlier. She popped by and I introduced her to the children."

Hugo finished his whisky.

Dana caught the use of the word *children* again, and could well imagine the reception Miss France got when she popped by. Why were men such fools? Were they really that blind that they couldn't see what everyone else could? They pull in their stomachs, puff out their chests, smooth back their hair, and exude charm from every pore whenever an attractive, younger, unattainable woman crosses their radar. She'd seen even the most committed husbands perk up at the sight of a dolly bird. Now she sounded like her mother. But it was true. It was what kept – for the most part – the matrimonial department at her law firm very busy. And one might have thought that Hugo had learned that hard lesson from his father, whose friendship with their music teacher had extended beyond a mutual appreciation of Chopin.

According to Hugo's sister, with whom they were now

also estranged, Hugo's father had been energetic in all areas of his life. During a rare, slightly tipsy, tete-a-tete at Dana's wedding, Hugo's sister had revealed that their father, a prolific genteel action man: patron of the arts, workaholic, theatregoer, dinner party thrower, countryside rambler, bridge player – had found that his energies were not entirely spent in completing the renovation of The Old Rectory.

Neither were they matched by his long suffering, albeit difficult wife, in the bedroom, according to Hugo's sister.

And when they enjoyed an affluent patch in their lives – promotion at the bank, small bonus allowing the renovations to be completed with a flourish – Hugo's father took a fancy to installing a music room in the The Old Rectory. It was decked out with a grand piano, flutes, harp, cello and Stradivarius violins. The latter were an investment, as Hugo's father had an eye for antiques and beautiful things. And which latter his father insisted the children learn to play.

And so Fräulein Reichenbach was installed. At least part-time. To teach the children to play and to prepare them for their examinations.

Unfortunately for all concerned, most particularly the Fräulein since she ultimately lost her employment, Hugo's father also had an eye for a well proportioned – if slightly stocky – Bavarian piece of skirt, who, it might be added, wasted no time in reciprocating the attention.

It was eventually revealed, when Hugo's mother discovered a picnic hamper, rugs and empty champagne bottle in the boot of the car upon her husband's return from a "bridge" game. The pheasant pie in the hamper had been reduced to mere crumbs – they certainly worked up an appetite – and the rugs were covered in grass and twigs. And oh yes, Hugo's sister had continued, a certain pharmacy item, rudimentary in nature – this was the sixties – had been concealed under the spare wheel. It had been used. Hugo's father was many things, but a litter bug was not one of them.

The fact that the children never seemed to progress beyond chalking their bows, also lent some weight to the notion that the Fräulein's attention to the music lessons was somewhat distracted.

Curiously though, apart from "throwing" Hugo's father out of the house on discovering the affair – which consisted of a token attempt at packing a small suitcase of a few of his clothes and then pushing it out of the bedroom window, which he retrieved, carried back into the house and unpacked – Hugo's mother did nothing more about it.

And the matter was never raised again.

There was no lingering elephant in the room, no resentment – at least not from Hugo's mother – no bitterness, no accusations. It seemed not to make the slightest difference to anything. And according to Hugo's sister, the Anglo-German Alliance had not been the only one.

Dana later worked out why. Hugo's mother was not being stoic, or putting up with it for the children's sake, or even turning a blind eye over one slip-up. Neither was she being Victorian about the matter and accepting that men will be men – as some might have supposed a woman of her era would have believed.

It was simply that Hugo's mother had been lazy. And selfish. She didn't want the burden of a husband, and all that "business in the bedroom", as she once put it. She had never wanted the children either. It was Hugo's father who had insisted on having a family. Left to her own devices, Hugo's mother would have been perfectly happy spending her days watching television and eating cakes. She had once remarked to Dana, after Hugo had brought her breakfast in bed when staying at their house on holiday, "I'm fond of him, you know." It struck Dana that a mother, at the very least, loved a son. One was fond of one's acquaintances or one's cat. But one *loved* one's children.

Initially Dana had been tempted to feel sorry for Hugo's mother, but as she got to know her better she realised the empathy had been misplaced. Then Dana had considered whether Hugo's father was the one who had suffered: a difficult wife – cold and unemotional – could he be blamed for seeking comfort elsewhere? The reality was that they were both selfish, unpleasant, self-centred people who deserved each other to the bitter end. Which was exactly what they got.

The question Dana now asked herself was: like father, like son?

Or did Dana herself have more in common with her late father-in-law than even she would admit?

Despite outward appearances and a certain Cockney Barrow Boy persona – adopted from an appreciation of Guy Ritchie's films: *Lock Stock and Two Smoking Barrels* in particular – and then adapted to suit his own ends, Alex was very much at home with fine dining. And the etiquette required – no mean feat when faced with four sets of matching cutlery and several wine glasses – to carry if off. Apart from the formal House Dinners at school, Alex had made careful study and observation of the correct manner in which to conduct himself at events, and knew not only which side to pass the port, but what would be expected at a white tie, let alone a black tie, dinner. His knowledge in such matters would now put a large percentage of the names in *Debrett's Peerage* to shame.

But there was method to his madness. On two counts. First he rather fancied himself as a member of an organisation such as The Bullingdon Club, popularised in the film *The Riot Club* and infamous now with the likes of jolly old Boris and our dear leader Dave, when he got to university. It was one of the things he relished about the prospect of Oxford or Cambridge, or indeed even a red-brick, where he planned to start his own version of the club. His interest in such institutions was simple – booze, and lots of it.

The second count was women. They loved a bit of posh. Or so he believed.

So when in the company of girls who never used the word "gosh" but often used the word "fuck", he would be all *Brideshead Revisited* and ever so dapper.

It also worked the other way – hence the Guy Ritchie cockney rebel approach. So with girls who often used the word "gosh" as well as the word "fuck", he would ditch the manners and become a bit of rough.

At least that was his plan. In truth he hadn't really had the opportunity of testing either approach, but confidence was everything, or so his old man kept telling him.

Either way Alex had plans to try one, or both approaches this weekend in Brighton, when the old folks had bedded down for the night. He'd asked Cressida if she fancied hitting the bars, but she'd told him she had to go and buy something to wear first so would probably join him on Saturday night. That suited him very well because the kind of places he planned on going would be likely to frighten Cress, and plus she probably wouldn't get in without ID – although even in Alex's limited experience, girls who flashed a bit at the bouncers didn't really need to back it up with a hard copy to get inside the joint. In any case Alex was planning on hitting the heavy metal places tonight, not the sort that would appeal to Cressida.

Alex smiled sweetly at his mother across the dinner table.

He nodded politely at his old man beside him, lecturing him on the bottle of wine he had just ordered to complement their starters. He'd been promised a glass or two with dinner. Just one or two though Dad had cautioned again – don't want you getting tipsy Alex! Unlike his old man, who was grinning like a Cheshire Cat now after several whiskies.

The wine would make an excellent hors d'oeuvre to Alex's drinking plans later. And warm him up for a bit of a smoke too.

The waiter arrived with grilled crevettes for Mum – happy now after her Martini, Sussex Smokie for the old man, and venison pate for Alex. Cressida had forgone the starter so as not to spoil her appetite for her main course. Not that Alex could understand that notion, the more food the better as far as he was concerned.

Alex waited politely while the sommelier poured a small drop of wine into his father's glass. Hugo, to Dana's surprise – Alex had caught his mum with raised eyebrows

– took up the glass, swilled it around, sniffed it and swished it about in his mouth like Mighty Mint mouthwash.

Everyone smiled good humouredly. Watching Hugo, the wine buff, pondering.

The sommelier stood politely by. Also smiling.

Hugo finally pronounced the wine acceptable.

Everyone relaxed and the sommelier poured each of them in turn a glass.

Alex had already caught the latter's eye – and spotted the chasing-the-dragon tattoo, just visible on his arm when the cuff of his white jacket rode up a little – and the sommelier had winked at him.

Alex was poured a very generous glass. Hugo was too busy lecturing them, on the small producer of this particular bottle from the Loire Valley, to notice.

Alex winked back.

With a drink assured and more to come, Alex relaxed.

"So how can you taste the wine Dad?" he asked.

Hugo puffed out his chest.

"It is all a matter of executing the tasting procedure correctly young man. You don't just glug it. You take your time. Swirl it around in the glass, inhale the bouquet, then sip, let it pervade your taste buds, back and front of the mouth and tongue – that is what gives you an appreciation of wine."

Hugo sat back. Smug.

Alex cracked a roll and piled on a generous amount of pate.

"But how can you appreciate it? If you've been drinking lots of malt whisky?" Alex asked.

Hugo bristled.

"Nonsense, an aperitif before dinner makes no difference at all, I got all the notes, particularly the top note of cinnamon."

"Oh," Alex continued, "it's just I thought that grape and grain should never mix. That if you drank whisky then you should never, ever drink wine or vice versa. I'm sure you told me that Dad. It was a lesson to learn the hard way, you said. So I just thought, that if you were drinking whisky and then wine, there was no way you would be able to appreciate either. And you do say that drink is to be appreciated if one is to learn anything."

Alex plastered the last of his pate on his bread and shoved it in his mouth.

Cressida was grinning at him.

His mum was grimacing, waiting for Hugo's response.

Hugo put his knife and fork down very carefully. Wiped his mouth with his napkin. Placed both hands on the tablecloth, face down. Much like his late grandfather when about to give a lecture, Alex thought.

"Alex makes a fair point," Hugo said.

Everyone exhaled.

"It is true that some people say grape and grain should not mix," Hugo continued.

He held up a finger and wagged it.

"But, as with everything there are exceptions to the rule, as in this case. Now take this bottle of wine for example." Hugo held up his glass.

Everyone watched.

"This wine is earthy, heavy, a little peaty even – and therein lies the clue!"

Hugo took up the bottle, examined it and then set it down, quite forcefully.

Everyone jumped. Alex pretended to jump.

"The clue is 'peaty'! Like the malt whisky, as Alex quite rightly points out" – Hugo turned to Alex and took his hand, this was awkward, but no going back now – "that I was drinking was Highland Park, and that is a peaty malt, and so it complements the wine here perfectly," Hugo continued.

He took up his glass again. Let go of Alex's hand.

"And to prove the point, we will order not only another bottle of wine – but Alex shall have a malt whisky, Highland Park of course, with me after dinner in the lounge!"

It was like the end of a symphony, it had built up to a crescendo, and it was almost as though applause were expected.

Dana smiled lovingly at Hugo.

Hugo smiled benignly at Alex.

Cressida continued to smirk.

The sommelier, who had heard every word, caught Alex's eye again and high-fived him from across the room.

The sommelier was also French, but of a different variety than Veronique. It was his accent, and so his assumed nationality, that had got him the job at the hotel. He did indeed come from Marseilles. Via Colombia.

Cressida now smelt blood. If she were to sit here enduring Dad getting sloshed and watching everyone eat themselves into a grave, then there would have to be some reward for it. I mean, look at them all. Okay Mum's got fish, grilled, so that's not too bad, but still gross if Cressida had been forced to eat it. Dad's eating lamb shank with those blobby bits of fat. It made Cressida shiver just to imagine it, without actually looking at it. It was like that advert for the Stop Smoking Campaign, where the cigarette grew a tumour while the man was dragging on it. All those yellow fat globs on Dad's plate. Jesus, she should just call the surgeon and the operating theatre now, save him the trouble of waiting for his arteries to finally give up the ghost.

And Alex! Tucking into a rare steak. Rare! Who is he trying to fool? Bet he doesn't even like it. Just trying to look sophisticated, or more likely, wangle some more wine if he has it done the way Dad advised him, so that he could appreciate the flavour of the meat. Yuck. Disgusting. It could have been even worse though. Alex wanted to order the steak tartare. Jesus H Christ! That was raw! Mum had shaken her head, and even Dad suggested it might be an acquired taste.

"Leave that particular delicacy until I take you to my father's old club for lunch one day," Hugo had advised.

Mum had laughed at that one. So Alex had the rare steak to compromise.

Alex was always so extreme. Trying everything weird, pushing everything to the limits. She knew it was because boys had some part of their brains hard-wired to danger, or was that teenagers in general? No, couldn't be because she liked trying different things, but not extreme things like Alex.

Just look at it. Pulsating there on the plate. In a river of blood. Like a transplant victim where they forgot a bit and left it on the operating table. Mind you, he got another generous glass of wine she noted.

Cressida's plate of vegetables arrived and were placed

on the table in front of her with a flourish, like a magician conjuring a white rabbit out of a hat. The waiter almost bowed. He'd said that he would "see what he could do" when she had announced that there was nothing suitable on the menu for a vegan. Then he came back with a plate of vegetables – Kenya beans, baby carrots, peas, broad beans, parsnips, sprouts. Her mother had looked cross and Dad had asked if she didn't want some roast potatoes or chips with it. Chips! What planet was he on? Planet sloshed, that's what.

But how could she eat anything fried? Jesus she wouldn't be able to get up from the table. I mean look at all these people in here – they'll be injecting insulin before they even make it upstairs to bed. And it wasn't just her opinion. The government said so all the time. It was always on the news. The country was buckling at the knees with obesity and diabetes. Even her mother commented on it. No thanks. Cressida would stick with her vegetables, thanks very much.

Truth was, Cressida's appetite, such as it was, had died at the sight of Dad's lamb shank and Alex's rare steak. But she made a huge deal out of cutting up her vegetables and clanging her cutlery to give the impression of eating vigorously, aided by slurping lots of water. Another appetite suppressant, but it gave the impression of washing down lots of food.

Hugo smiled at her and patted her hand.

"Daddy?" Cressida speared a carrot.

"Yes darling?"

"Please may I have my ear pierced tomorrow?" She swallowed the carrot whole.

"Of course darling. Where do they do that?" Hugo

patted her hand again while mopping up the meat juices on his plate.

"There's a place in the North Laines, it's called The Needle and it—"

"Absolutely not. No way," Dana's voice was raised across the table.

"Don't be silly Dana darling, all girls have their ears pierced, and after all Cressida is no longer a baby, she's 16-years-old now," Hugo remarked.

He patted her hand a third time and glugged some more wine.

Dana sighed loudly and put her knife and fork down. Solicitor mode was coming up, Cressida noted.

Alex gave Cressida a sarcastic look, which said – thought you'd nailed it didn't you, with the old man?

Cressida remained neutral – all was not lost yet. Alex's eyes, she also noted, were a little glassy now too.

"Hugo," Dana said, in a voice that would not have been out of place addressing a High Court Judge, one who was claiming not to know who Leonardo Di Caprio was. "Cressida, as you very accurately state, is no longer a baby: she is indeed sixteen and more than old enough to have pierced ears."

Dana took a sip of water and continued with a languorous intake of breath.

"The only flaw in your summation is that Cressida, as she well knows" – Mum looked at her now – "already has pierced ears and has done for the better part of five years."

Cressida pulled a face and looked down at her plate.

Hugo looked confused.

"Well perhaps she wants new ones?" he suggested.

"No Hugo, she is pulling a fast one and playing you for a fool," Dana explained. And Cressida, being the only one sipping and not gulping her one glass of wine, thought she caught her mother mutter under her breath, "Not that that would be difficult."

Hugo looked hurt, or at least the alcohol-induced version of him did.

"You failed to catch her reference to ear singular and not ears plural. What she really wants is a third piercing in the cartilage of her ear at the top, which is absolutely disallowed, vetoed. Full stop." Dana took up her knife and fork and resumed her meal.

Hugo still looked confused, but made no reply.

Cressida skewered another carrot, this time savagely. Bloody Mum, always interfering. I had Dad nailed there.

Everyone ate in silence for some moments. The clamour of the dining room continued around them. The room was growing warm, the windows steamy from the guests, the heat, the food, the rain still *pitter-pattering* outside.

The grape, and grain, were taking further effect.

Alex polished off the last of his steak and looked up.

"Dad?"

Hugo looked at him.

"Can I have a tattoo?"

Cressida led the chorus of response, "No!"

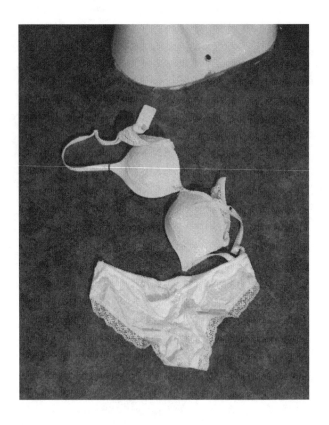

EIGHT

Dana had meant to make a note of the restaurant and bar bills after Hugo had signed for them. Just so that she had a running tally as the weekend progressed. But the mellow afterglow of the relatively calm family meal, and Hugo's flourishing dismissal – as she'd gone to peek at the bill when he'd signed his name with aplomb – had put an end to that idea. She usually recorded such important elements of their travels so as to ensure that one, they had enough money set aside to pay the final bill and two, it wasn't a nasty shock when they did so.

But, well sod it. It was all Hugo's idea, so let him worry about it for a change.

Everyone seemed to have had a nice time, that was the main thing. Alex and Hugo had got on well, although that last whisky in the bar after dinner had perhaps been a mistake. For Hugo at any rate, he'll regret it in the morning. And Cressida had eaten. Without protest. That in itself was a minor miracle, and had made unexpectedly plain sailing through dinner. It had taken the edge off what was usually now a stressful event – family meals.

It had not always been like that. Dana thought back to the early years. Everyone carefree and happy. Family holidays and eating out. The worst that happened then would have been a toddler tantrum. That was normal. Noisy, but normal. And controllable. Or an eyes-bigger-than-belly event, usually when Alex had wanted too many chips, or ice cream for pudding. Even Cressida had sometimes eaten too much and been sick in the car on the way home. How things had changed. What a joy it would be if Cressida was sick because she had simply eaten too much now.

Dana sighed. All that happiness, mundanity, normality of previous years. All taken for granted. All gone forever. Although, come to think of it, if Cressida was to throw up now after eating, then Dana's logical conclusion would be another eating disorder: bulimia. Dear God, how had they gone from toddler belly ache to bulimia? Where did it go wrong?

Hugo and Dana had been happy. Happy together, happy with the children, happy with life. Getting up, living the day, going to bed. Happy. Dana couldn't remember any unease, any tension, any stress. Of course there had been disagreements, rows even. Huffs, sulks and sometimes raised voices. But never with any underlying tone. Never with things left unsaid. Everything that had needed to be said had been. Out in the open. Nothing concealed. Nothing hidden. No false pretences. No rose-tinted glasses. No pretence of anything. Just normal happy family life. Just the four of them. No one else.

Even with their respective parents – difficult as Hugo's had been – there had been acceptance, mutual understanding. It was probably only now, looking back, that Dana felt the latter element had been her compromise. At the time it was just accepted that Hugo's parents were, well, awkward. His father had been tyrannical and exacting. And demanding. And a downright bloody bastard in retrospect.

His mother had been initially sweet, scatty, muddled, placid. Only later did it emerge that she was in fact sly, duplicitous, manipulative, selfish, demanding. Trouble.

But none of that had seemed obvious, or insurmountable, back when they had been happy. And normal. They had enjoyed each other's company, relishing an evening together, unlike now when it was to be endured, or even, sometimes, dreaded.

Dana remembered back to their courting days – or rather, living together days, before they got married – before the children came along. They'd lived in a little cottage in a quaint medieval village. The house was tiny: little kitchen, narrow stairs up to two small bedrooms. Pretty sitting room at the back of the house overlooking the garden. With a real log fire. In the early days, when they were in love, they'd get a take-away from the gourmet Chinese down the road, nice bottle of wine, sometimes two, light the fire, put the duvet on the floor in front of it, eat, drink, laugh and then spend the night lying there together.

But that had been twenty-two years ago.

And now.

The children were no longer a joyous adjunct or delightful enrichment of Hugo and Dana's happy union. Now, the children were, at best, the cohesive glue that kept them stuck together, and, at worst, buffers between them. Dana even admitted that she had used them as shields, "Not tonight Hugo, Alex has a temperature, I think I'll bring him in here to sleep in our bed, you go into the guest room," or, "I'm too tired Hugo, I've been up since six with Cressida and have to be up again at five tomorrow, better if she sleeps in here with us tonight."

How had it come to this? Dana realised that she would not be the first, or last, wife to ask this question.

But for now she pushed it aside. For now, there was the weekend to get through, no – to enjoy, she insisted. And it was late and she was tired. So to bed.

Yes, bed. When exactly had that become something to be dreaded rather than welcomed?

Still, she told herself, she was not a child-bride in some God forsaken third-world country, or pushed into an arranged marriage with an elderly ogre, or a victim of abuse. She chose to sleep next to the man she had married. It was her decision. And it remained her choice.

Notwithstanding that in reality there was nowhere else to go when the house was mortgaged to the hilt, in negative equity, the bank account was in overdraft, and the cards were over their limits every month. She daren't step off the treadmill because to do so would crystallise her debt, and a bankrupt solicitor was no longer a solicitor. And although the termination of that particular career might be what she ultimately sought, it needed to be on her own terms, on account of the fact that this current activity kept the wolf from the door.

Still. It could always be worse, as her wonderful dad had counselled her. Always look at the positives and you can work out the negatives. Count your blessings. There is always someone worse off than you. So she did just that now. Alex was getting on with, and talking, again to Hugo, Cressida had eaten her dinner, Hugo was in a good mood, and might write something productive tomorrow – and she was in a luxury hotel for the weekend.

Dana washed the last vestiges of makeup and face cleanser off at the marble sink – Nivea now rather than Eve Lom of her more financially prosperous years – and patted on some eye and night cream.

Then she flossed her teeth.

Then folded the towels.

Then ran the tap to sluice out the remains of the toothpaste from the sink.

Then she sat on the loo seat and looked out the window at the coal black night and the little glints of rain reflected on the panes of glass. She waited a few more minutes, hoping to hear Hugo snoring from the bedroom.

No sound. Eventually she pulled the light cord and tiptoed out towards the bed.

Just as she got into bed Hugo reached out a hand for her.

Dana froze. Fuck it. Thought he was asleep after all that whisky.

"Darling, give me a cuddle." Hugo fumbled a hand towards her, groping blindly in the dark along the pillow.

"Go asleep Hugo, it's late and you'll have a sore head in the morning."

Dana turned on her side and pulled the duvet up over her ears.

Hugo continued to fumble. Now under the covers.

"Sweetheart, we're on holiday, come on."

Dana was irritated.

"No, we're on a weekend break with the 'children' as you keep calling them, so go asleep."

Dana yanked the duvet and tucked it under her bottom between them, demarcating their respective zones of the bed.

Hugo was soon snoring, snorting and puffing.

Dana's thoughts drifted away to an uneasy sleep, inhabited by the dark, handsome stranger in the lobby. And her text message correspondent. Lunch probably. Dinner maybe. And the red dress.

In the *children's* room, Cressida counted calories and the number of H & M branches in Brighton, as she lay alone in room 421.

Back home, Oscar lay sleeping contentedly on their bed. His tummy full of Bella's home-made curry.

Alex counted the cash in his wallet as he stood waiting. In the rain. Outside the staff entrance to the kitchen of the hotel.

NINE

Something, somewhere was making a sharp rapping sound. Oh God, Hugo thought. Not Bella at the bloody door again. He lay very still. Listening.

Pat. Pat. Pat. That seemed to be coming from the window. Rain, he deduced. And then *rap, rap, rap.* But this time it was very close, almost in the bedroom with him. He was vaguely aware of his head. It ached. And it felt fuzzy for the second morning in a row. Oh God. Have I overslept again?

He tentatively opened one swollen eye. It hurt. He closed it again. Had he finished that bottle of Highland Park in his study last night? He tried opening the other eye. It also hurt, but was less stuck together than the other one.

Slowly, his surroundings came into focus. It was unfamiliar.

Jesus! Did he have Alzheimer's already? Wait. No. Slowly, it all came back to him. He opened both eyes. Not entirely unfamiliar. The hotel. They were in a hotel for the weekend. Hugo breathed a sigh of relief. Lifted his head off the pillow. There was a shaft of weak sunlight through the gap in the curtains. He sat up on his elbows.

Something in his head was hammering. He remembered. Four, or was it five or six, large whiskies? And two bottles of wine. From the Loire Valley. Christ. What had that cost? The rapping noise continued. What the hell was that?

Rap. Rap. Rap.

Hugo tried to marshal his thoughts and focus. He looked towards the door and followed the sound. It was coming from the other side. Someone was knocking at the door.

Hugo turned to Dana. The bed was empty. Except for him.

"Excuse me?" a voice enquired from the other side of the door, "room service."

"Room service? What?" Hugo asked aloud.

He gathered himself together.

"Just a minute, just a jiffy," he said, voice raised, his head thumping.

He managed to get out of bed, still wearing his boxer shorts he vaguely observed. His attempt at amore had been unsuccessful then. He grabbed a towel from the bathroom – his bag sat unpacked on the valet stand – and ventured towards the door.

"Yes?" he asked the door.

"Room service sir, I have your order," a foreign voice responded.

Polish, Hugo thought.

"My order? But I didn't order anything."

"Yes please sir, I have your breakfast if you would be so kind sir," the voice insisted.

God sake. Hugo opened the door, and a small man with a bald head stood there holding a silver tray with a tall glass on it.

"Thank you so much sir, sorry for the disturbing of you."

The man bustled into the room, drew back the curtains – which made Hugo wince like a vampire exposed to high noon – and placed the silver tray and drink on the table in the middle of the room.

"What's that?" Hugo asked.

"Prairie Oyster sir."

The man walked back to the door.

"But who ordered that?" Hugo asked, as he stared at the glass.

"Your wife sir. She said it might help. I believe it is very good for the hangover."

The man's expression remained blank, and with that he left the room.

Hugo sat on the edge of the sofa and stared at the drink on the table. His stomach was queasy and his mouth felt like the inside of a bird cage.

He took a final look at the oily, urine yellow liquid in the glass, and the embryonic egg sac floating in it, and then made straight for the bathroom.

The air inside the gym was refreshingly cool, although not as cool as it would have been outside, had Dana done her run along the seafront, instead of on the treadmill. She hadn't fancied a head-on collision with storm-force winds, or the spiky pricks of rain along the promenade. Mind you, a few pricks in here, she thought, as she dripped sweat after her forty minute running session.

There was the usual mix of silver-haired off-peak members having their Saturday morning constitutional; an overweight woman, with a very wobbly bottom, labouring uphill on the inclined treadmill, in the tightest of lycra; a young chap who was clearly out of shape, but who had youth enough on his side to heft a heavy weight up on the bench press; and a man in his mid-fifties who – her mother would have said – didn't half fancy himself. Along with any marginally decent looking woman in a tight top.

Prick. Dana pulled the zip right up on her post-run fleece top. She'd noticed the man – black shorts, GB vest top, dark hair flecked with grey – looking her up and down with a smug smile, as she'd been nearing the end of her run. He was in good shape himself: muscular legs, tanned, good looking. But. Too good looking. He knew it. And with that came arrogance, smugness, conceitedness. Which in turn made him very unattractive. So in fact his looks were, ironically, his undoing if he was looking to pull anything other than a muscle in a gym.

Of course, there was always the clueless type of woman – shallow, dim, dizzy, call it what you will – who would be attracted to this type of man. Usually because she was flattered by the attention, even if she was attractive herself. And gyms were the ideal place to find such types, both types: the prick in the shorts, and the dim women.

Dana cast her eyes around, mind you, he had slim pickings in here today. I wouldn't spit on him, and the wibbly-wobbly woman looks like she might expire at any second. The Prick caught her eye as he stretched his hamstring. He smiled at her. Dana gave a terse upturn of her mouth in reply. It was difficult to be openly rude in such a confined space. Might encounter him in the steam room. Then it would be awkward.

She wasn't sure why she was in such a bad mood.

Probably because it was her birthday. And the last year of her forties. God! How had that happened? It seemed like only yesterday that she was leaving her thirties. In fact, she could still remember being twenty-nine. Dana involuntarily looked in the huge, floor-to-ceiling mirror. Slim, toned, firm. Okay, so I don't look it, she thought. But looks aren't the point really. She caught the Prick watching her look at herself in the mirror. Oh dear, now he thinks I'm shallow, dim, dizzy – and therefore his kind of woman.

Where the fuck was Hugo? I hope he got that message I left for him on the table. He can get his arse down here and have a swim with us before breakfast. That'll teach him to get drunk, have a hangover, and forget that it's my birthday.

Dana mopped her brow with a hand-towel, and was just picking up her locker key from the floor beside the exercise mat, when she noticed that the Prick was now smiling and salivating at something on the other side of the half-open door behind her.

Dana shook her head in mild amusement, and pulled the door the rest of the way open.

Cressida stood on the other side in her speedo swimsuit, with her waist length, baby-blonde hair flowing like a mermaid behind her, and pulling an agonised face.

"Mum," she hissed through clenched teeth.

"What? What's wrong?"

"I've been standing here for hours waiting for you," Cressida said.

"Well hardly, I've only been in here forty minutes. What's the problem?"

Cressida grabbed Dana's hand-towel and held it up in front of her, like a shield.

"I'm naked, look at me!" Cressida was almost squealing.

"You're wearing a swimsuit."

"Exactly. Everyone can see me. It's beyond embarrassing."

"But you're going swimming, what did you propose to wear? A diving bell?"

"Course not, but I was going to cover up the swimsuit with a big fluffy towel. That was the agreement we made. You said if I came into the spa with you then I could cover up with a big fluffy towel."

"Oh for goodness sake, what a fuss. Well why didn't you get one then, from reception?" Dana asked.

"Because they said I had to have my room key to leave as security in exchange for towels and locker keys and stuff, and I didn't bring it down with me. So I had to dump my stuff in a locker with no key, and stand here like a retard waiting for you while you indulged yourself in there!"

Dana threw her eyes up to the ceiling and caught the Prick watching them out of the corner of her left eye. He was standing smiling and looking Cressida up and down.

Dana scowled at him and made what she hoped he would understand to be a warning stare. She took Cressida's arm and guided her towards the changing rooms, making sure that she walked close enough behind her so as to obscure any glimpse of Cressida from the back.

"Paedophile and a Prick," Dana muttered under her breath.

Where the fuck is Hugo?

On their way to the changing room, Alex came bounding down the stairs in rugby shorts and sweatshirt.

"Hello darling." Dana hugged and kissed him. "Did you sleep well?"

Dana caught Cressida laughing, but the latter said nothing.

To his credit, Alex stood stoically firm as the hugging and kissing took place. His good nature enhancing, rather than detracting from, his manliness.

"Sort of," Alex replied.

Then Alex took his mother's hand and kissed it. "Happy birthday Mum!"

Dana beamed. She was very proud of Alex, and very touched.

"Thank you darling. We're just off to the pool and sauna, any sign of Dad?" she asked.

"Dunno. I'm gonna do a weights session with Juan." Alex nodded in the direction of the gym.

"Juan?" Dana asked.

"Yeah, I went – I mean met him last night, don't you remember? He's the wine waiter?" Alex made for the gym door.

"Oh, right. Okay. Well don't overdo it, you had a drink or two last night as well," Dana cautioned.

"Or nine or ten," Cressida mumbled.

"What?" Dana asked.

"I said it's after ten Mum, so let's get into the spa," Cressida said, smiling.

"Okay," Dana said. And then to Alex, "See you later. If

you see Dad tell him we've gone for a swim, and then we all need to get to breakfast before it finishes."

This is just – magical. Dana decided, as she floated in the agreeably warm pool. Just perfect. Relaxing. Just what I needed.

The pool area was decorated in a mock Grecian style with pillars and murals and ferns. It was dimly lit with underwater lights that made the pool glow a luminous, azure blue. One could almost be on a Grecian island in the summer. Well, pre-immigrant Grecian island at any rate. Lovely.

"Come on in Cress," Dana shouted. "It's lovely."

Cressida hovered at the edge, now concealed head to foot in the much coveted huge, white, fluffy towel with the discreet Metropole Hotel logo at the edge. Neither the Speedo swimsuit, or indeed Cressida, were to be seen as a consequence.

"I can't go in there can I?" she responded.

"Why on earth not?" Dana asked, as she treaded water.

"It's not vegan is it? Chlorine."

Oh for God's sake, thought Dana.

"What do you mean, not 'vegan'?"

"All those nasty chemicals. You know what they are designed to do?"

"Not really Cressida, no," Dana responded, "keep the water fresh?"

"Er no! It's obvious, isn't it?"

"Is it?"

"Yes Mum, don't you get it?"

"I have to say that I don't Cress, no."

Dana dived under the water, feeling goddess-like now,

with the azure water and Corinthian columns.

Cressida continued to hover.

"Well, it's a hotel pool Mum, so you should know."

"Sorry but I don't, and the water really is lovely."

Cressida sighed loudly, much like a primary school teacher telling the class that two and two made four.

"Chlorine kills the organic matter," Cressida explained.

"Organic matter? Like what?"

Cressida sighed again.

"Like urine and worse." Cressida peered into the water, as if she could see just such a thing in the pool now.

"Oh." Dana had a look too. "Worse?"

"Yes. It's a hotel pool. Babies and toddlers go in there. And you know what nappies are for. As I said it's not vegan. Not even vegetarian."

Cressida sauntered off and lay down on a wooden steamer chair with a deeply padded royal-blue cushion.

Suddenly Dana had had enough water for one day. As she emerged from the pool she saw the Prick coming out of the men's changing room in orange Yves Saint Laurent swim shorts. His torso was muscular and golden, Dana observed in spite of herself, but then he ostentatiously flexed the muscles on his back, ruining any attractive spell he may otherwise have cast. He threw his towel on the sun lounger next to Cressida and winked at her.

He walked to the edge of the deep end, sprung forward, and dived under the water in one fluid movement.

Just then a boisterous and loud family of five crashed through the doors into the pool area, in a tangle of floats, balls and snorkel masks.

Dana smiled as two chubby toddlers, in swim nappies,

and armbands, were launched into the water.

Fortified by two co-codamol painkillers − ostensibly for his "bad back", but now serving a secondary purpose − and three strong black coffees, Hugo made his way tentatively down to the leisure club in search of his family. Dana, he knew, would have completed a strenuous run, and Cressida might be in the sauna, as long as her hair didn't get wet. Alex, he felt sure, would still be sleeping off the effects of the whisky and wine from the night before. Not likely to see him much before sundown he decided.

The humidity from the pool area hit him like a tidal wave when he opened the door, making his head lurch. He had intended going for a swim, but then he caught sight of a family of sumo wrestlers, who had turned the pool into a white-water, rapids hazard, and promptly gave up that idea. A nice chap in orange shorts commiserated with him while nodding in the direction of the pool, telling him that the kids-free time was after four. Hugo thanked him profusely and said he'd return then.

He had no such idea.

If he managed to get through the morning's shopping and a spot of lunch, he intended to be napping by mid-afternoon, if he were to have any chance of being in shape for the birthday dinner later.

First, he had Dana's wrath to deal with. He felt bad about the way the day had started. He had intended to order a nice breakfast in bed for Dana, with a red rose on the breakfast tray. And a birthday card. But he had forgotten to put out the order for breakfast on the door handle the night before, and by the time he had realised, Dana had already got up and then it was too late to even phone the order down to the kitchen.

Interesting touch, the Prairie Oyster. Slightly out of character for Dana. But then one never knew quite what was going on in women's minds, Hugo thought. All those hormones. Made better, or worse, by that TRH thingy she took? He didn't know either way. Although, if he'd had to guess, he would have said women were better off without hormones, giving them more of the stuff seemed akin to putting a migraine sufferer in a disco with flashing strobe lights. Surely taking yet more hormones only made her even more moody?

But perhaps today she is just emotional about her birthday. Women can be sensitive about their age. Not like us chaps, who take it on the chin. It's a natural process, ageing. Might mean we get a few less runs in when batting, but we just accept it. We don't try to hide it. Still, perhaps he should have made a bit more of an effort this morning.

Never mind. He'd make it up to her later. Buy some nice presents, with Cress's help. And then a good dinner in the French restaurant down Ship Street. He'd already requested a nicely situated table when he'd made the booking a few days ago. Hope the plastic's up to it. And that thought made his head pound even further.

Hugo couldn't see any sign of Dana or Cressida, and the chlorine fumes were stirring up his tummy again. He gave up, left the pool area and wandered off looking for the gymnasium.

The clanging sound of metal being banged up and down, and loud pop music, led him to a room he took to be that very place. He popped his head around the door in search of his wife. Dana wasn't in there.

To Hugo's amazement, Alex was.

Stretched out on the floor, drenched in sweat, banging out a series of full, very fast, push-ups, with some other man along side him, counting in a foreign language, and high-fiving each other with every fifth push-up.

"*Veintiuno, veintidós, veintitres, veinticuatro, veinticinco,*" the man lying beside Alex exclaimed.

They high-fived each other in mid push-up. Leaning the entire weight of their bodies on one hand.

"Twenty-six, twenty-seven, twenty-eight, twenty-nine, thirty!" shouted Alex, who slapped another high-five at his companion, jumped up and stretched his back.

Christ! Where's his hangover gone? Hugo asked himself in astonishment. Sweat had now broken out on his own forehead, but was the result of a thumping head and dehydration rather than exercise.

"Hey. All right?" Alex asked when he saw him.

"Perfectly," Hugo responded.

"You okay?" Alex queried.

"Never better. I was just on my way to the pool actually," Hugo lied, looking at the foreigner standing with Alex.

"You look a bit – clammy, that's all," Alex continued.

"Not a bit of it, just overdressed. These gyms are always too warm, they never turn on the air conditioning, too expensive I suppose."

The gym was like a fridge, and Hugo was wearing swim shorts, a vest top and flip flops.

"Yeah. Right," Alex said. And then turned to his training partner. "This is Juan, we've been working out for the last couple of hours."

A dark, wiry young man in his late twenties extended a

hand to Hugo.

"Pleased to meet you Juan. Have we met before?"

"*Si Señor*, I work in the restaurant, I am the sommelier."

Juan's handshake was like an iron vice, gripping despite the sweat.

Hugo wasn't sure why, but Juan looked, well, shifty. His eyes were dark, and seemed to cut around, as if wary of his surroundings or the natives.

Hugo observed him for a few seconds until Alex roused him from his contemplation.

"Mum said she and Cress were going for a swim, and then we all need to get to breakfast."

"I've already looked and she isn't in the pool, so I guess they must be getting changed," Hugo replied.

"Oh, thought you said you were just on your way to the pool for a swim? Are you sure you are okay Dad?"

Hugo was irritated, but determined not to let it show.

"I just popped in there first, and then here to find your mother. I'm going back for a good workout in a second," he said.

Hugo stretched upwards and then bent down to touch his toes. His oesophagus backed up like a blocked toilet as he did so, and he feared he might vomit on his flip flops.

Then a voice from behind exclaimed, "Ah ze Mister Hugo, bodybuilding!"

Hugo observed a pair of shapely ankles and black high heel court shoes in front of him.

It took every reserve of strength and will-power that he possessed to repress his nausea, and straighten up without needing the assistance of an orthopaedic surgeon.

Veronique was standing in the doorway of the gym smiling at him. Rivers of sweat trickled down Hugo's cheeks and pooled under his chin. A similar cycle was being repeated under his arms. He knew that if he looked in the mirror his pallor would scare a medical professional.

"Ah *bonsoir*, er *bonjour* I mean, madame, or mademoiselle, I mean. Ha!" Hugo responded in greeting, forcing a jovial mood.

"You are doing ze workout this morning?" Veronique asked him, still smiling.

"Just supervising the children in the gym!" He laughed out loud.

Hugo hoped Juan's English wasn't up to much.

Alex stood closely observing him.

"You show ze little ones how it's done, how to build ze big muscles."

"Ha! That's right." Hugo laughed, and made a muscle with his right bicep.

Veronique stepped forward and patted his arm. Hugo made another exaggerated muscle, mimicking Popeye, and Veronique patted it again.

As before, Alex found the exchange hysterical, and even Juan was smirking.

Everyone was laughing.

Except Dana. Who had walked up behind them a few seconds ago with Cressida.

"Hugo?"

Hugo jumped involuntarily when he heard Dana's voice behind him. He swung around.

She was standing there with pursed lips.

Cressida was scowling at Veronique.

"Darling! Didn't see you there. I was just with the boys in the gym." He nodded at Alex and Juan.

"So I see. And with an audience." Dana smiled tersely at Veronique.

Veronique smiled at her, flicking her lustrous black hair back over her shoulder and almost brushing Hugo's face in the process.

He sneezed.

Veronique said, "*Vos souhaits!*"

Juan exclaimed, "*Salud!*"

Alex shouted, "*Gesundheit!*"

Hugo laughed.

Dana didn't bless anyone, she just said, "Goodness, it's a regular United Nations in here this morning, anyone know the foreign words for 'Happy Birthday'? No, don't bother, you can make it up to me later. Shall we go for breakfast now?"

She left the leisure club with Cressida striding after her.

TEN

"I think I've put my back out. Might need a massage later," Hugo said, as the remnants of breakfast were cleared from their table near the window. They were the last of the late morning stragglers, and had had to pick their way through dried up croissants, rubbery bacon and plastic looking fried eggs.

Dana ignored him. She looked out at the insipid wintry day. The sea looked fierce. Crested waves crashing onto the orange pebble beach. It was still raining, and difficult to determine where the sea started and the sky ended, there being no horizon visible in this weather. Should have brought those yellow, full-length cagoules we got in Disneyland Paris, Dana thought. Be about right for this weather.

Dana vaguely remembered Camilla remarking that Tristram had taken her to Antigua for her birthday. The only umbrella you'd need there would be of the sunshade variety.

Alex came back to the table with another plate laden with yet more food. Hugo shook his head.

"Don't know how you can eat all that," Hugo said.

"That's what a good workout does for you Dad. Gives you an appetite," he responded, as he tucked into more bacon and eggs. "As well as a *muscle*."

Alex smirked and winked at his mother, who, in spite of herself, smirked back in solidarity.

Hugo glared at him.

Cressida nursed her orange juice, not having done anything "worthwhile" she said to justify a breakfast.

"By the way, thank you for the 'breakfast in bed' Dana. Very amusing, if not very expensive too." Hugo held up his glass of juice in salute to her.

Dana was puzzled.

"What breakfast in bed?" she asked.

"My Prairie Oyster. Very funny."

"Prairie Oyster? What are you talking about Hugo?"

Hugo leaned forward.

"You ordered me a drink for breakfast? It was brought to our room after you had left for your run," Hugo explained.

"I did no such thing! You must be joking. Why should you get breakfast in bed on my birthday?"

Dana shook her head.

"Well I can assure you a waiter knocked on our door, and delivered a Prairie Oyster to me with your compliments, well not compliments exactly, but he said that my wife said it would be good for my 'hangover'. Not that I had a hangover…" Hugo's voice trailed off.

"You must have been dreaming, or ordered it in a drunken stupor before you went asleep. I most certainly did not."

"What's a Prairie Oyster Daddy?" Cressida asked.

"It's a drink for—" Hugo stopped, having caught the use of the word "Daddy".

That'll be Cress gearing up for her shopping, thought Dana.

Hugo resumed, "It's supposedly a hangover cure, Worcestershire sauce and raw egg and things, it's a drink. Utterly vile, and guaranteed to have you heaving into the toilet if you look at it with even the vaguest of sore heads and—"

Hugo stopped short.

Alex had his head down and was vigorously cutting up his bacon and eggs, and being quite unable to suppress his mirth.

"Alex!" Dana and Hugo shouted in unison.

Having cost his father the better part of £12.50 plus room service charge for the ill-fated hangover cure, Alex was unable to extract any pocket money from him for a morning's jaunt in his heavy metal vinyl music shops, or worse.

However, Hugo did catch sight of Dana slipping him thirty pounds as they stepped out into the February weather.

Alex immediately took off towards the town centre, promising to meet them later outside – at his suggestion – The Cricketers pub in Black Lion Street.

How he knows these things is a mystery, Hugo thought. I'll bet the little devil looked it up on the internet before we came down here. As Hugo had said before, and would no doubt say again, they get up to all sorts on the internet, teenagers. We don't know the half of it.

The rain had stopped, and the wind died down, by the

time Hugo, Dana and Cressida hit Churchill Square. Cressida practically squealed in delight when she saw all the shops on Western Road – Gap, New Look, Reiss, French Connection, not to mention her beloved H & M.

Hugo vaguely suggested that they split up – Dana and Cressida head off to the clothes shops, while he made for Waterstones and the excellent City Books, a bit further down Western Road, or that little antiquarian bookshop, Colin Page, just off Ship Street.

That idea was swatted like a fly by Dana.

"Hardly. Be rather letting you off the hook, wouldn't it?" she said.

Hugo had accepted it stoically, and also had the good sense not to venture an opinion as to why Cressida could not just wear some of the clothes that her mother had brought with her for the weekend.

Western Road thronged with Saturday shoppers: gaggles of women, couples – with the male half usually trailing a few steps behind, and men on their own walking with purpose and military precision in order to get the errand over and done with and so to the pub. Oh God, Hugo groaned. The pub – that'd be nice, hair-of-the-dog, peace and quiet. Read of the paper. The crossword. Maybe watch a bit of sport. He had rallied slightly since early morning, might just manage a half of something.

Hugo stopped at the top of the steps outside the shopping centre. There was a pub, bit gaudy admittedly, with huge outdoor heaters – but people drinking outside. He wondered if perhaps he might sit there while the women looked inside the shopping centre. Perhaps he could be called when needed to deal with the business end of the shopping expedition? Dana gave him a hard stare, and he was dragged across the road.

Bloody dangerous isn't it? Giant double decker buses coming in all directions, hundreds of bus stops lining the pavement − well seemed like hundreds − and hoards of people waiting in lines, while the buses thundered past at break-neck speed, no warning except a deafening blast of a horn if you didn't hurl yourself out of the way.

And into the infamous H & M.

Cressida could hardly contain her excitement. The place was enormous: miles upon miles of rails, shelves, mannequins, or so it seemed to Hugo, floors up and down. And packed. To the hilt with teenagers, pushing and shoving and grabbing. Signs everywhere announced a Mid Season Event. Whatever that meant.

Discount I hope, Hugo thought.

Hugo examined some price tickets on a rail marked "£10 and under". Looks reasonable enough, he decided. A decent selection of garb. He gestured to Dana and Cressida.

"Look at this − all sorts of lovely outfits and such a bargain too," he told them.

That was a good choice of word. *Bargain*. People are always attracted to the idea that they are getting something valuable for next to nothing.

The two women immediately headed in the opposite direction, towards New Season Collection, and ignored him.

He was left standing, holding an acid yellow T-shirt with beads dangling from the bottom, marked up at £4, until a 13-year-old with pink hair and wearing her mother's lipstick, grabbed it from his hand and made off towards the cash desk.

Goodness. I'll just wait by the door, he decided.

The throngs continued to converge on the shop while Hugo stood by the fire extinguisher, next to the entrance.

The security guard had him in his sights. Probably thinks I'm a paedophile. Hugo made a big thing of looking at this watch, shaking his head and sighing. Much as to say, "Huh, women! Never to be rushed!" The security guard didn't crack a smile or nod in sympathy. He just continued to keep Hugo under observation.

A woman approached the door from outside, struggling with a buggy and M & S shopping bags. Hugo stepped forward to open it for her, that'll show the security guard. He held the door open, smiling benignly. The woman backed in with the buggy and swept past, not so much as a thank you. Well. How do you like that? Then a swarm of other people traipsed in, pushing and shoving, while he continued to hold the door open, taking full advantage. Not one person thanked him.

The security guard smirked. Hugo glared at him. He let go of the door in protest and let it slam. Straight into the face of an elderly lady being guided into the shop by a girl who looked like her grand-daughter. The elderly lady shook her head at him, the grand-daughter muttered, "How rude!"

The security guard resumed his hard stare, and his observation became surveillance.

After about eight hours – in reality about forty-five minutes – Hugo left his post at the fire extinguisher in search of a chair. His head was throbbing again and the sausage he had eaten at breakfast, behind Dana's back, was repeating on him.

Not a sign of them. Bloody hell. What are they doing?

He was about to lose his cool, when it occurred to him that they had gone up to another floor, found everything that Cressida had wanted and Dana had paid for it all.

Ah, well okay then, he thought. He relaxed a bit and waited.

Ten minutes later he was irritated again. Surely they were finished by now? Even if they had paid for the stuff they'd picked out. Hugo ventured towards the escalators. He looked up and then down. Which way? He had no idea. A tall woman in hipster jeans made the decision for him when she pushed forward behind him, forcing him onto the up escalator. It laboured uphill to the top floor at a leisurely pace. Hugo got off. Looked around, or at least tried to.

It was a needle in a haystack. Bodies everywhere. Rails of clothes everywhere.

No sign of Dana or Cressida.

Maybe they are in the changing rooms. Brainwave. He made his way towards an assistant.

"Excuse me, where are the changing rooms please?" he asked a young woman by a rail of dresses.

"How the fuck do I know? Do I look like I work here?" snapped a skinny woman in black with a pierced nose.

Christ! Hugo was stunned. He didn't know what to say in response so he stumbled away towards the safety of the cash desk. At least he could be certain of correctly identifying a member of staff there.

There wasn't a soul behind the cash registers. He peered at them. Every display on the tills announced "An assistant nearby will be happy to help you". He looked around. There were no assistants nearby.

Hugo went down the escalators again. Resumed his

place by the fire extinguisher.

The security guard was holding the door open for the woman with the buggy as she left the shop, she was laughing and joking with him. And thanking him profusely.

No sign of Dana or Cressida. It was now an hour since they had first entered the shop.

Sod it. I've had enough of this.

Hugo strode up to the security guard. His neck was thicker than Hugo's thigh. If he had been American he would have been a quarterback. He stared Hugo down.

With what might have been a gulp – after all Hugo had a very dry throat on account of the dehydration – he asked, "Excuse me, where are the ladies changing rooms please?"

Hugo stood on the pavement outside the shop. Still waiting. And now fuming.

At the suggestion of the security guard, he had decided to leave the shop and wait outside.

I'm giving it five more minutes then I'm heading to that pub, he decided firmly.

"Hugo!"

"Dad!"

Dana and Cressida shouted at him in accusatory tones from across the street.

He looked over at them between the passing buses and held up his hands.

"What the bloody hell?" he mouthed to them.

They dashed over when the coast was clear of traffic.

"Hugo! What are you doing standing there?" Dana snapped.

"What? Are you joking? What do you think I am doing?"

"Dad! We have been looking everywhere for you!" Cressida said.

"How the hell can that be? I've been standing in that shop, where I might add I was nearly arrested as a Peeping Tom, for the better part of an hour! Where the bloody hell have you two been?"

Hugo was in no mood to be trifled with.

"Cressida tried on a couple of outfits, but couldn't find anything suitable, so we came back down to where we left you, but you'd disappeared," Dana explained.

Hugo couldn't even begin to get his head around this and was about to launch into an admonishment when Cressida reminded him, "Well, it's Mum's birthday so it's not fair to be standing here arguing."

Dana smiled lovingly at Cressida and said, "Come on, let's try Zara, they've got more selection."

The women headed back across the road to the shopping centre.

Hugo wondered if they served alcohol in the food court, as a bus swerved to avoid hitting him.

Alex slipped the guy behind the counter a crisp fifty. The young guy, boasting impressive ear stretchers, held it up to the light and and squinted.

"It's all right mate, it's kosher. Only printed it this morning." Alex laughed, as he read the back of the vinyl he'd just bought – *Dying Foetus: Live In Concert*.

The young guy laughed back. "Ha! Yeah right!" Then slammed it in the cash register and counted out Alex's change.

"To be honest mate, I wouldn't know a dud from a fake!" the guy said, and laughed again.

It struck Alex that the two words he had used amounted to the same meaning, but since he had just passed what he considered to be a dubious note that fell into both categories, Alex took the change and then headed out onto North Street.

Although his old man wouldn't part with any money to give him a sub for the weekend – probably on account of not trusting what Alex would spend it on – Alex still had money in his pocket. He had a stash back in the hotel for emergencies that his grandma Bella had given him, and Juan had loaned him the fifty he had just used, on the strength of getting it back tonight, when they met up at another pub and gig venue, that Juan had promised would be *malvado* – wicked.

This roused even Alex's suspicions as he didn't know many people who tossed you a fifty pound loan on the basis of only a few hours acquaintance. Not unless they were the kind of people who made you offers that you could not refuse.

Unless of course it was in fact "manufactured", and so, in essence, worthless.

Shopping accomplished, Alex now turned his attention to the serious matter in hand – a tattoo.

He had made careful study, and had carried out extensive research on the matter. Several places had been recommended, via both the internet and his heavy metal gig colleagues.

Juan had sealed the deal though with his recommendation of Jonnie, his mate in the North Laines. He did killer tattoos and piercings. Juan's own chasing-the-dragon tattoo had been Jonnie's handiwork. He'd cut Alex a good deal as well, just mention Juan's name.

As Alex pushed through the shoppers lolling on the pavement and part of the road along Bond Street, he consulted a napkin, upon which had been scrawled, "Blood of Satan – Tattoos and Body Piercing".

Never, ever, take a man shopping with you, Dana decided, as they had to wait yet again for Hugo to catch them up walking through the shopping centre. Even if he is paying. Because regardless of how much is spent, you pay for it yourself in the end anyway in terms of sulks, moods, huffs, irritability, and general dragging of feet – which latter takes an age to get anywhere or do anything.

Hugo had even tried to skulk off to the food court for a cup of coffee. Well, Dana wasn't having that. He'd made his bed when he'd left Cressida's suitcase behind, and now he'd have to lie in it. And that meant going from shop to shop with them until Cress had found what she wanted, and Hugo had borne the brunt of the financial consequences. In fact, in Dana's opinion – which was growing ever more hardline and militant with every obstacle that Hugo attempted to put in their way – he was getting off lightly. She could have insisted that he drive back home for the suitcase.

She was no fool. She had realised straight away that he was on a mission to thwart his participation in the shopping expedition, and that he had used every possible weapon in his armoury: wandering off and pretending he couldn't find them, hiding so that he couldn't be found, and then even telling them he was thirsty and needed a coffee. Well, he wasn't going to get away with it. In fact, he ought to thank his lucky stars that he was only being required to replace what had been left behind at home in Cressida's suitcase, and not what he had offered originally: to give Cress some money to embark upon an entirely different type of shopping trip. That first offer would have been a treat. This one was a chore, because it was now born out of necessity, and so the enjoyment and gloss that it might otherwise have had was absent.

No, Hugo should be grateful and stop sulking.

Dana and Cressida bounded into Zara, and Hugo treaded heavily behind them, lagging. They parked him beside the door, next to a rail of large fluffy scarves and wraps, and gave him strict instructions to remain precisely where he was and that no argument would be brooked on the matter. Dana didn't care whether the fire alarm went off, an armed robbery took place, or even if he suffered a fatal fit – he looked wounded at this suggestion – in no circumstances, whatsoever, was he to leave that area. They would be back to fetch him, as soon as they had found what they wanted.

Cressida immediately headed for the young fashion department, and was soon engulfed by leather mini skirts, skinny jeans, Afghan gilets, pleated chiffon dresses and parka jackets.

Hugo looked aghast as she carried an armful of garments towards the changing room.

Dana looked through rail after rail of evening dresses, having decided to treat herself to a new outfit for dinner tonight. Black, black, black – navy. No, not the latter colour, she firmly decided. Might look nice on Kate Middleton, or, Windsor, now, but not a middle-aged woman trying to look younger. That gave her pause.

Jesus. *Middle-aged.* Since when did I start thinking of myself as middle-aged? Dana asked. One thought of one's parents as middle-aged. Certainly not when one's parents were still alive. Or her mother at least. Jesus. How depressing. The kids had skipped any notion that Dana and Hugo were middle-aged. They'd gone straight to "old". And presumably by that token Grandma Bella was "ancient". It was all very depressing. Is Hugo middle-aged? Umm. She stood surveying the clothes with this thought in mind.

Yes. He is. Hugo has always been middle-aged. Even when he was young. It is all simply a state of mind, Dana decided. And numbers. Essentially it was how you felt. How you felt about yourself, and how others felt about you. But anyway, middle-aged is the new sixty. Years ago, Dana's parents would have been middle-aged at forty. But now people lived to ninety or one hundred! You were still young at fifty. Middle-age only began at sixty.

And with that Dana turned to face a rail of body-hugging, short lace dresses. She went to reach for a bright red lace dress. Her hand wavered. She left it hanging there. Instead, she picked up a very short, emerald green lace dress, with scoop back and off-the-shoulder sleeves. Perfect for tonight, she told herself.

She left the red-for-danger dress where it was. For now.

Despite the fact that this shop was smaller than the previous one – and therefore the press of bodies all vying for a finite number of covetable items was even greater – Hugo found Zara to be a most agreeable shopping destination, all things considered.

Firstly, there was no burly, aggressive, security guard

threatening, with his eyes, to rip off Hugo's head and feed it to his dogs – or so it had seemed to Hugo in the last shop at the time. Less so now, since the guy was just doing his job. And, to be fair, Hugo probably did look like a Peeping Tom, or whatever passed for a pervert these days.

Secondly, and much more importantly, this shop had the most attractive, enchanting, young lady shop assistants, made all the more exotic by the fact of their all being Spanish, or Latin of some variety at any rate. And this was an important consideration for a man banished to the front door, and charged with the task of remaining there for what could be an hour or more.

And as he stood in exile by the fluffy scarf rail, he amused and entertained himself with the observation of these young ladies, all curiously bearing the same name of "Monica". He knew this because every so often a call would be made on the shops PA system, beseeching, "Monica to the cash desk," as the queue grew ever longer at the tills.

Monica – how enchanting, Hugo thought, as he watched a very shapely young lady dressed in black, with hazel eyes, fold and refold a table full of jumpers.

Jolly nice.

And another young assistant of the same name, with shoulder-length, chocolate-brown hair and olive skin – in a short black skirt he observed – bend down and re-match each shoe to its partner under the coat rail.

And, as he cast his glance towards the tills, yet another lithe, long-limbed Monica strode behind the counter with a very big smile.

Just lovely! Hugo grinned. And smiled. And grinned

some more, as he day-dreamed of all the lovely Monicas in the shop.

It never occurred to him that it was an improbable coincidence that all the girls were named Monica, that according to Spain's National Institute of Statistics, *Maria* was the nation's most popular girl's name, and therefore the likelihood of a Spanish shop full of Monicas was about a million-to-one. Or, that the call "Monica to the cash desk", was a generic, catch-all demand for an assistant, any assistant, to get her arse over to the till.

As Hugo stood in his rose-tinted, romantically smudged, halo-rimmed, reverie, he saw Cressida emerge from the changing room, and stand to one side with her mother, as they decided which of the mountain of garments to hand back to the assistant in the changing room, and which to keep. Hugo held his breath for a minute or two as several outfits were held up and examined by the two women. Cressida shook her head and held three outfits, on their hangers, out in the direction of the sales assistant. Good, he thought. But at the last minute, Cressida changed her mind and snatched them back, holding the entire shop, or so it seemed to Hugo, clutched to her chest.

Hugo exhaled violently. Right. Whatever, he thought. Although, "whatever" was the last benign thought on his mind.

Dana, he observed, also held an item in her hand. Some teal coloured curtain, or table cloth. Although, even to Hugo's limited knowledge of shopping, the latter seemed an unlikely item to have been sourced in here.

Dana caught his eye and waved with a smile. Hugo waved back, not quite matching her enthusiasm in the smile department, as he patted the wallet in his back pocket.

Cressida, he noticed, eyed him with suspicion and wariness. Probably thinks I am going to make a fuss about all that stuff. Well, I'm not. I'll show them. I'll take it on the chin. Like a man. His new-found iron resolve called to mind a scene from a Clint Eastwood film – he was a big fan of Clint Eastwood – when Clint said, "A good man always knows his limitations."

Mind you, he still had Dana's present to buy. That dampened his spirit just a little. And then, when he thought about exactly what to buy his wife for her birthday, his shoulders slumped. Always so difficult. Especially with limited funds. Bet Camilla's husband, Tristram, has no such worries. Just sends his secretary out to Asprey or De Beers for a trinket or two. It's easy when one has money.

Still, it's the thought that counts. Money can't buy everything. Better to buy a single red rose, if you've gone out and picked it yourself, rather than a diamond you sent your secretary to select.

Mind you, a rose wouldn't cut the mustard today, certainly not tonight.

As Hugo debated these weighty matters, he saw that Dana was engaged in trying on a brown, fur jacket thing near the changing rooms, and Cressida was smiling and nodding at her mother, and holding up the lace curtain thing beside it. Cressida turned her mother around to face the mirror. They both nodded their heads.

Then Dana took off the fur thing, and looked at the price ticket and scowled. She showed Cressida and both women shook their heads. The fur thing was put back on the hanger, and they made their way towards Hugo.

Aha! Right! Spot on. Hugo thought. Problem solved. Dana wants a fur jacket, and that is exactly what she will get for her birthday. She won't be expecting it – since she obviously thought the price was out of her league, oh yes, he had seen her reaction to that. Birthday gift idea problem solved, and a happy Dana in one fell swoop. With the added bonus that Cressida would not have to trawl the streets with him looking for the present, now that he had found what to buy her. Cressida would now be free to continue shopping – there were plans to visit makeup and cosmetic shops he had heard with growing horror and alarm – with her mother.

Excellent. Hugo could grab the fur thing, pay for it. And then off to the pub, leaving the women free to do what they liked until lunchtime.

In Hugo's relief at having sorted out this irksome chore, he'd forgotten his real purpose of being, until he was summoned towards the cash desk, as the mountain of clothes was packaged, wrapped and bagged, and a delightful *Monica* told him, in sweet Latin tones, that that would be £182.67 please.

Fuck Clint Eastwood, Hugo thought. I'm obviously not a good man, since I didn't know my limitations, £182.67 is way beyond them.

Or was it though? Hugo remembered his platinum card, the one he kept in reserve. He'd just paid the bill, so he could use the credit that accrued to the balance as a result of his payment, before it was depleted by the addition of next month's interest.

Monica's smile was actually a little too sickly sweet, Hugo decided as he handed over the plastic.

Once the shopping mission had been duly dispatched, and the women – and more importantly Hugo – were safely out of the shop, Hugo announced that he had things to do.

"Well we've still to get the cosmetics, and bits and bobs," Dana advised.

"And I need knickers from Primark," Cressida added.

Hugo held up both hands. "No, absolutely not." He shook his head as well. "There is no way on God's green earth that I am going into Primark, no way, not on a Saturday at midday, in fact not any day."

Hugo remembered the last expedition to Primark, to kit out Cressida for a school skiing trip. It still brought tears to his eyes. God Almighty, it was like a pilgrimage to Mecca, one where they all stampede and people die.

"And, if I might add," Hugo continued, "it is hardly appropriate that I come with you to purchase intimate apparel."

Well thought of, that one, he congratulated himself. That should floor them.

Cressida nodded her head vigorously in agreement as the notion just dawned on her.

"I suppose so then," Dana reluctantly agreed, "we can do that bit ourselves."

Hugo perked up, let off the hook, and in his anxiety to keep the momentum going he added, "Of course, I will pay you back for whatever – essentials – Cressida requires."

The women agreed. Decision made. Almost.

"But Dad, don't you and me have to go and, you know, get something?" Cressida spoke out of the corner of her mouth, inclining her head towards her mother.

"Ah yes, but no actually. That is very firmly in hand, sweetheart." Hugo smiled.

Cressida moved around to her father and whispered in his ear.

"Are you sure Dad? What are you going to buy her? Don't you need my help?"

Hugo have her a hug. "Not at all, I've seen something that will be just perfect, and I assure you Cressida, that you in particular will be very pleased with my choice of gift. Not only will your mother love it, but you will approve it wholeheartedly yourself."

With that, Hugo guided them to the doors of the shopping centre and waved them off down Western Road, towards the delights of Primark on a wet Saturday morning.

Hugo now strode back towards Zara with determination and purpose. He was very pleased indeed with himself, on two fronts: he'd extricated himself from the agony of having to do any more shopping with the women, other than this one little task, and he'd saved hours of trouble later in searching for a present for Dana. And, as a bonus, he would be sitting with a pint in hand – he felt that he could now manage a whole one, instead of a half – and *The Telegraph* crossword, in less than fifteen minutes.

Back inside the store, Hugo made straight for the changing room and the rail of fur things. A gaggle of girls stood in his way. He waited politely for them to shift. Then a stout woman barged in front, with a tent-like garment on a hanger, on her way to the changing room. He waited a little less politely for her to pass. Then a male

153

assistant – where had he sprung from? Hugo hadn't noticed any men before – pushed a consignment of new stock across his path, blocking his way to the rail of furs. Can it never be easy? Hugo asked himself. Still, he could see the fur jacket sitting on the rail, just out of reach. That made matters even easier. Just the one jacket – the others were scarves and collars, so no problems about having to negotiate sizes and things.

The male assistant parked the new clothes rail, impeding Hugo's progress, while he chatted with the girl outside the changing room. The latter laughed and joked, and continued to process the women coming and going with clothes through the changing rooms, handing out little plastic numbers, and taking back unwanted clothes, as they passed through on their way out.

"Come on!" Hugo said under his breath.

The assistants continued to chat. Oblivious.

"Excuse me?" Hugo asked.

They ignored him.

Hugo cleared his throat. "I say, excuse me please," he said, a little louder this time, over the rail of clothes in front of him.

Both assistants now looked up at him, irritated by the interruption to their conversation.

"I'm just trying to get to that jacket, just there." Hugo pointed to the brown fur jacket, on the rail to the right of the assistant, as he leaned over the clothes that blocked his path.

"Which one?" the female assistant asked him.

"That furry jacket, just there beside you." Hugo stabbed his finger, and then his whole hand, towards it.

Just then, a woman with several other coats under her

arm, swept it off the rail, held it up to the light, looked at the price ticket, smiled, added it to the pile under her arm, and marched off to the cash desk with it.

The shop assistants both looked at Hugo.

He stood panic stricken – the afternoon's quiet enjoyment, the pint, the crossword – everything hung in the balance. Not to mention Dana's happiness. Or at least her birthday present.

"It's gone," the male assistant informed him.

"Well I can see that, if I'd have been able to get to the ruddy thing without all this" – Hugo waved his arms at the clothes rail – "obstruction, then I could have bought it."

Hugo glared at them both.

"Do you have any more?" he asked.

The male assistant smirked at the female assistant, and went off with his consignment of clothes, clearing a path to the rail that Hugo had sought, now minus his jacket.

"No. Last one." Monica smiled.

Bloody marvellous, Hugo thought, as he stomped towards the door.

Suddenly the Latin exoticism had lost its charm. He'd always preferred an English Rose anyway. Just like his father.

As the seconds turned to minutes, and the minutes threatened to turn to hours, Hugo realised that he was practically jogging down towards the Lanes in a blind panic. Mission Present remained unaccomplished. As his mind raced wildly, and he struggled to marshal his thoughts, he was unable even to remember any comforting, or inspiring, Eastwood quotes.

He swung down the steps past the gaudy pub, now bursting at the seams with midday drinkers – don't know they're born, he thought – sprinted down Cranbourne Street, now pedestrianised, but might as well be a Formula One racetrack, the amount of baby buggies he had to dodge, straight over the traffic lights, without even waiting to see if they were green, flew down Duke Street, swivelling his head right at the Pandora jewellery shop as he did so, and continued towards Ship Street, seething as he passed Colin Page bookshop and craning his neck left to see what he was missing.

Truth was, all thoughts of pints, *The Telegraph*, and books were long gone.

He had only one purpose in life now – to find Dana a present.

Fuck. But what? As he stood at the intersection of Duke Street and Ship Street, he looked back at Pandora. Jewellery? He was useless at that sort of thing. And anyway, he wasn't in Tristram's league. Pandora wasn't Asprey, but he was pretty sure it wasn't cheap either.

There was always lingerie he supposed. Something black or red. What about that Ann Summers shop? Dana always liked pretty lingerie. Women did, didn't they? Once, when they'd been in Selfridges, or was it Harvey Nichols, years ago, well anyway, Hugo had noticed a lingerie shop where the assistants had all dressed up in the gear. Bit racy, he'd thought. "Provocative" something or other. No, that wasn't it. "Agent Provocative". No, it was French, like the phrase. "Agent Provocateur". Yes, that was it. Dana had liked that, years ago, or at least she had looked at it.

Was Ann Summers the same thing? He had no idea.

But he had spotted an Ann Summers shop up on Western Road. Yes, Hugo decided. That was it. He'd go back up there and buy some red lingerie. Just like Agent Provocateur. And be done with the present business.

Christ, he wished Cressida was there with him.

Just as he turned to go back, someone came out of the bagel shop, and bumped into him.

"Sorry mate," a man said to him, in a smear of bagel and cream cheese.

"No, no, my fault entirely. Wasn't concentrating. Which is the easiest way back up to Western Road?" Hugo asked the man.

"Straight along here, Ship Street, and then the road at the end is North Street, both ways, turn left and North Street becomes Western Road." The man wondered off chewing his bagel.

Hugo realised he was now hungry. And thirsty. That spurred him on. Right, let's get this over and done with, he thought, as he marched down Ship Street.

He had progressed only a few hundred yards when he caught up short, and stopped in his tracks. To his right, a tiny shop – nestled between TK Maxx Discount store and a sweet shop – caught his eye. It was painted black, with a sign in purple, swirling lettering, that proclaimed – Penelope's Portmanteau Vintage.

And sitting smack in the middle of the window, on a mannequin, was a brown fur jacket.

Bingo!

Hugo hesitated for only a second as he put his hand on the door – it looked a little pricey, but to hell with it, the pint was practically shouting his name by now – and went in.

Excellent. Just excellent.

"A lovely little shop." Hugo was astonished to hear those words uttered from his own mouth in reaction to a retail establishment, hitherto anathema to him.

A very attractive blonde lady looked up from behind a small purple desk and smiled at him.

"Thank you," she said.

My word, what an attractive lady, Hugo thought, not sure if his excitement at being so close to his goal was getting the better of him.

"Can I help you with anything in particular?" the lady asked him.

Hugo advanced towards the desk, looking around at all manner of glittering jewellery, exotic handbags, and quite a few fur coats. He nodded at his own discerning taste. And for his Zeitgeist.

Fur is obviously à la mode, de rigueur, very now, the New Look, and so on as he ran out of adjectives. In short, it was obviously very much in fashion, judging by this shop.

Well Zara's loss was, what was this place called? Portmerrion? No, Portmanteau, Penelope's Portmanteau, Vintage – whatever the latter meant – gain.

"You most certainly can," Hugo gushed in excitement.

The attractive lady stood up.

"Are you looking for a present?" she asked him.

Goodness. Serendipity! Hugo thought, on exactly the same wavelength. This bodes well.

It didn't occur to him that men in shops like this were either transvestites, it was Brighton after all, or looking for a present. Hugo did not look like a transvestite, the incident with Bella in the hallway notwithstanding.

"I most definitely am." He beamed.

Hugo strode towards the mannequin in the window and pointed.

"And there it is!" he said with a flourish.

The assistant smiled and went over to the window.

"What size are you looking for?" she asked him, as she began to unbutton the fur jacket on the mannequin.

"Umm, well I'm not exactly sure to be honest. Small I think." Hugo still spoke with purpose, but he was on slightly uneven terrain now.

The assistant however, obviously a master of managing nervous male shoppers, was very helpful.

"Would you say a ten or a twelve?" she asked him, as she removed the fur from the dummy.

"Ah, well now, you see again I'm not so sure."

Hugo racked his brains. What size was Dana? Bigger than Cressida, and much smaller than her mother Bella. But that was a useless analogy since he knew no more about the sizes of the other two than Dana.

Hugo had a brainwave.

"I reckon that the lady in question is about your size," he told the assistant.

She smiled.

"Would you like me to try it on so that you can gauge it better?"

"That would be excellent, if you don't mind?"

The assistant nodded her head and took off her own jacket.

Very shapely, Hugo observed. And about Dana's size too.

Things were looking good all around.

The assistant put the fur jacket on, and stood in front of

Hugo. She turned this way and that, put the collar up, the cuffs down, buttoned it and unbuttoned it.

"How's that?" she finally asked him.

"Perfect, just perfect." Hugo beamed.

"Would you like to take it?" the assistant asked, as she took the fur jacket off and handed it to Hugo to examine.

"Umm, yes I think so. How much is it?" Again he waited with inhaled breath.

"£125," she said, smiling.

Now, ordinarily Hugo would have exclaimed, "Christ!" However. He had observed Dana's reaction to the price of the other fur jacket in Zara, and how she had baulked at that. Therefore this one must be a fraction of the cost!

And therefore an absolute bargain. Dana would be pleased.

"Definitely. I'll take it, thank you so much." Hugo handed the fur jacket back to the lovely assistant, who whipped it away to the desk, and started to wrap it up in elaborate tissue paper, suit cover and fancy pink paper carrier bag.

"How would you like to pay?" she asked him.

"Platinum MasterCard." Hugo handed over his credit card with a flourish, but who was he kidding, he admitted, as the payment went through.

As the assistant wrapped and processed the transaction, she told him about the fur jacket.

"Specialist clean obviously, but as it is natural fur it can get wet – just make sure the lady lets it dry naturally," she explained.

"Yes, yes, got that." Mission accomplished, he was now anxious to get to the pub before meeting up with the others.

The lady continued, "And the recipient might be interested to know that the fur is from a big cat, and is dyed to look like mink." She handed Hugo the bag.

"Cat, big, dyed, yes, yes, got that too." Hugo took the bag as he looked at his watch – twelve thirty.

"You have been a great help – Miss?" he asked her.

"Fiona, I'm the owner," she smiled in reply.

"Well thanks again Fiona, I think I will be in the good books with this." Hugo laughed and nodded, as he walked towards the door.

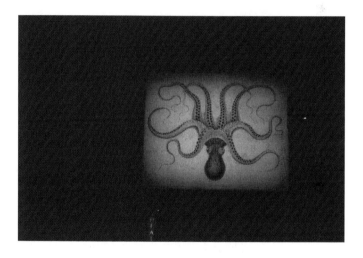

ELEVEN

Alex gulped the last of the Red Dog local ale that he was drinking, in the back of the pub, near the vintage jukebox, just as he spotted his old man walk in the front door and stride up to the bar.

Shit. Nearly caught there. The old man's on a mission, isn't he? Alex thought, as he watched his father drain nearly half of the glass put in front of him before the barman had even given him his change.

Alex laughed. That'll be shopping with Mum and Cress. Still, he looks relaxed enough now, as Alex spotted the Penelope's Portmanteau shopping bag that his father had plonked down under the bar by his feet. Probably got Mum's present out of the way.

Alex was feeling smug too. He'd been down the North Laines – after making an appointment at The Blood of Satan for later on – to Snooper's Paradise, a kind of indoor vintage market place, where Alex had haggled hard for a very pretty silver necklace for his mum. Turned out the bloke on the stall had roadied for a band that Alex liked, and after talking for a bit, Alex had

162

secured a thirty per cent discount. Good result all around, since his grandma had given him the money to buy it in the first place. Still, it was the thought that counted, and he knew what his mum liked. Alex was good in that way. First class taste. Like his dear grandfather, Grandma Bella always told him.

Alex went out the side door, round to the front of the pub, and came back in to where Hugo was standing, feigning arrival.

Stealthily, Alex picked up his dad's pint and took a gulp while Hugo was engrossed in a crossword.

"Hey. You cheeky little bugger!" Hugo said when he saw him.

"Sorry Dad, couldn't resist that."

Hugo playfully slapped him away.

"Yes, well. No more. You're not old enough to be drinking in pubs, and you had more than sufficient last night."

Alex winced, not at Hugo's comment, but at the aftertaste of Hugo's drink. Lager. Nasty stuff. Alex was an ale man, and the lager jarred horribly with the Red Dog he had consumed before his old man showed up.

There was, however, method in his madness. Any whiff that Hugo got of Alex's beery breath would be chalked up to the gulp he had taken of Hugo's pint, and nothing else.

For a man treading a fine line in deception – and his ongoing plans for the weekend – Alex could afford to take no chances.

"Where's Mum and Cress – still shopping?" Alex asked.

"By any luck they should be just finished. I left them about forty minutes ago heading in the direction of Primark." Hugo took a sip of his drink and looked up.

Both men shared a mock grimace at this thought, relieved that they were well out of it.

"They should be here any minute and then we can go and get some lunch. I promised Cressida somewhere called 'Yo Sushi', and as it is your mum's birthday I don't want any complaints from you about it, whether it's fish or not." Hugo's look was resolute.

"That's cool. Yo Sushi's fine. Lots of chicken there too." Alex shrugged his shoulders.

Hugo looked relieved and returned to his crossword.

"And sake," Alex added.

Hugo looked up sharply.

Alex held his hands up in a surrender gesture. "Joking!"

Just then Dana and Cressida bustled through the door of the pub, weighed down with innumerable paper and plastic shopping bags.

"Bloody hell – the charge for the carrier bags alone must equal a third-world country's national debt," Hugo said, as he got up to help them and pecked Dana on the cheek.

Dana hugged Alex and tousled his hair. "Don't be so dramatic, it's just a couple of bags. We got some things. But in the end it was a bit chaotic, even for us," Dana remarked.

The men exchanged another smug nod of the head.

"What you been up to?" Cressida asked Alex, trying to grab the carrier bag that he had folded down over the handle, rather than carry properly.

"This and that," he replied, tapping the side of his nose and smiling at his mum.

Dana smiled lovingly back.

"Right then," Hugo said, gulping the rest of his beer

and tapping his empty glass down on the bar. "Let's go and find Cressida's sushi restaurant!"

"*Yo Sushi* Dad, get it right," Cressida corrected, as they all traipsed out of the pub and down Black Lion Street.

It was just after one thirty, and the trippers were out in force in the Lanes. Heads bobbing up and down everywhere, mirroring the waves on the sea that was just visible through the narrow streets. People were shopping, browsing, window shopping, bustling about with bags and boxes, walking hand in hand, eating take-aways, a few brave souls with an ice cream – it was the seaside after all – cyclists on bikes weaving in and out, people walking on the edge of the pavement, then in the road, then hopping up again on the pavement when a car hooted its horn.

They sauntered down past The Friends Meeting House, at the other end of Ship Street, and onwards past the council offices. As they passed the Town Hall, a wedding was in full swing. Well, post-wedding, the business end of the event having been transacted inside the building. Now the fun part was taking place outside. Brighton style – which meant a brightly coloured Cadillac, brightly dressed wedding party, retro fashion. A flash of bulbs popped as photographs were taken. Lots of guests, lots of flowers, lots of confetti.

Hugo had spotted the flurry of activity as they had neared the Town Hall. Saw the Cadillac festooned with white ribbons, and a Just Married sign with tin cans attached to the chrome bumper. Very traditional. He motioned to the women, assuming they would want to stop and have a look, as women do. All that Cinderella, white spun, candy-floss lace, wedding gowns and veils, it always stopped women in their tracks.

Hugo was a few paces in front, he turned around and came back to Dana and Cressida.

"Look darling, it's a wedding, do you want to stop and look?" he asked them.

He led them over. A group picture was being organised by a harried looking photographer, who was trying politely to herd them all in front of the Town Hall steps, and kept pushing two small children together who were holding baskets of flowers. The children, trussed up like something from *My Big Fat Gypsy Wedding* – that reality programme on television, looked like they were having none of it, although they also looked like they could have been persuaded for a tenner apiece. Five and six-years-old, going on thirty.

Someone produced a bottle of champagne and two glasses. Someone else threw more confetti. The photographer finally stood back to take the photograph. Hugo positioned the women behind the latter.

"Lots of colour!" Hugo remarked. "Gosh look at that Cadillac, bet that cost a pretty penny!"

Someone interrupted the photograph by holding up the champagne bottle and glasses. The groom stepped forward to take it.

"Ha! They nearly forgot the champers," Hugo commented, smiling good humouredly after his pint of beer.

The photographer waited, pretending to be patient.

"Hang on, ha! They've forgotten the bride too!" Hugo laughed. "They'd better get her in the picture, there'll be hell to pay if she's forgotten!"

As he said this, the "groom" turned to another man in

identical clothes and buttonhole standing beside him, handed him the other glass of champagne, looked into his eyes, smiled and kissed him full on the lips, to a loud cheer from the crowd and flashing bulbs from the photographer.

"What?" Hugo murmured.

"It's Brighton Dad. Get over it," Cressida said, as she put her arm in her mother's and walked off down towards East Street.

At least the rain has stopped even if it is not sunny, Dana decided. Although she had had visions of sitting outside English's Fish Restaurant under blue skies, sipping a Pinot Grigio, and eating a nice sea bass. But there were no seats and canopy umbrellas set up outside today, and it was not, after all, Yo Sushi. One remained a mother, even on one's birthday. Life was always a compromise.

As they walked on, Dana chuckled at the wedding incident, so like Hugo to miss the point, jump to what he considered the right conclusion. Goodness knows what he'd say if Alex was gay. Hugo's generation, no wait, stop. Hugo's generation is my generation, she reminded herself. Except that it isn't, not really. Even though Hugo was only five years older than Dana, he was a different generation in mindset.

He was also his father's son.

Hugo's father would not have understood the gay wedding.

And so therefore neither did Hugo.

Alex wasn't gay, but if he had been then Hugo would just have had to deal with it, or get over it, to coin Cressida's phrase.

Anyway, the incident had been highly amusing. Bet they have a great time at their reception, Dana thought. Wish I could go. Dana had a colleague at work who was gay, he always seemed to have the most fun and the most parties.

Having recovered from the others' mockery of him, Hugo now asked, "So where exactly is this restaurant Cressida?"

They had been wandering about for a little over twenty minutes.

"I don't know, do I?" she responded.

"But I thought you said you did. It was your idea after all," Hugo reminded her.

"That's not true! You said Brighton had Yo Sushi. You said, and your words were, 'Brighton has a Yo Sushi'," Cressida said.

"No I didn't. I said I'm *sure* they have a Yo Sushi, which is entirely different to saying that I know where it actually is!" Hugo responded.

"Well I don't know. I didn't look it up because you said we would go there!" Cressida was getting worked up.

"Well neither did I!" As was Hugo.

"Okay. Stop. This bickering isn't getting us anywhere," Dana interrupted. "Right. Cressida do they have lots of branches everywhere?"

"Well, I suppose. I don't know. I only know the one Emma goes to," Cressida replied.

"That's hardly helpful as it's sixty-five miles away, is it?" Hugo chipped in.

It started to rain again. People scattered. Umbrellas went up. Hoods were pulled over. Collars turned up. The rain pelted down. The paper carrier bags mushroomed with splotches of rain, and then turned a darker colour.

Cars splashed by, a taxi hit a puddle near the pavement and sent a muddy spray of water perilously close to them.

They huddled under a tree, without leaves, and therefore useless, in the rain. Bickering.

"Cressida, Google it please," Dana commanded.

"My battery is dead," she replied.

"Hugo?" Dana looked at him.

"Left my phone at the hotel, where's yours?" Hugo asked her.

"Same place," Dana responded. That was a lie. There were too many messages on it to risk getting it out now.

"Alex. Please find the restaurant on Google," Hugo in turn commanded.

"No signal, otherwise we would be there now," he replied.

Hugo glared at him.

"This is insane. Standing here in the rain, speculating and arguing. I'm going in there to ask." Hugo strode off towards English's Restaurant, leaving the others stranded under the tree.

A few minutes later he was back.

"When you want a job doing etc, right, let's go. Got the directions, it's just around the corner, come." Hugo took Dana's arm.

Just then, the heavens opened, and they were lashed soaking wet with a torrent of freshly squeezed Brighton rain.

"My hair's getting wet!" Cressida cried, as they all dashed across the road and down a narrow side street.

"We're all wet Cressida, stop complaining," Hugo shouted over his shoulder, as the deluge continued.

It's all right for you Dad, Cressida thought. You haven't got much hair to worry about. How can I go into a packed Yo Sushi with hair like this? Everyone will look at me. And then I'll have to sit there while it frizzles up and dries, making me look like some sad, 1980s pop star. It is so embarrassing. Cressida also had another much more serious concern – she could feel a funny taste in her mouth when she licked her lips. She knew that the moment she looked in a mirror her worst fears would be confirmed.

Her mascara had run.

She tried to shield her face and head from the elements by holding up the Primark carrier bag, but that was perilously close to disintegrating itself, and anyway, the gale-force winds that accompanied the rain threatened to whip it out of her hand and carry it away on the thermals, like the smaller seagulls floating in the sky above.

"Thought it was just around the corner," Alex shouted above the wind.

Hugo stopped and glared at him.

"I'm not a bloody sat nav am I? I'm simply following the instructions that Italian chap gave me in that restaurant."

They redoubled their efforts by bracing against the wind, heads down, shoulders low, like frontiersmen in the wilderness.

They trudged on down towards the Old Steine.

"Ahh!" Dana exclaimed as her green silk scarf was whipped off her shoulder and whirled around in a flurry. Alex ran to catch it.

"For goodness sake Hugo, we won't be worth tuppence if we have to keep walking in this, let's go back to the hotel and get a sandwich and some hot tea," Dana pleaded, as she stuffed her scarf, now sodden, inside the Zara bag.

Hugo looked around in desperation. Consulted a scrap of paper, written partly in Italian.

"Bingo!" he shouted, as he pointed to a discreet building, clad in dark wood, with a small chrome sign over the door that read – Tako.

"That's it. Over there, come on," he shouted above the elements.

Alex crossed the road with him, Dana moved forward a little. Cressida stood rooted to the spot.

"What? Come on, let's get inside before we melt in the rain," Hugo said.

"That's not it!" Cressida cried.

"Yes it is, it states quite plainly here" – Hugo waved the scrap of paper in the wind – "*Tako.*"

"It's not Yo Sushi is it Dad?" Cressida cried again. "It doesn't state quite plainly *Yo Sushi*!"

"She's right Hugo," Dana added.

Hugo fought the wind as he trudged back across the road.

"Look, I know it's not the actual name of the restaurant that you wanted darling, but I have it on very good authority that this is exactly the same as Yo Sushi, it is in fact the Brighton version, but the same, if not better, in all respects."

Cressida looked unconvinced. Remained standing where she was.

Alex stood in the doorway of the restaurant. Heeling

and toeing and whistling.

Dana stood watching all of it.

Hugo was on the spot.

"Okay, here's what we will do. It's pissing rain, it's your mother's birthday, we are all likely to get pneumonia if we don't get out of this weather in a moment. In addition, it is now one fifty-five and our luncheon options are limited on a busy Saturday, when all restaurants, including very likely this one, will be jam-packed. So. I will go inside to the restaurant and explain the situation, need to be careful as can't insult them obviously by telling them they are second choice, but I will explain that you have particular dietary requirements, and that your heart was set on Yo Sushi, but in fact this place looks better. How's that?"

Hugo was giving it his best shot and smiling hopefully.

Cressida looked at her mother, damp: her lovely scarf all wet and rolled up in a ball in the carrier bag, her nice Gucci handbag getting all wet too. Poor Mum.

Cressida had also confirmed her worst fears when she tentatively touched her index finger to her left cheek, and it came back black as ink.

"Well, okay, but I'm only going in there if you can sort it out Dad. And I didn't have any breakfast, and it's against the law to neglect your children and let them starve." She added the latter for good measure.

As Dana and Cressida huddled together in the door recess of a dental implant surgery, Hugo strode across the road again back to Tako restaurant. He went in the door, followed swiftly by Alex, who had clearly made up his mind about his lunch.

A few minutes later Hugo was standing in the doorway

of the restaurant waving them over.

Dana and Cressida dashed across the road, dodged a puddle, and were ushered inside by Hugo.

It was like dusk inside Tako. A very long, low, room crouching in the half-light, and set with long, low tables against each wall. Dark, mahogany wood furnishings, rich chocolate brown leather seats, some sort of tiled, fossilised sandstone floor, low, dark ceiling. And a huge gold leaf mural or wall hanging, like a setting sun, running the entire length of one wall.

The tables were set with one bone-white linen napkin, a pair of chopsticks and a crystal clear glass tumbler.

A row of tiny candles were laid out, flickering, along a narrow shelf on the wall under the mural.

In muted decibels, a series of clangs and clashes – traditional Japanese music – played in the background.

Given the lavishness of the decor, a quartet of musicians might well be hidden away in some recess, rather than any notion of the musical ambience emanating from a CD player.

An enormous tank of exotic fish was embedded in a rocky recess, smack bang in the middle of the back wall. All manner of creatures swam around, but taking centre stage was a huge, pink octopus with rubbery tentacles, which lashed out in all directions at the other fish dodging its embrace. It would not have been out of place in the Sea-Life Centre. Or a Jules Verne novel.

The candles flickered, the music clanged, the fish swam.

But. They were the only diners in there. The place was completely empty.

Dana had misgivings immediately. She cut her eyes in all directions looking for a menu, or rather a price-list. It was not too late to retreat. But, typically, there was none to be seen. She was reminded of that television series from the 80s – Tenko – set in Japan in the Second World War. Both the music and atmosphere were similar.

Alex was sprawled on a luxurious, chocolate brown leather bench seat at a table in the middle of the room. He had his phone out.

Hugo ushered Dana and Cressida to seats, anxious to please, despite the cost, Dana thought.

"Put that away please Alex, the Japanese are a very correct race of people. Meals are important ceremonial-like times for them, and it would be a grave insult if they saw you looking at that contraption." Hugo took Dana's coat and laid it over the back of her chair as he spoke.

Alex looked around the empty restaurant.

"Must be having a ceremony somewhere else today then," he remarked.

Hugo prickled, Dana could sense it.

"They probably dine later. And anyway thought your phone had no signal?"

"Free wi fi," Alex responded.

Dana wondered how they knew these things, but then supposed that Alex had just searched for it, as teenagers do. They expect to be connected. It doesn't occur to them that they wouldn't be.

Connected. Like us. A connected family. Stop it, she decided. We're here and we will enjoy it.

"Do please put your phone aside though for now Alex," Dana urged.

"Just Facebooking. Keeping our family adventure

published on social media." Alex tapped in something to his phone and then put it in his pocket.

"Well I sincerely hope you don't 'post' the minutiae of our confidential lives young man. Some things are private and not for public consumption. All that drivel people post, all those irrelevant details that no one is interested in." Hugo looked around for a waiter.

Not a soul had been in sight since they had walked through the door.

Mind you, Dana agreed with him about the social media point. She did have a Facebook account, but it was only to share the odd photo or message with friends or relatives in far-flung places. And she posted the odd legal snippet too, when the fancy took her. Usually only if it was derogatory about some revered judge or celebrity lawyer.

A certain Hollywood star's new wife had come in for comment from Dana too – she was puzzled by the concept of her being a "high-flying lawyer", and trotting the globe in designer outfits, attending various glittering events with her husband. In Dana's experience, most high-flying lawyers she knew worked a minimum of eighty hours a week. Lucky if they made it to the South of France for ten days in the school summer holidays.

But she never put anything private or intimate on the social media domain, and was amazed, and horrified, when some of her friends did. The most solemn and private of family matters were posted, liked and favourited. Deaths, illness, births – a friend of hers actually detailing her birthing experience, and a photograph of the child emerging from, well, where it emerges from. And another friend announcing the death of his mother. Dana hadn't known whether to "like" it or not. She had debated for hours. If she "liked" it then surely that was disrespectful, surely she was saying she was glad the woman was dead? And if she didn't "like" it, then surely that was saying she wasn't interested enough to "like" it?

In the end the dilemma had been solved by, of course, her teenage daughter, who informed her it was cool to like a post announcing a death, because you were evidencing your sympathy by the "like".

Dana still wasn't convinced. What irritated her the most was indeed the drivel that people posted. What they had for dinner, what their cat had for breakfast, what their Christmas tree looked like, how they were feeling – Jesus that was the worst one, surely? Why announce to the world that you are feeling tired, fed-up, upset, angry, depressed, happy? Would you pick up the phone to everyone in your address book and say, "Hi, this is Dana, I just want to say that today I am feeling fed up." Or would you write to them, or email them and say, "Dear So and So, I just want to tell you that today I am very happy. Kind regards, Dana." Of course not. They would think you were a lunatic. And, come to think of it, when people posted all that nonsense – and there were even little apps or avatars or whatever they were called to illustrate your feelings with a cartoon picture – they never said, "I am fed up. *How are you?*"

It was all self, self, selfish. Dana was working herself up into a very bad mood.

"When can we order some grub? I'm starving," Alex asked across the table.

Hugo looked around.

"The waiting staff will be out in a minute, they don't rush things in Japan. Tranquility and calm is the key to their culture. That's where the reference to 'Zen' comes in," he lectured.

"I have to go to the ladies and sort out my hair and face," Cressida announced.

"I wouldn't bother Cress, you fit right in here. You look like a Geisha Girl, or a panda, with all that black stuff around your eyes." Alex laughed.

Cressida threw a chopstick at him.

"Now now, come on, stop making nasty remarks Alex." Hugo turned to Cressida. "I think the ladies toilets are in the back darling, I saw a sign when I spoke to the waiter earlier."

Cressida got up, hauling her oversized handbag with the little pink kitten keyring, and made off in the direction of the toilets.

"Pandas come from China anyway, not Japan," she said to Alex, before she disappeared behind a huge silk screen with a painting of a red bonsai tree on it.

Just then, a man in a black silk suit with a Mandarin collar, appeared, approached their table, bowed, handed them four parchment scrolls, bowed again, turned around and went back where he had come from.

Dana and Hugo exchanged a look. Dana was relaxing a little and found the brief interaction with the waiter amusing. Hugo, she supposed, was now weighing up the financial implications of their splendorous surroundings.

It did strike Dana as a little odd that the waiter had uttered not one word. Still. Hugo had already been in and spoken to them, so clearly they had the necessary information and full brief.

Dana unrolled the scroll. It was ragged at the edges – or made to look worn and old – and the menu was printed, or possibly hand-written, in a flourishing Japanese-style calligraphy in red ink. It wasn't quite the Hiragana Japanese alphabet. But it may as well have been.

The menu was totally unintelligible.

Dana looked at Alex. He had his phone out again and was taking pictures of the menu surreptitiously under the table.

Alex looked at his phone as he did so and smirked.

Hugo was studying the menu very carefully. He was frowning and his lips were pursed. He didn't look very calm or tranquil to Dana.

Dana tossed her menu on the table.

"This is pointless. I can't understand anything on the menu. I'll just ask for some teriyaki chicken and rice when the waiter comes back. And a glass of green tea. That will set me up for later." Dana looked at Alex again.

"What's teriyaki Mum?" he asked.

"It's grilled meat, chicken in this case, with soy sauce, it's very tasty." Dana proceeded to roll her menu back up.

Alex slung his menu down. "I'll have the same."

Hugo didn't say a word.

"And a beer," Alex added.

Hugo looked up. "You will do no such thing. We will all have a drink tonight. But for now, we will enjoy some culturally traditional Japanese cuisine, and I applaud your mother's choice of green tea, very traditional and very cleansing to the system."

"So what are you going to eat Dad? What takes your fancy on the menu?" Alex prodded Hugo's scroll.

Hugo cleared his throat and straightened the menu.

"Well actually, I am torn between a few dishes detailed here," he responded.

He hadn't got a fucking clue then, Dana thought.

"But I think, in retrospect, that teriyaki chicken is an excellent choice. With rice."

Hugo laid his menu down.

"Is that on the menu then Dad?"

Hugo bristled. "Of course. All Japanese restaurants serve that as a basic dish."

"Of course." Alex smirked.

Hugo bristled again.

"But Cress won't eat that, will she?" Alex goaded.

"You heard my conversation with the waiter when we came in the first time Alex, I have organised Cressida's menu request already. Don't you worry, that is all taken care of. Now - what shall we do tomorrow? Brighton Pavilion?"

"Well actually Hugo, I was thinking – why don't you and Alex go up to the new Amex Football Stadium and have a look, while Cress and I go and visit the Pavilion and the museum?" Dana said.

She was hoping that a visit to the new stadium would serve a dual purpose – one, cement the new-found cordiality between father and son, and two, spur on, or at least inspire, Hugo to get cracking with the book.

Hugo nodded his head slowly.

"That is certainly an idea," he agreed.

"They have a state-of-the-art gym there, and maybe Alex could get some ideas for his business studies project for A-level?" Dana said, encouraged by Hugo's response.

Alex shrugged his shoulders.

"Yeah, I don't mind. Mr Stonewall said I needed to get cracking on that, gave us all the Big Lecture in our house meeting last week, said all the money our parents were paying, we needed to keep up our end and get on with the work," Alex said.

Hugo stiffened his back as Dana looked at him, she imagined that his enthusiasm for the teriyaki had been dampened by mention of the school fees.

Still, at least they aren't chasing for them. That's a good sign. I'll worry when that happens and not before, she decided.

"Well, yes, quite right," Hugo said, blustering.

"I'm not the worst though, some others haven't even started," Alex explained. "Where's Cress? Has she been abducted and sold into slavery as a Geisha?"

"Alex. Please, that's in very poor taste. You really cannot say things like that," Hugo said.

"It's all right, I won't mention The War either."

Hugo glared at him.

A waiter appeared, as if from nowhere – this was starting to feel a little like Mr Ben – that children's cartoon from Dana's youth – the one where Mr Ben goes into a changing room, tries on a costume, usually an exotic one, and is then transported off to another land for adventure.

This time the waiter was younger and dressed entirely in white. He approached the table, didn't bow, took each of their glasses, turned them over and disappeared.

Hugo held up a hand. But the waiter was gone.

Cressida finally emerged from the ladies. The black smudges were gone and her hair was slicked back. She sat down.

"What's up? You all look very odd?" she said, smoothing back her hair.

"Nothing darling, just discussing what we are doing tomorrow, tell you later." Dana patted her hand, and then removed it as the waiter returned.

The waiter in white now held a jug of clear liquid, which he poured into their glasses.

Then the waiter dressed in black came back, bowed and smiled.

Hugo sat upright, cleared his throat and said, "Thank you. We have looked at your impressive menu, and whilst we are very taken with a number of dishes on it, we were wondering if we could please have three of the teriyaki chicken with plain boiled rice, and four green teas to drink. Please. Thank you."

The waiter in white withdrew. The waiter in black took their scrolls, smiled, nodded, bowed again and retreated.

Hugo exhaled and relaxed back in his chair.

"You see," he remarked to Alex, "as I say, the Japanese culture is to please the guest, make them feel totally at home, tranquil and calm, nothing is too much trouble for their guests."

"We're not guests if we are paying though, are we Dad?" Cressida said, as she took a sip of the liquid.

Dana did the same, it was, she was relieved to note, water.

"That's not the point, it's all about respect with the Japanese," Hugo replied.

Cress has a point, Dana thought, I wonder what the bill will be? The prices looked steep on the "menu", unless it was in Yen, which was less than a pound. Well, there must be a limit to what they can charge for chicken in soy sauce and Cress was eating, essentially vegetables and rice, so that couldn't cost the earth either.

"So, what is everyone doing this afternoon?" Dana asked.

"Well obviously I have to deal with this" – Cressida pulled at her hair – "and then these" – she held up her fingernails – "and then I have to sort out my clothes for tonight. What do you think I should wear Mum?"

Cressida started rummaging in the carrier bags under the table.

"What about that little cream floaty dress with the corset waist?" Dana responded, "that looked very pretty?"

"Maybe." Cressida continued to rummage in the bags. "Is it posh tonight Dad?"

"It is an upmarket French restaurant, if that is what you mean by 'posh'," Hugo responded.

"Understated elegance then," Dana advised.

"I can't find that dress, is it there in your bag Mum?" Cressida asked.

Dana bent down under the table and retrieved a carrier bag from Zara.

In the background, a waiter emerged and moved things around behind them.

"I think so." Dana put the carrier bag on top of her lap and started going through it.

God, I hope we didn't leave it behind, she thought, as she looked through the bag.

Dana was interrupted in her search by the waiter in white, who carried a tray of steaming glasses to their table. She waited politely while he placed one in front of each of them.

Alex sniffed his and winced.

They looked – interesting. But not at all like green tea.

There was some shuffling behind their table, as the waiter in black and a man in white overalls, pulled the silk bonsai screen across, cutting the room in half.

Hugo looked up. "Great. I suppose now they are having a private party or something. It'll mean a lot of noise no doubt." He sniffed his tea and also grimaced.

"Don't be such a misery guts Hugo," Dana said, "it might be very entertaining if it's Japanese."

"Yeah, specially if it's another wedding," Alex added from across the table as he pushed his "tea" away.

Hugo glared at him again.

The waiter in white had withdrawn to assist with the preparations for the party, or whatever it was.

"I assume that is the reason the restaurant was so quiet," Hugo said, "they probably didn't want to take any bookings if they had a large party later, probably thought we'd be quick."

"Is it there Mum?" Cressida asked

Dana fiddled about and finally extracted a cream, chiffon, very short, floaty dress, and handed it across the table to Cressida.

Hugo took a sip of his water, Dana did the same, the "green tea" being very unpalatable. They were used to the sanitised, Westernised, Waitrosed version. The traditional reality was always something else.

Just then, there was a loud splashing sound and at the same time Cressida shouted, "Oh no!" And flung the dress down on the table.

"What's wrong now?" Hugo asked.

"It's gigantic!" Cressida shouted again.

"What? And please keep your voice down Cressida,"

Hugo said, pursing his lips.

"It's the wrong size. Look, it says 'UK 10'. It's enormous! I can't wear that, I'll look like a wigwam."

Dana took the dress and examined the label. It was indeed a size ten, and to be fair to Cressida, much too big for her, as she was in reality more like a size six.

"Oh for goodness sake, it's not a catastrophe, is it? I thought you'd lost a leg or something with that reaction." Hugo sat back in his chair.

"Not a catastrophe for you Dad, but it is for me. We'll just have to go back to the shop and change it. Won't we Mum?"

"Well you can count me out. You women can return to that purgatory, but I for one will be in the hotel pool this afternoon, and maybe even in the sauna getting some heat for my back." Hugo sat resolute.

"Fine. We'll do that then, we'll nip back after lunch, put the dress back in this bag Cress or they won't change it if it gets mucky," Dana said.

Dana handed the dress and carrier bag to Cressida, and as she did so the waiter in white appeared at the edge of the bonsai tree screen and started pushing it back, opening up the room again.

Hugo looked up.

"You see? All that fuss and shouting has probably stopped the preparations for the party. Don't blame them. They probably want us out of here as quickly as possible." Hugo shook his head.

"I need the loo now." Dana got up. "What's taking them so long anyway, surely they have teriyaki chicken in the fridge or something?"

"I'll come too Mum." Cressida jumped up.

"Why do girls always go to the toilet together?" Alex asked.

"Indeed, why they do anything is a mystery to me," Hugo responded.

Dana followed Cressida to the ladies, the latter now leading the way on the strength of her knowing the layout. As they passed the screen, Dana had to side-step a large wet patch on the fossilised, sandstone floor. Jesus. What a family, she thought. All our bickering and shouting. We've even made the tranquil Japanese nervous, not only have they abandoned their preparations, we've made them drop things.

The music in the ladies room sounded more like a spa to Cressida. Compared to the racket in the restaurant, it was soothing and relaxing. Like the music they had played when she and Mum had gone for facials once, as a treat for her fifteenth birthday, to the Champney's salon in Tunbridge Wells. This was similar: all waterfalls and raindrops and flutes. And the toilets were lovely too. If she ever had her own bathroom, she would decorate it like this, she decided.

Crisp, white, bamboo rice-paper screens at the window. And little white linen towels to dry your hands.

"Look Mum, the hand cream is in these little dishes and it smells gorgeous." Cressida held up a little pot to Dana.

"Lovely. Like ginger and something else." her mother sniffed the pot.

"Lime," Cressida said, "I think it smells like lime." She took a dab and rubbed it into her hands.

Dana gave her a hug, brushed a stray hair from her

cheek, and kissed her on the top of her head.

"Are you okay darling? Are you having a nice time?" her mother asked.

I will be when I get my hair and clothes sorted out, Cressida thought. But it's Mum's birthday, so I won't complain.

"Yes Mum, I'm just hungry!"

"Now that is good to hear," Dana responded, "so let's go and eat!"

They walked back to the table, Cressida jumping over the wet patch on the floor, horrified at the thought of getting her little velvet pumps wet again. She'd only just managed to dry them out on the hand dryers in the toilet earlier. Wonder if I can wangle a taxi out of Dad back to the hotel? Yep. Definitely worth a try, she decided, as she sat down again.

The music had been turned up for some reason. Cressida found it irritating, and difficult to concentrate on formulating her makeup and outfit plans for later, with all that racket. Her tummy was starting to rumble as well. She wasn't sure she could wait much longer for something to eat. Wished she had eaten some breakfast now. Still, she couldn't have gone shopping with a full tummy, so it was worth the sacrifice. But she was more than ready for her vegetarian sushi now. It was yummy. She had first had it with Emma when they had stopped by a Yo Sushi, after a shopping expedition. Lovely little rolls of rice, wrapped in maki seaweed, with wasabi and pickled ginger. Yummy. Not fattening, and very vegan. The Japanese – or was it Chinese – Cressida was not clear on the point, knew all about being vegetarian. And vegan. And even the supermarkets did it now – those little cartons of sushi with those little itsy-bitsy tubes of soy sauce, sachets of wasabi paste, and slivers of pickled ginger.

The more she thought about it, the more her tummy rumbled.

God knows what the others are going to eat, but at least I'm safe.

Teriyaki chicken! How can they? They don't even know where it's come from. Probably kept in cages behind the kitchen, like in those films. If it even is chicken. Cressida had heard nasty things about dogs and cats on YouTube, when Emma had asked her to support an animal rescue charity in Korea. All those poor little dogs and cats, she'd said. We have to stop it. We have to help them. When I'm older I'm going to go and work in an animal rescue centre in one of those places, she decided. During a gap year. Mind you, it might be a bit, well, not very civilised, what with no electricity or hair dryers or stuff.

Well at the very least she would volunteer to help in one at home. Or maybe send them money. When she had it.

The lights were turned up a little, making them all blink.

The waiter in white appeared, took their napkins from the table, flicked them out, and then laid them carefully over each of their knees.

"Thank you very much," her dad gushed.

The waiter was expressionless.

He disappeared, and then came back with a tray with four large, white porcelain plates on it. He proceeded to lay a plate in front of each of them. He withdrew again.

Dana looked at Hugo, who looked at Cressida.

Alex smiled.

The waiter in white reappeared, and snapped their chopsticks apart, and placed them diagonally across their plates.

Dana shifted uncomfortably in her seat.

Hugo grinned and thanked the waiter again. The latter still said nothing.

Again the waiter withdrew.

Alex laughed.

Hugo shot him a warning look.

The candles flickered, the music clashed and clanged, a little louder this time. Cressida noticed her mother looking over her shoulder to the back wall. She saw Dana involuntarily jerk her head. What's up Mum? She pondered. Hope Dad hasn't upset you again. Cressida was no fool. She knew her parents argued. She knew her mum worked very hard. She knew there were tensions, not exactly sure about what, but parents never gave their kids any credit for knowing stuff. As she said, Cressida was no fool.

Just then, the waiter in white slid quietly over to the table and stood silently to one side, like a sentinel. Cressida thought he looked very funny and wanted to giggle. There was a flurry of activity from the back of the restaurant, as doors swung open and the waiter in black appeared smiling and nodding, and he too stood by the table to one side.

And then a very fat man, with a shiny bald head, staggered in from behind them with a massive platter, held high above him, and laid it down in the middle of the table.

All three men stood back and bowed.

The waiter in black extended his right hand with a flourish towards the dish in the centre of the table.

Dana sat open-mouthed.

Alex fought, physically, to suppress laughter.

Hugo asked in a very weak voice, "Is it − is it − vegan?"

The waiter in black smiled, nodded, and said in a thick, heavy accent − a kind of East-West dialectic fusion, "Yes, yes, sashimi. Fish. And speciality of house *Tako* − you call, octopus!"

Cressida looked at her mother.

Her mother was looking at the back wall.

The back wall had a trail of water leading to the wet patch on the floor.

Cressida followed it to the fish tank.

The fish still swam, more happily this time, and with more space.

The octopus had gone.

Cressida screamed, jumped up, sent the platter flying onto the sandstone floor, and ran out the door.

TWELVE

"How was I to know that *Tako* meant octopus in Japanese?" Hugo said, as he, Dana and Alex hurried back to the hotel, juggling the shopping bags between them.

"Well that bloody great slimy thing with tentacles in the fridge fish tank should have been a clear indication of the type of food they served," Dana shouted back.

"There is no need for foul language Dana, thank you very much. And if I may say in my defence, I did consult with the waiter, and told him of Cressida's requirements, while you waited outside, and Alex" – Hugo turned to Alex, who was smirking at the exchange between his parents – "will back me up on that point, won't you Alex?"

Hugo stopped on the corner of West Street just as they were about to turn onto the seafront. He searched Alex's eyes for confirmation.

Alex was laden down with Cressida's shopping bags, and, despite his initial glee at the cock-up in the restaurant, was now feeling very hungry, and very pissed off at missing out on his teriyaki chicken.

"Well you didn't exactly make it clear, did you Dad?"

"What are you talking about? I made it abundantly clear that Cressida did not eat meat, that she had hoped to go to Yo Sushi, but that we had spotted their restaurant instead and it looked better, and that we had a special requirement if the house could provide it." Hugo was red in the face, what with the wind and defending his position.

"That's not the same thing as saying she is a vegetarian. Or a vegan. Is it?" Dana shouted again.

In spite of his hunger, Alex continued smirking as he thought back to a few moments ago. The look on Cress's face. Fuck! It had been priceless, almost as priceless as his old man's. When his dad had looked at the platter of raw, sliced fish, mountains of it, surrounded by little curly, hairy mollusc-type things – sea urchins it had turned out – and the gigantic, slimy, suckery octopus plonked in the middle, he had gone a shade paler. Alex couldn't work out if that was because of the cost – Alex was no expert, but he'd been in enough fine dining restaurants, mostly with Tristram, Camilla and Lucas – to know that fish was sold by weight. And that octopus thing had been fucking massive!

And then Cressida screaming, while the sushi chef stood there bewildered, and then Cress jumping up and knocking the whole lot to the floor, and the octopus flailing around on the sandstone tiles. Well, all right, it wasn't flailing because it was dead. But ha! It looked like it should still have been swimming. And it had been. That was the hysterical bit. The waiters hadn't been setting up for a party when they had pulled the silk bonsai screen across.

They were murdering the octopus!

It was the best fun he had had in years. And he'd caught it on camera. Video. Thank God for Apple iPhone.

Soon it would be on social media.

Probably go viral.

And then his old man apologising profusely, rushing off to pay, leaving a big tip.

And now they were practically jogging back to the hotel to look for Cress.

Wicked!

"You see what I reckon happened is this" – Alex held his parents attention – "I reckon what you said sounded something like, 'my daughter doesn't eat meat, so we want sushi and the house speciality', and sushi – to a Japanese person – is after all, raw fish. It was your mention of 'if the house could provide it' that sealed the deal. That's what I reckon anyway."

Hugo glared at Alex.

Dana glared at Hugo. "Well quite obviously the reason that no one spoke to us was because they hardly had a word of English. And equally obviously Hugo, your meaning was lost in translation."

Dana turned to walk on. "Either way, we have a very distraught daughter."

She marched on up the seafront towards the Metropole.

Hugo followed, shoulders slumped, weighed down by the bags, the weather and the misery of it all. Or so it seemed to Alex, who brought up the rear, glancing at his watch.

* * *

Hugo followed the others back into the hotel. The rain shower, typically, stopping immediately he went through the door. And yet, he was no sooner through it, than gallantry and his upbringing forced him to trudge back down the steps again to assist an ancient lady who was emerging from a white and blue Brighton and Hove taxi. He'd spotted her out of the corner of his eye as he had gone up towards the revolving door, hoping he could just breeze past pretending not to notice. Conscience had got the better of him though, and he'd been forced to retrace his steps, take her bag, one of her sticks and hobble up the marble steps towards the foyer, where he hoped some other good Samaritan would relieve him.

In truth though he felt like he deserved it. He'd been an utter cad over the luncheon fuck-up. Entirely his fault. He had taken at face value what an Italian had told him in a French restaurant – come to think of it, what the fuck would an Italian know about Japanese sushi anyway? And he'd been too keen to get out of the rain and wind, without making proper enquiries, or handling it correctly. And then he'd gushed forth to the poor chap in Tako when he first went to enquire, and didn't bother to question why the waiter hadn't responded, other than with a nod of his head, or to take the trouble to ask if he understood the request.

So it was really all his fault. And now he would have to take his medicine. And most likely it would cost him more money – in bribes to Cress, not to mention a slap-up room service lunch for the rest of them. The only thing that had passed their lips in Tako had been obscenities.

Oh well. Better face the music.

Mind you the Italian had been perfectly correct as it had turned out – Hugo had asked for a sushi restaurant and that was exactly what he had got. Fucking Italians. Should stick to pizza.

To his relief, the ancient lady was handed over to a waiting receptionist who had apparently been expecting her. Hugo imagined that she was filthy rich, stays there for six months every year and has a brass plaque outside her room. Christ, I bet she doesn't have to worry about the bill. Or school fees, probably pays the great-grand children's boarding school fees up front, in advance, on the day they are born, for the next eighteen years or whatever.

Oh fuck, he thought. The school fees. Alex had mentioned them in the restaurant, can't blame him of course, he wasn't to know. But Hugo had noted the sharp look that Dana had given him. Still. Best not to worry about that now. Don't want to spoil things. Hugo attempted to muster some meagre comfort from his surroundings. It's only half way through the weekend and I will make up for the shortcomings so far with a sumptuous meal tonight in the French restaurant, the bestowing of the birthday gift, and we will be a happy family again.

But for now, Hugo was anxious to locate Cressida and deal, swiftly and however painfully, with the consequences.

The hotel was busy. Guests and staff criss-crossing the elaborate reception hall in all directions. The dining room in full swing with post-lunch coffees. The bars full, the stairs looking like an escalator with the numbers of people going up and down, guests checking in, coming and going with shopping bags. In short, a sea of bodies. No sign of Dana, Alex, or, more to the point, Cressida.

Hugo stopped at the reception desk and waited politely for his turn. He asked a Scottish girl with short blonde hair for his room key – despite the modern use of plastic key cards, Hugo still insisted upon leaving his with reception when he went out – then, if there was any message for him, and then, if she had seen any member of his family. She had not, she confirmed when she handed over his key.

He assumed that Alex would be using his mobile phone to call Cressida. Except, now that he thought about it, Cressida had said her battery was dead.

He decided to go up to the room and wait for news. Nothing he could do running around like a headless chicken on his own. Truth was, he had absolutely no idea where Cressida would be, or indeed where a girl would go after suffering a, well, a fright, he supposed. The others will look for her in the room of course, but after that, well who knows? Shopping? Might she conceivably have gone back to the shops to console herself? Is that what women did? Probably, he decided. Although, in her fright, Cressida had left her handbag behind. Not that that mattered. She didn't actually pay for anything she bought.

Deep in thought, he walked towards the stocky, pink marble staircase. Truth was, if Hugo was allowed his own opinion, which he wasn't – not on this occasion anyway – he couldn't really understand what all the fuss was about. Not now, when the dust had settled. Okay, so Cressida didn't eat fish, fair enough. She was a vegetarian – sorry, a vegan. But after all, it was only a plate of fish. Wasn't it?

It's not like it was a sucking pig or something. Was it? And she hadn't been asked to eat it. Just, sort of look at it, for a few minutes.

It was just a plate of fish, Hugo thought, as he remembered back to the centrepiece on the table.

Just an octopus, well, all right, a large one. But it was dead, it's not like it was still alive and wriggling around.

For goodness sake! What was all the fuss about? It had been alive and swimming about in that tank thing, but by the time it was on their table, it was dead.

It had been killed.

Just a few yards from where Cressida had been sitting.

Unknown to her.

Smiling. And waiting for her "yummy" rice and vegetable sushi, as she called it.

Oh fuck. Hugo glanced, surreptitiously, and just for a second, over his shoulder, back in the direction of the bar. Thought better of it, and walked on.

As he reached the stairs, the corridor snaked around to the left, and he was just about to keep walking, when he saw what he thought was Cressida's down-turned head and the back of someone else's in a blue suit jacket.

"Cress?" he ventured.

The head bobbed up and he was overjoyed to see his daughter look up at him, albeit with the black panda eyes again. Ah, tears, Hugo immediately registered.

At the same time, Dana and Alex appeared behind him.

"Thank God. You've found her," Dana exclaimed, as she rushed over to the two figures seated on a cream linen sofa in the corridor recess.

Hugo was about to feel a tinge of pride at being

congratulated for finding Cressida, until Alex told him, "We went up to our room to see if she was there first. Mum wasn't half slagging you off for dawdling when Cressida could be lying in the bath with her wrists slit."

Alex was finishing the remains of a packet of salt and vinegar crisps, with another packet tucked under his arm.

"I—" Hugo stopped in his tracks, and his mouth fell open. Christ Almighty, he thought. Talk about kicking a man when he's down.

Hugo continued to shake his head as Alex went over to the women and stood while his mum knelt down beside Cressida, stroking her hair gently and murmuring to her.

"Ze little one has 'ad ze most terrible shock to ze system," the person in the blue suit jacket said.

Hugo sprung forward.

The blue suit jacket held out a little lace handkerchief and was dabbing it at his daughter's eyes.

"Thank you so much for looking after her," Dana said, continuing to stroke Cressida's hair.

"It is my pleasure. Ze little one was in such a terrible state when she run through ze doors. Crying and sobbing and so desperate. So I think, my God! What 'as 'appened to ze family. And so I rush from ze office where I was and I carry her here" – the blue suit jacket patted the sofa – "and we talk and she tell me everything and all ze terrible truth of ze day!"

As this torrent of despair went on, Hugo started to edge ever so slightly backwards. He was starting to feel like he had burned Joan of Arc at the stake, such was his growing guilt.

Dana looked up. "Hugo!"

She was not smiling.

He felt he needed to say something. Anything in fact.

"Cress. Darling. We've found you!" he said, albeit a little late to the party, as his daughter would have said – if she were actually still speaking to him.

Cressida looked up at him, her eyes betraying nothing but tears.

Veronique, being the person in the blue suit jacket, swivelled her head around, and swung her mane of black hair over her shoulder, as she too looked in Hugo's direction.

Not knowing what version of events she had been given by Cressida – Hugo conveniently forgetting that there was, in effect, only one version – he took the decision to brazen it out.

"Such an unfortunate mistake. Such incompetence." He looked at Veronique. "The French of course would never insult their diners in such an appalling manner. So barbaric these Far Eastern races."

No one said a word. Alex, now starting in on his second packet of crisps – prawn cocktail, leant against the wall and smirked.

"Part of the problem of course is the language barrier. Lost in translation, as Dana put it." Hugo looked at his wife, who had raised her eyebrows. "One can have the devil of a job ordering in these places when the foreigners don't speak the lingo."

Veronique stopped dabbing at Cressida's eye.

Hugo instantly regretted this. Bollocks. He realised what he had said. Didn't really mean that, he thought. Actually, the truth was he did mean it. Sod it, after all, they were in England. If they wanted all that foreign muck then they would go abroad. What he wouldn't give for fish and chips in newspaper for supper.

What he absolutely didn't want to do of course was insult Veronique.

"Ah, *mais oui, pardon Madame,* er *Mademoiselle! Je n'ai pas,* er, offend! Ah, er *pardon! Merci beaucoup!*" he said.

Hugo was getting very pink in the face.

Alex nearly choked on his crisps.

Dana still frowned.

Cressida had the beginnings of a tiny smile on her very tear-stained face.

Veronique got up and turned to Hugo.

"Ze mister Hugo should not worry. I am made of? How you say? Ze thick skin! No offence: we 'ave, with mister Hugo ze *Entente Cordiale!*"

A wave of relief washed over Hugo, as he stood like a schoolboy, having given his teacher his apple.

Veronique turned to embrace Cressida as she stood up, kissed her on both cheeks, and told her to keep the little handkerchief.

"And now I must to work. I am always 'ere if you need a *mon ami* – a friend," she said to Cressida, who was all smiles now, and off she went, *click-clicking* in her high heels, towards the reception desk.

Cressida, with her mother's arm around her, made her way towards the lifts. Hugo and Alex followed.

As they waited for the lift to come, Alex held out his hand.

"Anyone for a prawn cocktail crisp?"

THIRTEEN

Dana never ceased to be surprised – in the main pleasantly – by her children, she thought, as she walked back down, yet again, from the city centre, having been to change Cressida's gigantically-sized dress from Zara.

After getting Cress propped up on the bed with an assortment of nail polishes, files, buffers, glitter, a plate of hummus with carrot sticks, an almond milk hot chocolate – Dana didn't point out that the chocolate might be dairy – and a re-run of *The Big Bang Theory* playing on the television, she had set off on the dress errand.

Alex, to her surprise, had insisted on accompanying her. "After all it is your birthday Mum," he had said. He'd even gone into the shop, and waited patiently for her while the dress disaster was rectified. Then he'd offered to buy her a coffee, so sweet of him. But Dana had urged him instead to go and browse in HMV, when he'd casually mentioned that he was looking for another Tarantino DVD. Not fair to drag him around. Let him go and look at his films and music. He was a good boy at heart. And poor old Cress – such a sensitive little thing.

Always had been. Nearly went to pieces when that kitten had been killed on the road. Such a dangerous road, should not have had a cat living there anyway. And too many gaps in the fence that had needed fixing. She'd been saying it for months. It was just a matter of knocking some new close-boarded fencing in here and there. Should have done it herself.

Anyway, Cressida was sensitive. And it was, in its way, very sweet. She was a gentle girl and she treated both animals and people very kindly. It was a lovely trait, and it pained Dana when it was so brutally abused and offended. But, she would get over it, and indeed, it was part of the process of growing up. However much Dana yearned to shield them from it, her children, like everyone else's, would have to go through much worse in order to become well adjusted, resilient adults. Not quite "ze thick skin" Veronique spoke of – hers was more like a jockey's arse, as her mother would have said – but certainly they need a layer of resilience to fortify them against the slings and arrows etc of life.

Dana wondered exactly what Veronique needed her thick skin for. Surely not the fact that she was French in England? Men just loved that, the exotic accent, the little girl lost, it was all very sexy as far as Hugo and the rest of the old fools were concerned. Mind you, in some cases it proved to be a costly mistake. The matrimonial department in Dana's law firm evidencing the point on a daily basis. More particularly in the case where one half of the marriage contract involved an Eastern European lady. It all started out very rosy. He, always the one with the money, was speared by Cupid's arrow often unexpectedly. Lust hit hard. Sometimes followed by love, but always by a wedding. And unfortunately for the clients – almost exclusively men – the wedding ceremony had not been preceded by a Pre Nuptial Agreement. This was a costly oversight. And one that the exotic ladies took full advantage of.

Sometimes, and Dana wasn't being unduly harsh, she thought that the old fools really did deserve it. They never stopped to question why a very young woman – who would make Marilyn Monroe look jaded and plain – with legs a mile long and boobs a mile wide, was telling a middle-aged, or much older, man that he was a god in bed, and the most fun she had had for years. Except, the Eastern European lady would swear, that the fun she had had elsewhere had been purely platonic. She being white as the driven snow.

And so there would be wining and dining, and shopping, and sex, and lavish gifts, and more sex, and shopping, and a lot more sex, and an awful lot more shopping. And then the proposal. Followed, in a heartbeat, by the acceptance. And the wedding would take place, at great expense, in front of a vast number of guests – and one or two bewildered relatives flown in from Kiev or somewhere, not females under forty, as the authorities wouldn't chance even a temporary visa again – in some exotic location, often Monaco: it being both a hop, skip, and a jump from Heathrow, and usually where the old fool maintained an address for tax purposes.

Occasionally, all that activity – the sex, not the shopping – would produce offspring. Limited to one. The Eastern European not wanting to do anything to herself that would limit her prospects in the future.

Then gradually the sex would peter out. And then stop.

Pouts and sulks would set in. Disagreements. Discord. Then the old fool would be sleeping in one of the ten spare bedrooms in the mansion flat in Knightsbridge. There would be more pouts and sulks, but not less shopping, and often some erratic behaviour.

Then one day when the old fool was out, usually working, or working on his investments, or whatever, the locks would be changed and when he came home sometimes the police would be involved.

Occasionally a court injunction would be sought, by her, alleging some minor assault, this cemented and added weight to what was to follow.

The divorce petition. Usually based upon his behaviour. He'd made unreasonable demands – he wanted sex – and so on. But the divorce petition was not the important document, or indeed the end goal.

That was the Financial Settlement. And the little nipper, the fruit of the union and testament to their enduring love, and her enduring devotion and monumental efforts to keep her marriage alive, ensured that the Eastern European never had to work another day in her life. Which would be no different to any of the other days in her twenty-six, or twenty-nine, years on the planet.

So, Dana concluded, men could be fools. She may have gilded the lily a little in her mental summation of the cases that she observed in the office, and not all facts were the same. But there was no denying that even as the dark haired, sometimes blonde, exotic beauty with long legs, wide boobs and sexy accent tottered into reception in the office, even Dana's male colleagues – seasoned professionals and so presumably immune – were adjusting their ties, patting their hair down, and considering their options for a working lunch.

It's what made the world go around, she supposed. Sex, or the promise of it.

And money. In fact it was probably just money, because the old fools lost no time in replacing the word "beauty" with the word "bitch", testament to the depth of their own devotion to the end goal, and the ultimate removal of the rose-tinted glasses.

Who said all you need is love?

All you need, Dana decided, is money.

And maybe the marriages that went from Monaco to her firm's office were made in heaven. Perhaps everyone got what they deserved. Perhaps they deserved each other, one as bad, or as grabbing, as the other.

Dana thought about the Prick from the hotel gym. He paled into insignificance on the old fool scale, compared to the wealthy husbands of the Eastern Europeans. He just fancied himself, probably more than the women he was eyeing up. He had no illusions in his heart of hearts. He'd try it once, give it a go, make a pass. But, if he was smart, he'd have no illusions. He might attract a certain type of woman, but never the stunning beauty. He had no illusions.

Because he had no money.

Mind you, there was the odd case that was a bit different, or bizarre even. When she had been a young solicitor, newly qualified, Dana had been called to assist her senior partner with a couple of matrimonial cases, and she remembered one poor chap, who rushed in off the street without an appointment, and asked if her firm could take him on. Because he couldn't afford to pay much Dana was assigned the case – her fee-billing having the lowest expectations in the firm. She remembered sitting, wearing a sombre, charcoal-grey suit in the boardroom, taking notes, while the husband told his sorry tale. Apparently, his wife of many years announced her intention to join a gym, in order to get fit and lose some weight. Initially, he was not averse to this idea, on the basis that she enjoyed one too many fish suppers – of the chip variety.

However, after a few months, and a lot of gym visits, he noticed that his wife did not appear to be getting any slimmer, or indeed any fitter, since hoovering the stairs still winded her. His suspicions roused, he followed her one day when she said she was off to the gym. He saw her – since he was tailing behind in his white van – drive past the gym, and turn down into a residential street, where she parked up, got out and went into a terraced house with floral curtains.

He sat there fuming for two hours. Deciding whether to confront the bastard that his wife was obviously having it off with. What happened next though, floored him.

His wife emerged a little after four in the afternoon, opened the front door, and stood there while another woman embraced her and kissed her lips.

Dana remembered the husband sitting in her office relaying all this. Turned out that the wife had been having private sessions with the female gym instructor, only the sessions didn't include the type of exercise one would normally associate with weights, treadmills and exercise mats.

Dana's male senior partner took a sudden interest in the case when the husband produced photographic evidence, telling Dana that he thought it better that he should deal with it – man to man – and perhaps she might like to concentrate on conveyancing instead.

That suited her fine, since the husband – a fruit and veg trader – could only afford to offset the firm's fees in exotic fruit, which did nothing to swell her end-of-year bonus. And Dana preferred a Cox's Orange Pippin to a mango any day.

So, she decided, if it wasn't money it was sex, one or the other.

She walked past the hotel and crossed the road to the promenade. The rain had stopped, the skies had cleared, there was a hint of blue sky, and even a glimpse of the winter sun, lurking behind a white cloud.

Side-stepping bikes and joggers on the cycle path, Dana made her way down the steps towards the beach, the railings painted an odd shade of pastel blue-grey, a bit like the sea, not sure what colour it should be in February. The storm-like weather had washed up a lot of the shingle and large pebbles, which had spilled over onto the walkway that stretched for miles towards Hove and beyond.

Dana sat down on a blue metal bench – sheltered slightly by two wooden screens either side, which deflected the worst of the wind when it blew – facing the sea.

It was calm. She breathed out. Sighed. So tranquil here. Just a few people walking on a late Saturday afternoon. Most of the others were running around like mad things, desperate to shop, eat, drink, desperate to enjoy themselves, on their day out.

Dana stretched her legs out in front of her. Closed her

eyes and turned her face to the glimmer of weak sun. She could hear the waves on the beach. She breathed in, smelt the salt on the air. Breathed out.

Calm.

She thought about everything that was wrong, everything that had gone wrong. Things that could go wrong. How they got mended. How sometimes they didn't. But how it all carried on anyway.

How could she make it better? Would it ever be better?

A seagull cried, a long, low, desperate cry somewhere, out there.

Were they all happy – Alex, Cressida, Hugo? Would they be happier, or sadder, without her?

Soon – six months for Alex and less than two years for Cressida – they would be gone. Away to university. Gone.

Dana was suddenly gripped by the terrible realisation, that no matter how much they all bickered, no matter what had happened today, when the children left home and her mother died, Dana would be left alone with Hugo. Another bird screamed. She opened her eyes suddenly.

She sat and watched the seagulls. Screaming, screeching. A group of them pecked at some scraps from a discarded plastic take-away tray. One stood apart and came towards her in a shambling motion, with a hobbling gait, propelling itself forward in search of food. Dana saw that its leg was broken but it still tried to walk towards the tray of crumbs. It made her sad. For the brutality of nature: because the creature would surely die of starvation. And sad for other reasons she couldn't fathom. And then, quite suddenly, the seagull opened its wings and took flight, soaring up and away towards the sea.

It could still fly then. It still had the option of flight.

The weak sun sank a little lower, slinking towards the horizon. It promised a colourful display at sunset. To her left, Dana could see the metal skeleton of the old West Pier, which now sat, island like, cut off, out at sea, like a ghost ship. Shame it hadn't been allowed to sink like the *Titanic*. It served as a barbaric reminder of all that had been splendid and beautiful, but was now forlorn, neglected. And, for whatever reason, it remained so – silently sitting, keeping vigil over the seafront and the life that carried on regardless in front of it. It was depressing because it was a metaphor for how once good things could be ruined, and then left to further decay. Some people thought it looked beautiful even in its present rusty state, but when Dana had looked out of the bedroom window when they had first arrived at the hotel, she had seen it. And it had felt, in retrospect, like an omen.

Dana's phone pinged. Again. For the tenth time that day. She had not looked at it. And she would not. She needed to get through the weekend without distractions. On her own terms.

She got up, and climbed the incline towards the top promenade. As she walked and the sound of the sea and cry of seagulls receded, she tried to force her thoughts back to the present. It was her birthday. She should be happy. We are all here together, we are all safe, think about now – not the future, she willed herself. Take Dad's advice, dwell on the positives, not the negatives.

Walking up the steps towards the road, the smell of fried Chinese food from a nearby restaurant commingled with the unpalatable odour of urine – and worse – in the public toilet opposite, bringing her senses sharply into the present tense. As she crossed the road, dashing through the press of traffic and back into the hotel, Dana's phone pinged yet again in her pocket. Another message. She ignored it. Just then, the sun dipped onto the horizon, and Dana turned back to take a final look at the sea.

The West Pier was bathed in sunset, and the rust had turned to a golden glow, the metal skeleton to a magnificent ironwork, filigree palace.

Alex boasted an impressive collection of DVDs on the shelves in his bedroom at home. Not only did it encompass many Japanese horror films – and what his father termed "video nasties", although Alex had pointed out that Miss Wardle from film studies said that that was an 80s retro term, yet to make a come back – but the shelves also contained every one of the eight films made by Tarantino, including both a DVD and a video tape edition, and all of the other films in which the great man had had a hand either as writer, producer or actor.

Therefore, what had Alex sought in HMV when his mother released him from the strictures of Zara?

Not a goddamn thing, he thought, smiling, as he walked in the direction of the North Laines.

He was, however, carrying a small HMV carrier bag which contained the latest recordings of Ludovico Einaudi's hauntingly beautiful piano music on CD – the "hauntingly beautiful" term being his mother's reference, and not his.

Buying the CD had served a dual purpose: as well as loving his mum enough to buy her a second birthday gift, the appearance of both Alex and the carrier bag back at the hotel later would lend credence to his next mission, or at least conceal it.

Having made it through the scrum-like encounter of bodies that was Bond Street, Alex dodged the determined shoppers – shit the girls were the worst. Slam right into you with their suitcase handbags and shopping and didn't bat an eye, if the shoulder-barge had hurt Alex, then it must have hurt the girl, but she marched on regardless to her next shop. Must be like some sort of local anaesthetic, he decided – shopping: maybe they don't feel it till later.

A series of deft manoeuvres through residential streets – littered with cars, garbage, bikes chained to railings – and down alleyways, strewn with crushed beer cans and some Banksy-like decoration on the walls, brought him past Tidy Street, and around a corner with a pub hopping with punters like closing time on a Saturday night. It was called the The Leaping something or other. The thing doing the leaping having worn off the sign some time ago. Probably made for no end of speculation for the non-regulars. Alex broke his stride to have a quick look, wondering if he had time to sample one of their craft beers, but decided he had better keep his wits about him, just in case there were awkward questions, or serious decisions to be made a bit later. He walked on down a narrow, now deserted, street.

From the outside of the building it was not immediately apparent what manner of business was transacted inside. Although any number of possibilities were suggested from its appearance. The entire front was painted matt black, everything – bricks, windows, door, door handle, sign – even the glass was tinted to at least a forty-five per cent gradient.

What wasn't black – was in fact flame red – were two

small eyes and two small horns, painted onto the sign above the door. No name or writing. Just the eyes and horns.

One wasn't likely to mistake it for British Home Stores or a newsagents. And that was the intended purpose.

Alex peered through the window, cupping his hands to deflect the weak afternoon sunlight.

A large white skull sat in a display cabinet. Along with what looked like a long, twisted, horn pipe. And a dagger – silver, jewel-encrusted and encased in a sheath. The sheath, presumably like the dagger inside it, curved and curled to a sharp point.

Not a living soul was to be seen within the establishment.

Alex took a deep breath – wished after all he had availed himself of the craft beer opportunity at The Leaping something pub – straightened his back, put his shoulder to the door and entered, stuffing the Ludovico Einaudi CD into his jeans pocket as he did so. A powerful odour assailed his nostrils as he closed the door behind him.

Reminded him a bit of that stuff Mum and Cress used in the bath – what was it? Musk, that was it. And something else. Something sweet, but rotten underneath.

Alex wasn't one for all that girly, bath nonsense. But this was not at all disagreeable, he decided, as he stood and waited inside the building.

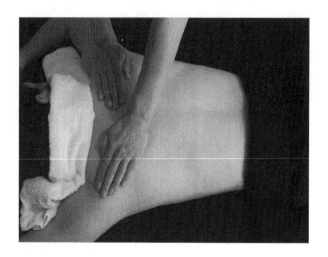

FOURTEEN

This. Is. The. Life! Hugo floated – in navy blue Speedo swimming trunks – in the middle of the swimming pool. He was the sole bather. That awfully nice chap in the orange shorts, that he'd met in the morning, had been spot on – the afternoon had indeed imposed a veto on children. So, no little buggers splashing about making a racket and spoiling the adult's fun. Yes. Lovely. Peace and quiet at last, he thought. Hugo exhaled deeply, and tipped over in the process, sinking a little under the water. As he swam over to the edge, he contemplated all the fuss of the afternoon – for the hundredth time. And the near brush with disaster, almost insulting that lovely girl, Veronique. How stupid of him. Sometimes I can be – no, not stupid, he decided – but people can often take things the wrong way. Yes, that was it. It was the way people misinterpreted things. Jumped to conclusions, got the wrong end of the stick. They didn't think things through, failed to grasp what was actually said, rather than what they thought had been said. Yes, people can be very stupid, Hugo agreed, as he paddled about.

Goodness, not that Veronique was stupid. Goodness no. She was far from it. Just a silly misunderstanding. That was all. Like the Tako restaurant incident. Hugo stopped his paddling and considered the latter.

Fuck. That had been a costly misunderstanding. He shivered. Not because the pool was cold, but because it had cost him the better part of − well, no sense dwelling on that now. And then the club sandwiches in the room to make up for what had happened: £21.95! For a sandwich! Each! Christ − how do they justify that? For three slices of bread, a rasher of bacon, a slice of tomato and some lettuce. And Cressida's didn't even have the bacon, or the butter. And then the extra plates of chips. And the Cokes. And the olives. And then Cress's hummus thingy and crudités. And the mini-bar was emptying at a rate of knots: between his whiskies, the kid's soft drinks, chocolate bars and crisps. He'd contemplated topping up the empties with water, and slamming them back in, but thought better of it, probably wired up to some device to detect that sort of thing.

Still, what was done was done. He'd given up totting up the damage on the plastic. Couldn't even start to fathom the end total.

But there was absolutely nothing to be gained from worrying about that now. In for a penny, in for a pound, was Hugo's jaunty motto today, as he sank to the bottom of the pool.

Still, Dana seemed to be having a wonderful time at least − all that shopping and luxury hotel. And a lovely dinner to come, and the presents.

And maybe, just maybe, a spot of the other, later. See how things went. After a nightcap. Maybe some dancing in the cellar piano bar – he had read that they had a jazz trio and a dance floor. Dana liked that, music, romance, that sort of thing. Women did. It got them in the mood, if it was on the cards to start with.

The spa and pool were deserted as Hugo emerged from the water and towelled himself dry. The lights had been dimmed around the pool so that the water glowed a kind of green, he noticed. Some sort of tropical music was playing. Very agreeable. Not that it would last beyond five thirty, Hugo conceded. That was when the child curfew ended and the little darlings would have full sway, be like the municipal baths or the lido during school holidays – kids bombing into the water, narrowly missing, or sometimes not, those already in. The older ones checking out the girls in their bathing costumes. The younger ones practising their front crawl, legs kicking up a flume in all directions. And some smart arse doing the butterfly – leaving a trail of destruction as tsunami-size waves rose up in his wake, and the weaker swimmers coughed and spluttered to keep their heads above the water.

Suddenly Hugo was 13-years-old again. He could smell the overpowering chlorine – more like bleach in those days, feel the ice cold disinfectant foot-bath you had to step through before you got near the pool, heard someone screaming his name.

"Veruca!"

Hugo froze. It was Mr Mulloney, head of sport. "I'm talking to you Veruca! Get that small, insignificant, good-for-nothing body over here now!"

The Voice boomed from the towering life guard's chair at the top end of the swimming pool. He had the megaphone to his mouth.

Hugo plunged blindly into the freezing foot-bath and walked falteringly over to Mr Mulloney.

"Where the hell do you think you're sneaking off to?"

"Nowhere sir. It's just that matron said I mustn't swim until my foot is cleared up." Hugo lifted up his right leg and wiggled his foot. It was covered in a rubber sock.

"You still got that nasty little disease, you nasty little boy? Don't answer that, I don't care. No more excuses. Get in that water now and I want to see ten laps, front crawl," Mr Mulloney's voice still boomed through the megaphone, despite being inches from Hugo's face.

Most of the activity in and around the swimming pool had ceased and all eyes were on Hugo.

"I haven't quite managed to do that in the deep-end yet sir."

Mr Mulloney looked at him. Got out of the chair, laid the megaphone carefully down on the seat, bent down, lifted Hugo's right foot up, looked up into Hugo's now terrified eyes, ripped the rubber sock off, picked Hugo up and hurled him headlong into the deep end.

Hugo shuddered. Even now. It was part of the reason he had paid – sporadically admittedly – for Alex and Cressida to go to a hand-picked private school. Not that any of the events of Hugo's childhood would be repeated nowadays – any hint of that would end in prison sentences in present times.

But one thing Hugo had never done was to tell his children that schooldays were the best days of their lives.

Anyway, all in the past. Can't blame anyone for all that, well apart from Mr Mulloney, he supposed. He had blamed his parents at the time. Had hated them for it in fact. Sending him away to a boarding school. But he came to realise that that was what parents did – things that they believed to be in the best interests of their children. Still, he found out in later life that his father had been savagely bullied himself at school, and so Hugo wondered why his father had then sacrificed his own son on the alter of a public school education. But no point either in dwelling on that now. They were all long gone – his parents, Mr Mulloney. Many years ago, Hugo had taken some trouble to find out about the latter's demise, and had intended to derive a measure of satisfaction – as you do when you are young – from hearing that the man had died a painful death, and endured great suffering. The curious thing was, that he'd heard from someone else at an alumni reunion that Mr Mulloney only bothered to pick on the kids that he actually liked. What he wanted to do was make a man of them. The ones he thought had no potential he left alone.

In his perverse way he was trying to help them. The irony of it all, Hugo thought.

Still, look how I turned out – perhaps old Mulloney wasn't wrong after all.

The intensity of the morning and afternoon activities – not to mention Hugo's bad back, brought on by leaping out of bed in fright to answer the door to the room service – suddenly gave him an idea, as he passed the reception desk on his way to the changing rooms. A sign on the desk proclaimed – Offer of the Month: Full Body Massage Half Price.

Gosh, Hugo thought, that would be nice. Work out some of those knots in preparation for the dance floor later. On a whim and spur of the moment – no flies on him, he thought – Hugo strode boldly back to the reception desk, and asked if there were any availability for a massage that very moment.

The skinny young girl behind the desk consulted a computer screen and frowned.

"Is that hot stone, aromatherapy, Swedish, shiatsu or Thai massage?" she said, in a vaguely Welsh accent, as she looked up.

Christ, thought a massage was a massage. Hugo was bewildered.

"What's the difference?"

"Well, your Swedish is good for stress relief, your hot stone massage is good for centring yourself and relaxation, your shiatsu fixes imbalances in the flow of energy in your body, your aromatherapy can help treat specific problems with perfumed oils and your Thai improves flexibility."

Hugo was no less bewildered.

Then he had another brainwave.

"The one mentioned here, full body massage," he said, pointing to the sign on the desk.

"They're all full body," the skinny girl responded.

Hugo looked around the reception for inspiration. What would Clint Eastwood choose? Wouldn't even be in a poncey spa in the first place. But if he were – which he wouldn't be – but if he were forced to be, then he would – be a man. Yes! He'd be a man about it. Which meant? What exactly? He wondered.

Hugo's gaze fell upon a well-thumbed copy of *Men's Health* magazine on the desk. It had a man smiling on the front in sports gear, in a gym.

"Sports massage please," Hugo announced definitively, smiling. Good old Clint, always came through for him in the end.

The skinny girl tapped away at her computer again.

She barely reached over the top of the counter. So waif-like, that a breeze could carry her away. Looked about 14-years-old, probably on work experience, he decided.

"And what would you like that combined with?" she asked him.

"What?"

The skinny girl sighed. "Do you want a hot stone sports massage, an aromatherapy sports massage, a—"

"Yes, yes, I've got the idea," Hugo replied irritably.

His enthusiasm for the event to come diminishing with every added option. He'd thought asking for the sports version would have been the end of it. Why is nothing ever easy?

"Whatever – er, Thai I suppose," he ventured.

Hugo had chosen this option because he couldn't pronounce shiatsu, supposed that the perfumed oils was for women, couldn't begin to fathom what "hot stones" meant – probably something uncomfortable if he had to lie on them, like a bed of nails, he speculated – and didn't want to sound like a pervert asking for a Swedish massage, as its subliminal meaning was Swedish *girl*. Ha! well he wasn't going to be caught out on that one.

Hang on – then what the heck did *Thai* imply? Oh God, that was even worse. Too late now.

Anyway, at the very least it would be relaxing: as all those brochures for exotic holidays, in far flung places like Phuket, always featured someone lying on a massage table, while a serene Thai lady, with a flower in her hair, stroked the recipient's back, and the latter lay there with a calm and tranquil face, in a blissful, massage-induced slumber.

He wondered, briefly, what Dana would make of it all,

as the skinny girl directed him down the corridor saying, "Treatment Room Two, where your therapist will be with you shortly."

As Hugo walked down the sand-washed golden walls – in reality painted magnolia – to the sounds of whales calling to each other underwater, not sure why they play that kind of thing, he was looking forward to having the knots eased out of his muscles, and, with any luck, a bit of a nap, before going back up to the room to make sure everyone was okay, and that the kids had written Dana's birthday cards.

But for now, it was Hugo time, and at £35 a pop – the price of the massage – he was determined to enjoy it.

A dark, mahogany door with a large white plaque proclaimed – Treatment Room Two. Hugo stopped, looked around and then knocked.

There was no reply. He knocked again. Still no reply. Tentatively he turned the handle and opened the door a crack.

"Hello?" he said.

No response.

"Can I come in?" he asked, as he opened the door further.

The room was empty. It was brightly lit and no whale music played. This was a little disappointing. But perhaps the therapist or massage person would sort it out when she came in, and make it a bit more relaxing.

In the centre of the room there stood a large, white, leatherette massage couch covered in white towels.

Hugo stood by the door and waited. Then he moved into the room and stood by the couch. No sign of anyone. Then he went out again and looked at the plaque on the door, just to double check. Treatment Room Two, no mistake.

Behind the door there was a white towelling robe, and on a chair behind it, a little see-through bag containing pair of white towelling slippers.

Hugo tapped his foot. And waited.

He sat up on the edge of the massage couch.

Perhaps this massage malarky wasn't such a good idea after all. Come to think of it, he'd never had a massage before. Well, not a proper one. In their early days together, Dana had not been averse to slapping on a bit of baby oil and rubbing his back – as a prelude to, well, the other. And he'd had a rub down on the side of the pitch, by the physio at a university rugby game, and a couple of times in the locker room afterwards, when he'd got an injury.

But never in a *massage parlour*, whatever that meant. Or a fancy hotel spa.

Or, he just realised to his horror, by another woman. No woman, other than his wife, had touched Hugo for the last twenty-three years. Even their GP was a man.

Hugo continued to wait.

The attraction of his spur-of-the-moment whim was rapidly receding.

And, come to think of it, £35 would buy a jolly decent bottle of wine for dinner. Or several large Speyside single malts.

Hugo jumped down from the couch – having decided to abandon the massage mission – not without a measure of relief, it had to be said, and walked over to the door.

He collided with the skinny girl from reception. Probably come to tell me there's no one to do the massage, he concluded. He begun to formulate his understanding and was about to say, "It's quite all right, no problem, I'll come back another day," etc, when the skinny girl came into the room and closed the door behind her.

"Sorry about that, I had to get Tony to relieve me at reception, and he was in the gym doing a session with a guest so I had to wait a few minutes, what with it being kids hour in a bit as well."

The skinny girl proceeded to take all the towels off the massage couch, and using the electronic control, lowered the couch several inches.

Hugo stood where he was. He was very confused.

"Where's the massage therapist?" he asked, with some trepidation.

"Here," the skinny girl replied, and laughed.

"Where?" Hugo looked around, cutting his eyes without moving his head.

"It's me, silly." The skinny girl was still laughing.

"You!" Hugo took a small, but to him significant, step back.

The skinny girl looked every one, but not more, than her fourteen years.

"Of course. You look surprised. How else did you think I knew so much about it?" She swung her long hair – plaited in a braid, like Cressida used to wear when she was younger – over her shoulder.

The skinny girl turned around and started fiddling about in a cupboard. She produced an oil burner, lit a candle and placed it underneath. A soft fragrance started to waft around the room.

Then she went over to the corner of the room and

turned on a CD player and suddenly flutes, pan pipes, waterfalls, and chirping birds sprung up all around him.

Hugo stood rooted to the spot.

"But, well, I thought it would be someone else, a therapist, a—"

"I am a therapist," the skinny girl said, as she went over to the light switch and dimmed the lights.

"Yes, but I thought when I booked it that it would be an adul—" Hugo was going to say "adult", but instead said, "an older person."

At this point every ounce of anticipated relaxation and enjoyment had been sucked, like a vacuum, from the event.

"I'm fully qualified, don't worry, I can't cause any damage." She laughed.

Hugo noticed that she still had spots, like an adolescent. And had he glimpsed a brace on her teeth when she smiled?

He remained rooted to the floor.

The sweet fragrance, the soft music, the dimmed lights, the candle burner – it all seemed so, romantic. Seductive. So wrong.

And it was a Thai massage.

Oh God, Hugo groaned to himself. I'm in a small room with the lights dimmed, and I'm about to take off my clothes and lie on a couch, while a child puts her hands on my naked body.

Jesus Christ! Men went to Thailand for that very thing! It was on the news regularly.

And then – they went to prison!

He was about to bolt from the room, when he heard himself asking, "Have you done, er many massages then?"

He immediately realised that he did not, under any circumstances, want to hear the answer to this question.

"Hundreds and hundreds. Probably late hundreds I suppose," the child replied, and then added, "now, I will leave the room for a few minutes while you make yourself comfortable. Just get under the towel on top of the couch and lie face down, and I will be back in a mo."

She moved towards the door. Hugo had decided that this would be his opportunity to escape before he was arrested, until she said, "I'll be just outside the door, call me when you are ready."

With that the child left the room.

Christ Almighty! Hugo ran from the door to the couch and back again, like a headless chicken.

He put his ear to the door and listened with bated breath. He couldn't hear a fucking thing with the birds chirping and the pan pipes blasting out.

He stepped back from the door and looked wildly around the room. There was no other exit. He took it all in, all of it, as the enormity of the situation gathered momentum and threatened to overwhelm him. Hugo sat down in the chair behind the door. Felt something uncomfortable underneath him. He reached around and pulled out the towelling slippers.

There was a knock at the door.

"Is it okay to come in?" the child asked from the other side of the door.

Hugo sprung up out of the chair.

"Er, not quite. Ha," he replied in desperation.

He was holding the bag with the slippers in it. He took them out, put them on. Not that wearing a pair of slippers legitimises any of it, he thought. An insane notion.

There was something else left in the bag. He rummaged around, and pulled out what looked like a white, transparent, paper cloth. He held it up, examined it. To his horror they looked like disposable paper pants. See-through. Was he meant to put them on? She hadn't said so.

And why were they "disposable"? Christ, what would necessitate them having to be thrown away afterwards?

Oh God, where was Dana? She always knew what to do in these ghastly situations.

And that thought sent another wave of terror through Hugo. How in God's name was he going to explain this?

Another knock at the door. A little louder this time.

"How's it going?" the child asked again, her voice seeming to become more juvenile with every question.

"Just be a jiffy," he lied.

Hugo was starting to feel a little numb. He wouldn't do well in prison. He was too soft. He'd never last the course. And it would be full of barbaric men like Mr Mulloney. Or worse. Mind you, didn't they segregate the sex offenders?

Oh God. Hugo took off his towel, revealing his navy blue Speedo swimming trunks underneath. He sucked in his tummy. Let it out again. He'd never realised how figure-hugging the Speedos were. Wished he had gone for Alex's surfer shorts instead. Regretted being so old-school now. Despite the navy Speedos, towelling slippers, and bit of a tummy, he didn't think that he cut too bad a figure. But now was not the time to admire his own physique. Much more pressing matters were to hand.

What should he do? He tried to think.

The child asked again, "Shall I come in? Are you under

the towels, can you manage okay?"

"No!" he cried, then realised what he'd just said, "I mean yes, yes I can manage, er, just, er sorting myself out."

Truth was, Hugo was starting to feel rather cold: what with finishing his swim, not having had a shower, the tepid temperature of the room – as he now realised – and the fact that the Speedos were still soaking wet.

Right. A decision needs to be made. He nodded his head. I either leave this room and explain firmly that I must reschedule for another time, or I get my kit off and get under the towel on that couch. Yes, that's the ticket, action. Either way.

Trouble was, what course of action to take. If he abandoned the massage goodness knows what the child would think of him, not that that mattered too much if he was clear of the situation, but she might make trouble if she was cheated out of the treatment and a tip. Or offended, the latter could be even worse. On the other hand if he stayed, well that was an entirely different set of circumstances.

Hugo looked around the room again, spotted the massage oil and little mixing pot that the child had taken out of the cupboard, ready and waiting. And beside it her jewellery. He'd seen her take it off earlier. Presumably so she didn't scratch him during the "procedure", as he now thought of it.

He picked up two bangles and a Tissot watch. And a small diamond and sapphire engagement ring. And a large gold wedding band.

A wedding band. Hang on – she was married! She wasn't a child, she just looked very young. Married.

Thank God. A wave of relief washed over Hugo. How utterly foolish of him to jump to conclusions based on appearances and supposition. How foolish.

Right, action needed. Massage will go ahead as the girl is clearly of age, and so nothing untoward can be inferred. So. I need to get under the towel on that couch.

He removed the slippers and looked down again at his Speedos. He pulled them down, looked at himself – horrified – and pulled them back up again.

Another knock at the door. "I don't want to rush you but I do have another massage booked in forty minutes," the massage therapist said.

"Righto, nearly ready!"

Should he keep the Speedos on, or take them off? What was the form? He didn't know.

Must be off, surely, if it's a full body massage?

Hugo pulled them down again and took them off. Stood with them in hand, wavering.

He looked over at the couch again to gauge the size of the towel, and then cast his gaze down towards his bits and bobs.

The obscenity of it hit him, and he stepped into the Speedos and pulled them up again.

Only they were wet. So down they came again.

Oh Fuck. On or off?

Another knock on the door. "Only I probably won't have time for the full body massage now, most likely just be a back, neck and shoulder massage," the therapist said, her voice seeming much deeper now.

The Speedos went up again.

That's it. They're staying put. Hugo went over to the couch, got under the towel and lay face down.

"Okie dokie," he called out.

He heard the door open and close behind him. The skinny therapist came over to the head of the couch.

"Sorry about that, I was fiddling with, I mean I was trying to, er" – shut up Hugo, he thought, you're just making it worse – "anyway better late than never!"

"That's okay, sorry to rush you, but the evenings are always busier than the afternoons on a Saturday," she replied.

She rubbed a liberal amount of oil between her hands as she said, "Now, it was a Thai sports massage you wanted, wasn't it? Which is my speciality actually. Now Thai is a very vigorous massage, and very deep tissue, so combined with the sports element it can work on specific areas. So two questions. One, is there any area you think needs work in particular, and two, would you like it firm or gentle – some people can find it a little uncomfortable?"

Hugo bristled at the idea of gentle – that was for the women, wasn't it?

"Well, my lower back has been causing me some discomfort after I, um, did something in the gym, as are my hamstrings, so if I could have the hamstrings rather than the neck say, as time is short. And very firm please. The firmer the better."

The therapist gave a little laugh and folded the towel down over Hugo's bottom.

"So how long have you been doing this then?" he asked her.

"About four years. I went back to college to retrain as a sports massage therapist after my last child was born," she said, as she began work on Hugo's back.

Hugo breathed a huge sigh of relief, now that the issue of her age had been clarified, and the horror of the Speedos sorted out, Hugo intended to lie back and enjoy the experience. Safe in the knowledge that it was legal and decent.

As the birds chirped, the water fell and the pan pipes echoed, Hugo began to feel a little chilly with the towel turned down. There didn't seem to be any heat in the room.

And the massage was getting more vigorous by the minute.

And Hugo's wet swimwear was beginning to feel icy cold. Not good so close to his nether regions. Any notion of a massage being remotely sensual had now well and truly been dispelled.

The therapist's fingers worked, her palms pressed and her fingers dug. Deeper and deeper.

Hugo realised that he was clenching his teeth. His jaw was locked shut. His arms clasped either side underneath the massage couch. His nails dug into the padding.

The massage continued.

Hugo suppressed a series of little gasps. Which he couldn't have uttered anyway as his teeth were clenched.

He began to hold his breath, letting it out only when the sadist therapist released her grip temporarily to move to another area.

He closed his eyes tight. Tried to focus upon relaxing thoughts. The joys of the evening to come. The delightful company of his family.

He breathed in, held it, gasped, released the breath. All he could think about were negative things. The front door lock, the partially written book, the cock-up in the

Japanese restaurant, the credit card bill, the letter from the bursar.

That was the clincher. Hugo didn't realise that he had been holding his breath the entire time, until he found himself turned over, on his back, with his knees raised, and the head end of the electronically-controlled couch lowered towards the floor.

"I think you fainted for a moment or two there," he heard a voice say.

He opened his eyes to see the sadist therapist standing beside him. The towel was pulled up to his neck. The massage apparently over. The lights had been turned up bright, the oil burner extinguished and the chirping birds etc had stopped.

"It can be a little too much for some people, especially when combined with the sports massage element," the sadist therapist said as she came into focus.

"Oh," was all Hugo could manage.

He felt screaming pain in every one of his muscles.

"Usually it's the men. Women have a very high pain threshold."

"Oh," Hugo said again.

He was breathing once more, although his knuckles were white from the pressure exerted clinging onto the underside of the massage couch.

The sadist therapist pushed a button, making the top end of the couch fly up and Hugo's head reverberated against the head rest. He now also had a throbbing headache.

"Right, I'll leave you to get sorted, and when you're ready just come back into reception. But drink this water first – massage can dehydrate you."

She handed him a white plastic cup of cold water. He took it and watched her depart.

Hugo wasn't sure how he had managed to get off the couch unaided, as he left the room and made his way towards the reception desk. He was limping in both legs. It felt like he had spent one hundred hours in the gym straight. Doing leg squats without a warm-up. He was certain that he would need painkillers to get through the rest of the weekend. The type you could only get on prescription. How he would manage to get his trousers and shoes on, God only knew. It was at this moment an utter impossibility. He'd have to throw a towel around him and go up to the room like he was. A hot bath might help. If he could get into it.

The sadist was waiting for him at reception.

"I'll just hand you over to my colleague to pay. It was lovely to meet you and remember to relax now and not do anything strenuous."

Off she went with a cheery smile.

Tony behind the counter said, with no expression, "That's £85 please."

"What!" Hugo replied, "it says here, 'half price massage', and I checked when I came in, and she said it would be £35!"

Although he was in no condition to argue, he couldn't help but point out the mistake.

"That's for the basic massage, you had the Thai, that adds another £50. It's very specialist and not everyone can do it you know."

Tony did not crack a smile. Deadpan.

Hugo slumped. Oh fuck it, he was in too much pain to dispute it.

"Just put it on my tab," he said, gingerly shuffling away towards the door.

Wonder if I can sue them, he speculated on his way out. Dana will know.

Second thought, better not to mention the incident at all. Women can be funny about these things. Could get the wrong end of the stick.

At least his back wasn't causing him any more discomfort.

The pain in his legs now transcending any other sensations in his body.

235

FIFTEEN

Cressida put the finishing, flourishing touches to her pink and very sparkly manicure, as she watched her third episode of *The Big Bang Theory*. And her nails set off her new silver bracelet, with the little kitten charm attached, just beautifully. Dad had bought it for her after their club sandwiches. She had spotted it while she was being consoled by the wonderful Veronique. It was in a display cabinet in the corridor, opposite the sofa they had sat on having their tete-a-tete. It matched the necklace that Dad had bought her yesterday. It was very nice of him to get it for her. And anyway, how could he refuse, after everything that had happened?

And Veronique was a dream! She loved her. Was in fact in love with this beautiful French girl. She understood Cressida like no one else did. Veronique had immediately just got it all, what the others had been so stupid about, what they just couldn't understand. And instead of trying to make it all Cressida's fault by saying that she was difficult, Veronique had said that Cressida was unique: special, discerning, sensitive, creative, and that sensitive and creative people were so often misunderstood by others.

She had a friend for life there. A soul-mate, someone she could turn to in trouble.

A *mon ami.*

And they had so much in common: they both spoke French, and English, Veronique had a brother too, and he was also a bit gross sometimes, and they both had such difficult parents, causing so much trouble and so many arguments.

On reflection things had not turned out too badly so far, Cressida decided. I got loads of clothes out of Dad, some lovely jewellery, some MAC makeup, I got some yummy room service, and got rid of Alex for the afternoon so that I could do girl stuff. And I've made a new friend. So, not totally crap in the end, all things considered.

Now, think I will get ready for tonight, Cressida decided, as she took the newly-changed, size six, cream, floaty dress off the hanger and went into the bathroom.

Dana decided that a deep, aromatic bath, filled with frothy bubbles from several of the mini-sized freebies in the bathroom, would be better than another swim or sauna. She had considered having a facial, or perhaps a manicure, as it was her birthday, but having looked at the prices on the treatment menu – and having attempted to tot up the expenses incurred so far that weekend – she settled for the bath. It was free – well, included in what they had already paid at any rate – and probably more relaxing than wrestling with locker keys, swimsuit and lotions and potions that she would have had to carry down to the spa.

Facials could be very much hit and miss anyway, depending upon the mood of the therapist, and the quality of the establishment. Mind you, Dana thought, as she poured another little bottle of bath creme under the hot tap, the prices charged did not always reflect the expertise, or otherwise, of the beautician or the results. She remembered once, when she was younger and money was not the issue that it had now become, going for a facial in a well-known health spa resort in Scotland, when they had been up visiting Hugo's father on holiday. After a lot of faffing about with filling in treatment cards and putting on and taking off fluffy bath robes, the beautician had gone through a long winded speech about the benefits of the oils she was about to use, and how they connected with the Chakras in the body and soul – or some such nonsense. She had then washed the soles of Dana's feet and anointed them with the oils – or something like that, cleansed her face with hot towels, carried out a manual lymph drainage – a facial and head massage as it turned out – then applied a healing face pack, swaddled her in blankets and hot stones, and said she would leave Dana to "inner reflection and contemplation", turned the lights off and left the room.

Now, Dana was not so easily taken in by such claims, basically believing nothing she was told until proven correct. After about fifteen minutes, she sat up, removed the hot towels from around her neck, escaped the strictures of the blankets, set the stones aside, got off the couch, went over to the door, and switched the light back on.

When she looked in the mirror she was horrified. Her

neck and ears were red and blotchy, her hair congealed with the hot oils from the massage, which had now dried a rancid but pliable lard colour, and the face mask had been slapped on in patches, not even reaching to her chin. She found a bottle of the "essential oils" beside a bowl near the couch which read "Asda's Little Angels Baby Oil". She tiptoed out of the room, expecting to encounter the beautician practising the Lotus Position and working on her Third Eye, but instead there was no one to be seen. Dana wandered along the hallway past treatment room after treatment room, but there was no sign of the beautician. Just before she got to the waiting area, she spotted a steel security door, with a sign that read Keep Locked Shut At All Times, standing ajar. She heard voices raised. Dana peered around the door which opened out onto a side alley piled high with boxes, empty vegetable oil vats and huge industrial blue plastic bins. Little weeds grew in the dirt that had accumulated in the corners.

Leaning against a bin was her beautician, dragging heavily on a Superking's Menthol fag, picking her nose, and making no attempt to stifle a loud, snorting laugh as she cackled into her phone, "Fuck off! He didn't!"

The incident would have been highly amusing, had the facial not cost £65, "with the option to buy products tailored to your needs by your therapist".

No, a bath will do very nicely, she decided, as she stepped into it, at least we are not wasting money on so-called luxuries in this hotel. Even Cress had done her own nails, and hadn't tried to wangle a manicure in the spa out of Hugo, although given recent events he would probably have agreed.

Poor Hugo. For a moment or two Dana felt a little sorry for him. Trying to please them all, not succeeding, but at least trying, a little.

And, to be fair, and with all his faults – of which there were many – Dana did concede that at least Hugo didn't indulge himself. He didn't spend all day in the pub or at the football – and Brighton and Hove Albion were playing at home today, she had heard him mention. But he didn't once suggest that he go and watch them, and he hadn't sat all afternoon watching Sky Sports either. Like some men do.

Dana ran a razor over her legs, and wondered where Hugo actually was, come to think of it. Maybe having a swim. Or a sauna.

Of course, she suddenly realised – he was probably wandering around, a bit lost and helpless, looking for my birthday present. And then she felt another pang of guilt. Here she was, lying in the bath, while he was out fighting his way through the shoppers in the growing dusk and cold, wracking his brains for a present, and on his own, since Cressida was in her room getting ready for tonight.

Oh well, it's only once a year. I might as well make the most of it, I suppose. Time for a large G and T, Dana thought, as she got out of the bath and pulled the plug. As she dried herself off Dana wondered which of the suggested gifts Hugo had got her. Long experience of ghastly underwear – that would look garish on a pole dancer – blouses even her mother wouldn't wear, and a wardrobe full of scarves which required an additional seventy-five years to be added to her lifespan in order to get around to wearing them all, had taught Dana to leave a strategically-placed list of suggestions.

The aforementioned list had been left on the coffee table in the their suite's sitting room this morning, for just that purpose. The suggestions were, as always, sensible and practical. The new John Connolly book, some running kit, new trainers, perfume, bath stuff. All useful.

Of course what Dana really would have liked money could not buy, and therefore she was not likely to get it.

And the things that money could buy they didn't have the money to buy.

Secretly though, Dana had always wanted – always yearned – for a beautiful piece of jewellery. Something gold, something with a green gem in it. An emerald. Every Christmas and every birthday since she had first met Hugo she had hoped to open a little box and find something beautiful inside it. But she never did.

And now they couldn't afford it. And now it was too late. And Dana wouldn't want it anyway. Not now. She had inherited a few trinkets over the years, all gone now, one way or another, although she still had Aunty Ag's platinum engagement ring, but it was hardly the same thing.

She sighed as she put on the complimentary bath robe and slippers, making a mental note to double check Cressida and Alex's luggage before they left the hotel – taking the little toiletries was one thing. Taking the textiles quite another.

Her mother had done that once, so the family story went. When Bella was younger, newly married, she and a group of friends were staying in a very smart hotel – a castle of some sort – which had a dungeon bar and restaurant, Killiney Castle Grill, she seemed to remember. And someone had felt faint, so they went outside, and someone else brought out a chair for them to sit in on the lawn. The chair was an antique, deeply padded, carved oak or something. And when it was time to leave they simply took the chair with them – threw it on top of the car, lashed a tow rope around it, and drove off. No one batted an eyelid.

Never get away with it now of course, apart from the fact that they would have been a menace on the road with several bottles of wine and spirits inside them. And the chair, sitting majestically, on the roof of the car.

Hadn't someone done that with a grand piano once? Famously stealing it from a hotel in New York?

Well anyway, a bath robe was not on the same scale as a chair or piano, but it was still wrong nonetheless. Dana would be doing a strip-search if necessary before they left.

She wandered into the little sitting room and opened the mini-bar, took out a miniature bottle of gin and a tonic, got a glass from the shelf above, and took it all over to the sofa.

Ah that's nice, she thought, as the bubbles from the tonic popped in her mouth and the sharp taste of the juniper berries hit her tongue. She sat back and relaxed. Looked around, decided to turn on the television to the mellow jazz channel. Dana put her drink down on the coffee table. And saw the birthday list peeping out from under that morning's unread, complimentary newspaper, along with the note she had left Hugo earlier, telling him that she had gone to the gym for a run.

She exhaled and took a long pull on her drink.

Cressida was putting the finishing touches to her green glitter eyeliner in the bathroom, when she heard the door to their room open and close. She had meant to put the safety chain across and lock it, but forgot, what with getting ready and trying to glue her false eyelashes on and everything. She waited a moment, held her breath. Could be that woman with the towels, Cressida thought. She's always trying to get in and snoop around. Oh, could be Mum too, she has a key.

Cressida slowly and quietly screwed the lid on her eyeliner, and moved closer to the door to listen. She heard footsteps and something being dragged, like the bed or a chair. Then silence.

Not Mum, she would call out, Cress decided.

Then more footsteps and a soft plopping sort of noise, like someone falling into a chair.

Her dad? Why would he be in here? No. Not Dad.

Cressida put her hand very gently on the door handle.

Could be a thief, or robber, or something.

She very, very quietly turned the lock on the door.

She heard something being picked up from a table.

Could be two of them. No can't be. They'd be talking if there were.

Cressida watched a lot of suspense films. She now thought of Jodie Foster in *Panic Room* – that film where those men break into her house in the middle of the night to steal the hidden millions, thinking that the house is empty, and Jodie Foster has to hide in the panic room with the steel door.

Cressida looked around the bathroom. There was no steel door. There was no panic button.

But there was water from the tap. At least she would not die of dehydration if she had to stay hidden in there for any length of time.

She put her ear to the door again.

She could hear drawers being opened and closed. It was a robber! They were looking for stuff to steal. Bastard!

Her phone, suddenly she remembered her phone, she would call for help. She looked around the bathroom. She'd left it outside in the bedroom, next to her bed. Just like in the film.

Shit! And her iPad, she'd left that there too. The robber would take that of course, both items.

Oh my God! My clothes! My new MAC makeup! Bastard.

Hang on, she thought, it's okay, the makeup is in here with me. But the kitten jewellery is still out in the bedroom. Robbers always take jewellery. And televisions and stuff. Well, probably not the television as otherwise they would look suspicious walking down the corridor with a television.

There was another dragging and scraping sound, like a heavy chair being moved.

Cressida's heart was beating very fast. She looked in the mirror. She looked frightened, she thought. And of course, the robber had come in smack in the middle of her makeup application, so that one eye was green, and the other still in its horrible natural state.

They could be a rapist or a murderer.

Cressida looked around for something to defend herself. All she could see was her toothbrush, and a hairdryer with a fat hose welded to the wall. And a toilet brush. Mind you after Alex had been in there this morning – "splashing the kids in the pool", as he put it – the toilet brush would probably do it.

There was a loud cheer from the other side of the door. Like a crowd, and then a football score was announced. The television. The rapist-robber had put on the television. He was taking a chance wasn't he? Hanging around. Why not just rob the room and clear off? Unless he was waiting for her.

Oh, where was Alex when she needed him? Useless. She knew where he had gone, he'd told her. Not that she could care less, except now she wished he was here. And he had said he would not be back until they headed out for the birthday dinner later.

So, in effect, she would be stranded alone there for an hour or more with the killer – the interloper now having morphed in her *Panic Room* imagination to a sadistic serial killer – and no one would know, until they found her mutilated body later that evening.

Veronique would care though. She would weep and be inconsolable about her new friend's tragic end.

The sound of the football match turned to a Formula One race-track, as the television channels were surfed.

Cressida sat down with her back to the door. She was tired standing on tiptoe, and she thought that if the killer tried the door then her weight against it would stop it opening if the lock failed.

Shit! What if he needed the toilet? He might come in here!

The killer was obviously restless, and therefore more dangerous, since the television channel changed yet again to a game show with Ant and Dec. Ah, she quite liked that show. This perked her up a little until Ant and Dec were unceremoniously swept off the screen with another flick of the remote control.

Then silence. Then another noise.

At first Cressida couldn't hear very much. Until she could just make out a breathing sound. Had the killer fallen asleep? The breathing got heavier.

And heavier. There were two people breathing. Very heavily.

Then there was a sort of groaning sound, "Ahhhh" – then more breathing.

Then more groaning. Which turned to moaning.

Then a woman's voice said, "Yes! Yes! Give it to me again!"

Then a man's voice said, "Don't stop baby, don't stop!"

Oh my God. I know what that is. Oh my God, that's disgusting.

What a pervert. On our TV!

Then the noise stopped completely, and another voice, one she knew, said, "Bloody hell, are they kidding? What do they mean pay at reception? How can they charge for that channel, thought it was included in the deal?"

Cressida unlocked the bathroom door and stormed out into the bedroom.

Alex sat in a chair he had hauled over in front of the television. He was holding the remote control and waving it around in front of the screen, like when the battery is running out.

"Alex," she shouted.

He jumped up out of the chair in a panic when he saw her.

"Bloody hell Cress, you scared the shit out of me!"

"What are you doing?" she shouted again.

"Watching the TV. I just got back."

"I've been locked in that bathroom, terrified for my life,

waiting while a killer-rapist was in here," she was still shouting.

Alex looked around the room.

"Well he's gone now," he said.

"Don't be stupid Alex, there wasn't really a killer-rapist, but I thought that it was you!"

"Not sure I follow all that Cress, but I do sleep here too, and this is also my room."

"Yes, well, you said you wouldn't be back till later and I thought someone had broken in." She calmed down a bit, sat on the edge of the bed.

"I had a change of plan. What were you up to in there anyway?" Alex looked around the room suspiciously, killing the television with the remote control.

"Me? Are you joking? You're the one who's been *up to things*," Cressida accused, looking at the television.

"Yeah, well – it was short-lived. Channel is blocked. You have to pay at reception or something. I'll sort it out later." Alex stretched, yawned and flung himself down on the bed.

"You will not. I'm not staying in here while you look at that nasty stuff."

Cressida went back into the bathroom, and resumed the application of the green glitter eyeliner. She stood back and looked in the mirror. She struck a pose, mimicking Jodie Foster in *Panic Room*. She'd be good in a crisis, she decided. Don't panic or jump to conclusions, that was how you survived. Just like Jodie Foster.

It did not occur to her that her own conclusion to the "crisis" of a few moments ago could not have been more outlandish or extreme if she'd invented it. Which of course she had.

Cressida was like concentrated orange juice – both need to be diluted to taste. She was what she was: a female, teenage product of the digitally connected, self-aware, social media age.

"So did you get what you wanted then, at The Blood of Satan?" Cressida asked Alex through the now open bathroom door.

"One of them. For now," he replied.

Cressida came back into the bedroom.

"So, what have you been doing all afternoon then?"

Alex sat up on one elbow. "This and that. Checking out some venues for later on. You coming out?"

"Dunno. Will that drug dealer be with you?"

Alex laughed. "He's not a drug dealer Cress."

"He's from Colombia."

"That doesn't make him a drug dealer."

Cressida didn't look convinced. "He's weird anyway. I wouldn't trust him."

"I don't have to trust him. I don't plan on marrying him."

They both laughed. Cressida thought back to the wedding incident.

"That'll please Dad at least," she said.

Alex got up off the bed and went over to his rucksack. Took out a can of beer. Held it up. "You want to split this before we go out?" he asked his sister.

Cressida went over to her handbag, with the little kitten keyring. She got out a miniature bottle of vodka.

"Nah, I'll drink this." She held it up.

"Where did you get that?"

Cressida unscrewed the top and took a swig.

"From their mini-bar thing. When I said 'Daddy?

Please may I have a chocolate bar from the fridge?'"

They both fell about laughing.

Dana finished her G and T and picked up her phone. Twelve messages. And one missed call. Despite her best intentions, she had to look at at least one message, or two.

"Very worried. Please respond," read one.

"Not heard back from you, everything OK?" read another.

"Brighton must be very alluring to have captivated all of your attention?" read the one before that.

Enough, Dana decided. They would all be along the same lines. She wouldn't look at any more.

The missed call would have been from him too, after the last message had gone without a response. Everyone else was here in the hotel, so it wouldn't be any kind of crisis that she was ignoring. Just another sort of situation.

There was a fumbling at the suite door and the handle rattled. Oh God, not the room service woman, Dana thought. She couldn't face her again, not after she had been so rude to her yesterday.

Instead, Hugo appeared in the open doorway. He looked very odd. He had a towel wrapped around his middle, and was naked from the waist up, and the towel down come to think of it.

"What on earth have you been doing?" Dana asked him.

Hugo looked startled, she thought.

"What? Oh, nothing," he said, limping through the door.

"Are you hurt?" Dana asked him.

He made his way into the room, holding the wall as he

went, as if to steady himself.

"What's wrong? Why can't you walk properly?"

Hugo rested at the bedroom door.

"It's a long story," he said.

"And I would like to hear it. I thought you were out shopping for my – well, shopping."

Dana got up and went over to him, looking him over, expecting to see a gaping wound or other injury.

"Do you feel ill? Faint? What?" she asked.

"Yes, rather. I, um, well, I went to the gym and did a bit of a workout, that's all."

"That's all? And yet you cannot walk now?"

"Well, it was a rather strenuous session and I'm not really used to it, truth to tell," he said, still holding on to the door.

"And did you do it in your underpants?"

Hugo looked up sharply. "What? Why?"

"Because you are naked."

Hugo pulled the towel away from his body, revealing the Speedos, now bone dry.

"No I'm not. I went for a swim afterwards, but when I got out I couldn't get dressed, couldn't bend down. Think I have injured my hamstring and back."

He inched along in the direction of the bathroom.

Dana looked at his Speedos and shook her head.

"Don't suppose I could prevail upon you to run me a bath? It might help ease the pain," he asked.

Dana continued to shake her head as she walked towards the bathroom.

"From the look of you it will take more than a bath. I'll get some pills."

In the bathroom she put the plug back in and turned

on the taps, then returned to the bedroom, where Hugo was still making his way along the wall.

She looked up at him as he did so and said, "You might want to take off your swimming trunks. Wouldn't want to get them wet. Again."

Hugo lay back in the soothing water. He'd taken a couple of co-codamol – the second set of the day as it happened – have to keep an eye on that, there's a limit to dosage he seemed to remember. He had some Vapo Rub in his bag which he used for his back, he'd slap a bit of that on when he got out of the bath, that, and a large malt, should sort it out. Christ, life was never straightforward. And just as well he had kept the fiasco in the spa under his hat, best to keep quiet about it altogether. At least Dana had bought the other version of events.

There was a knock on the door.

"Can I come in?" Dana asked.

His wife rarely ventured into any area where Hugo was undressed, so this was a pleasant surprise. Still, it was her birthday. Mind you, she probably considers it safe territory, what with my injury and that, he decided.

"Of course," he replied.

"What time is the restaurant table booked and how far is it? Do I need to order a taxi?" Dana asked, standing by the door.

"Eight o'clock and it's literally a few minutes walk from here."

Hugo scrubbed behind his ears.

"I thought we might pop down to the cellar bar after dinner, there's jazz on Saturday nights and a spot of dancing. The kids are allowed in if they are guests at the

251

hotel apparently," he said.

"Mm, that sounds very nice. Okay, let's do that. Give Cressida a chance to show off her new dress," Dana agreed.

Hugo splashed about trying to reach his toes with the nail brush.

"Can I bring you anything?" she asked him.

"A malt with lots of ice would be lovely," he replied, and added, "if there's anything left in that mini-bar."

"They replenished it this morning, so it's fully stocked again." Dana went off to make the drink.

"It'll also give you a chance to show off your nice outfit," Hugo raised his voice so she could hear him in the other room.

Then he added, "And anything else that you might wear with it." He smiled.

Rather looking forward to bestowing the gift, he thought. Old Hugo's not so clueless in the shopping department as they all think. I know what women like, and what my wife wants for her birthday. Yes, he congratulated himself, feeling just a tiny bit better after the pills.

Dana came back with the whisky, handed it to Hugo, whilst averting her eyes, he noticed, from his not entirely unattractive physique – even if he did say so himself – when she handed him the drink.

"Aren't you going to join me?" he asked her.

Dana stood back.

"I've already had a bath thank you and I've done my makeup," she responded.

Hugo held up his drink and chuckled. "In a drink." He rattled the ice in the glass.

Dana smiled. "Oh, no, I had a G and T earlier, thanks, I'm going to get dressed now, and then we should see how Alex and Cress are doing."

As she left the bathroom and walked over to the wardrobe, she asked Hugo about the progress on his book.

"I've been thinking about it rather a lot," he lied through the open door.

Truth was, it hadn't crossed his mind, other than in a blind panic down in the massage room, when all the issues in his life had conspired in a perfect storm of stress. He was a little behind schedule with his research and writing, but he had plans to knuckle down to it once the weekend was out of the way. And, come to think of it, he had come up with one or two loosely formed ideas – call it subliminal if you will – on weight-bearing exercises, brought on, funnily enough, by back and hamstring injuries. The irony was that his not actually going into the gym to exert himself had given him time to reflect upon the benefits, or not, of strength training.

Writing a book, he reminded himself as he savoured his malt, was not what people imagined at all. One didn't have to be tapping away at a keyboard, or making copious notes, or speaking into a dictaphone all day, to be doing the work of a writer. There was equal merit in thought. Just having some peace and quiet to think things through, formulate and refine ideas. Solve problems. Most of the actual work is done thinking up the ideas. Weighing their relative strengths, editing them, researching them. Only then could the writing be done.

Yes, Hugo decided, taking another sip, the actual typing up of the hard copy was just the finishing touch, the icing on the cake of the enterprise, so to speak.

For instance, I'm working just lying here thinking about the book, he told himself, as he sank back into the bubbles. Plenty of time for typing later. These things cannot be rushed. And anyway, he had more research to do, starting perhaps tomorrow.

"I was thinking that your suggestion to visit the Amex Stadium, and their new gymnasium, tomorrow is an excellent one. Perhaps I could speak to the coach, get his take on training young athletes. See how they put it into operation. Be a good resource for the book."

Hugo smacked his lips. Yes, good idea, good idea.

"Don't you have to phone ahead, make an appointment? Bit late now, isn't it?" Dana asked through the door.

"No, I wouldn't think so. The gym is open seven days a week, after all, a professional football team is always training. It shouldn't be a problem I wouldn't have thought. And anyway, having a look around the facility will be very helpful."

"Right. So what bit of the book will that fit into then?" Dana replied.

Hugo thought through the chapters. There would be ten or twelve. Not because he had ten or twelve topics to write about, but because they were nice round numbers. And several other similar books he had seen appeared to contain that number too.

"It will be the basis of general reference throughout the book darling," Hugo blustered, "strength training forms the central core of the whole topic, so it will be very relevant."

He wasn't entirely sure what it would be relevant to at

this stage, or indeed what the "central core" was – or, come to think of it – what the main topic actually was, but all in the fullness of time. It was early days yet. It would shape up in due course.

"I see," Dana said, "and are you going to do any writing-work as opposed to research-work tomorrow?"

Did he detect a hint of sarcasm, or irritation, in his darling wife's voice? He finished off his malt. No, she was just being supportive, and he should be grateful that she took an interest. A lot of men he knew complained about how their wives took no interest in their work. Just the pay cheque. Even Camilla, sweet as she was. Tristram had confided one night at a school dinner-dance – after a second bottle of Châteauneuf – that he doubted whether Camilla or Lucas would even notice if he failed to return home after one of his business trips, but they'd soon notice if his bonus wasn't paid. Poor chap, Hugo knew just how he felt, and he'd told him so. We toil away, earning a decent living – well more than decent in Tristram's case – and what thanks or interest do we get?

But in this instance Dana was being very supportive, taking such an interest, and Hugo should be more grateful, he decided.

"Yes darling, I am. In fact I have my manuscript with me in my briefcase, and I will be going through it in the morning, starting at breakfast, making amendments and revisions, and will take it, and my research notes, to the stadium later on."

Now that I have created the call to action, Hugo decided, I had better remember to get it out in the morning. But for the moment, more pressing matters were to hand. Hugo was not entirely sure how he was going to get out of the bath. He took a deep breath and cleared his throat, preparatory to calling Dana to assist him, but not wanting to spoil any slim chance he might have later on, he decided to clench both his teeth and his buttocks and ease himself ever so gingerly out of the bath.

That task, eventually accomplished, he managed to dry himself and put on another of the fluffy bath robes, and walk with a little more ease into the bedroom.

"My word. You do look lovely darling," Hugo said as he looked up.

Dana was wearing an emerald green lace gown – Hugo called any dress that a woman wore in the evening a "gown" – off the shoulder, quite short and rather racy. And high heels, and her hair was put up in a kind of knot. And she had on long, dangly bead earrings. No necklace.

Yes, he decided, the birthday gift will complement that outfit just perfectly.

"Thanks," she replied, "Zara."

"Yes, can't say I am their biggest fan, but nevertheless, you do look lovely."

"It's seven forty so perhaps you should get dressed too," Dana advised.

Hugo went to the wardrobe, peered inside, it was full of Dana's clothes. He looked across to the luggage rack. His bag still sat there unpacked. He was a bit miffed about this. Someone could have unpacked it. Wasn't that what the valet was supposed to do? Probably not, not here anyway. He fiddled about, found underpants, socks, a shirt – creased, a tie, trousers – also creased. He held them up and examined them.

Dana sat and watched from the window.

"So what was all that about olive oil and soap and

Provence?" she asked

Hugo shook the trousers, trying to remove the creases. "What?"

Dana got up and took the trousers off him, went over to the trouser press, opened it and put them inside.

"All that about importing this and that with Miss France downstairs?" she resumed.

"Thanks," he said, adding, "oh, just a new business idea, I have a lot more research to do on the topic."

He started getting dressed.

"I see. And do you think that there is a market for those products then?"

"Of course there is. France hardly exports any of its olive oil for resale here." Hugo fiddled with his shirt buttons.

"There might be a good reason for that." Dana stood by the trouser press waiting.

"There jolly well is. No one has bothered to import it, that's the reason, it's obvious," he continued.

"Is it?"

"I should say, all that lovely olive oil from the South of France, all that sunshine, all those olives, none of it available here. Blindingly obvious. Just needed someone to action it," he replied.

Having put on his socks with some difficulty, Hugo now stood in them, underpants and shirt tails awaiting his trousers.

"Right," Dana said, inspecting the progress of the trousers, "and you are going to start a French olive oil importation business on the strength of no one else doing it?"

"And soap, olive oil soap, also from the South of

France." Hugo thought that his new idea was growing in momentum, with all the interest that was being shown in it.

"But isn't that already available? Isn't that what Marseilles Soap is?" Dana asked again.

"Similar but not entirely the same thing darling. And as I say, it's early days yet, and more research is needed, but it's got legs, no doubt about that."

Dana snapped the metal lever back, retrieved the trousers, and handed them to Hugo.

"Well, better put your trousers on first, it's not just the Japanese who are very correct about manners. I believe the French prefer dinner guests to be suitably attired too. And potential business partners."

Ha! Hugo thought, now Dana was being just a little bit playfully sarcastic there, despite her obvious interest in his new venture.

"When you've done that could you rouse Alex and Cress while I put some lipstick on?" she asked, as she went into the bathroom.

With Hugo's slacks now pressed to a knife-edge, he was obliged to put on a jacket to avoid comparison with his creased, albeit Turnbull and Asser, tailored shirt. He knocked on Cressida's and Alex's door, while knotting his tie, which further concealed the deep furrows in the front of the shirt.

There was no response. Hugo knocked again. Still no response.

A third knock. Still nothing.

"I say, Alex, Cressida? It's your father."

No one answered, but he heard something falling over

inside the room.

He knocked again, more forcefully.

"Are you ready to go? You mother says we are leaving now."

He heard something open and close on the other side of the door.

"Can you hear me? Alex? Cressida?"

There was laughter from inside the room.

Hugo stood adjusting his cuffs. Becoming ever so slightly irritated.

He knocked yet again.

"What's going on in there? I can hear you, you know," he raised his voice a notch.

He heard what seemed to be a whirring sound within.

"Alex! This is your father. Please open the door."

More laughter, then, "We'll be out in a minute Dad," Alex said.

"Why can't I come in? Why won't you open the door?"

Hugo put his head against the door. The whirring noise continued.

"Cressida is getting changed," Alex responded.

"Oh. Well all right. But hurry up," Hugo said.

Then he heard Cressida laugh.

Hugo paused, thought about it.

"Hang on, if she's getting changed how can it be okay for you to be in there, but not me?" he asked.

No response. Then Alex said, "She's in the bathroom."

"Well then I can come into the bedroom." Hugo tried the door handle.

No response. Then Alex said, "I'm getting changed."

The whirring noise had stopped and Hugo heard them both laughing.

I'm not having this, he thought. Hugo banged loudly on the door.

"Young man open this door now. Do not force me to go and get the duplicate key from your mother."

There was silence for a moment or two, and then the door was unlocked.

Alex lay casually back on his bed, and Cressida was touching up her eye makeup in front of a mirror.

Hugo walked into the room, looked around suspiciously. "Thought you were getting dressed?" he asked Alex.

"Yeah, sorted now," Alex responded.

"And I suppose you just finished too?" Hugo turned to Cressida.

"Yes Daddy, nearly ready to go." Cressida's reflection smiled sweetly at him from the mirror.

Hugo saw that a large, floor-standing, chrome fan was plugged in near the wardrobe.

"Where did that come from?" he asked.

"It was in the wardrobe," Alex told him.

"Why do you need a fan? It's the middle of winter."

"Cressida was having a hot flush," Alex explained.

Hugo looked at Cressida. She smiled sweetly again, and put her hand to her forehead.

Hugo thought about it. "Nonsense, it's only ladies of a certain age who have hot flushes, like your mothe—" he said, stopping, no point in insulting Dana, "well anyway, it's nonsense. And why is that window open so far?"

The sash cord window was pulled up to its fullest extent.

"It was very clammy in here, and you are always telling us to get some fresh air," Alex said.

"Outside, when you exercise. Not indoors, catching your death while you sleep." Hugo strode over and closed the window.

He sniffed the air around it. Caught a whiff of something, not quite sure what.

"What's that smell?" he asked, looking from one to the other.

Alex looked at Cressida who looked wide-eyed.

"What smell?" they both asked back.

Hugo stood on tiptoe, despite his back, and sniffed the air again. He could detect something sickly sweet, musky perhaps.

"That" – Hugo sniffed and snorted, like a hog foraging for truffles – "smell."

Alex shrugged his shoulders. "No idea," he said, "must be something outside."

Hugo wasn't sure the smell was outside, but he wasn't convinced either way. He walked towards the door, spotting a box of matches on the table beside Alex's bed, a complimentary box upon which was printed "The Well of Wickedness".

Hugo picked them up, opened them, saw several spent matches inside.

"What's this young man?" Hugo asked, holding them up.

"Matches?" Alex responded.

"I can see that, the question is what are they for? And don't say 'lighting'."

"Of course not. They are for this," Alex responded by pulling out from under his bed, a ten-inch, plastic skeleton, in a prone position, with a large hole between the teeth of its skull, upon which rested, what looked like, a half-burnt Guy Fawkes sparkler.

It was still glowing red.

Hugo stood watching. Confused, suspicious, but confused.

"What is that?" he said, almost afraid to ask.

"Incense. It makes the room smell nice. Me and Cress like it. Got it in a hippy place down the North Laines. It's made from musk and cinnamon and herbs and stuff."

Alex held it up for inspection.

Hugo took the item and held it at arms length. Then drew it a little closer and sniffed it tentatively.

"So why did you conceal it then?" he asked.

"Thought we might get into trouble for lighting it in case it set off a smoke alarm or something," Alex explained.

"Right." Hugo continued to sniff the item.

"Presumably that is why you opened the window and put on the fan?" he continued.

"Yes Daddy. Didn't want to get told off by that room service lady. It's okay, Mum has incense at home, makes the house smell nice." Cressida smiled sweetly.

Hugo handed the skeleton and the embers back to Alex. He wasn't in agreement about the pleasantness of the odour, but supposed that if Dana had okayed it then it must be acceptable.

"Well run it under the tap before we go to make sure it is out properly. And whilst in principle it is probably all right, don't light it again here. I've enough to deal with without you two burning the hotel down and getting sued for every penny I possess."

Alex sprung up from the bed to take the incense stick into the bathroom, and in doing so disturbed the concealed empty beer can, which he accidentally kicked, causing it to roll into the middle of the room and come to a stop at Hugo's feet.

Hugo looked at the can and then up at Alex, the latter winced.

"And where did you get that?" Hugo asked.

Alex stood contrite in front of Hugo, with his hands behind his back.

"Lucas gave it to me a while back. He pinched it from his dad. We were going to share it at the end-of-term school party, but Lucas suggested I bring it to Brighton with me and drink it over the course of the weekend."

Hugo nodded knowingly and let out an exaggerated sigh. Boys will be boys he supposed.

Cressida was watching the proceedings like a hawk.

"I sincerely hope that you did not have any young lady?" Hugo asked her.

"No Daddy, and to be fair Alex has been sipping it yesterday and today, and it was only one can." Cressida continued to smile sweetly.

Alex still stood, meekly, with his hands still behind his back, holding the skeleton incense holder. Head down.

Hugo wagged a finger at Alex. "I knew you were concealing something young man, I'm not stupid. I've partied hard myself, back in the day. I know a trick or two, you'd better believe it. There are no flies on me."

Hugo smiled benignly and walked towards the door.

"As it was only one drink, not to be repeated, and as it is your mother's birthday, we will say no more about the matter. Now, run that thing under the tap and be downstairs in two minutes, and don't forget the presents!"

"I'm ready now Daddy, so I'll come with you," Cressida

said, grabbing her coat, and smiling at Alex, as they left the room.

As the door closed behind his father and sister, Alex did as he was told and took the incense holder into the bathroom. He removed the stick of incense and put the ember end under the running tap, as instructed, and left it to dry on the handbasin.

Then he tapped the skeleton incense holder against the side of the bin to empty out the incense ashes that had accumulated at the bottom, and carried it back into the bedroom.

Before he put it away, he turned the holder over, slid back the cover on a battery-like storage compartment underneath the skeleton head, and felt inside. The concealed space wasn't big enough to store an incense stick. It was more suited to storing gram and ounce weights.

Alex prodded again, smiled and slid back the cover.

Then he took a fresh stick of incense from a packet under the bed, and placed it in the holder. He'd probably have to adhere to what his old man had said, and not light it again in the hotel in case it caught fire.

But appearances, and apparently smells, were everything.

SIXTEEN

Dana's *Assiette de Fruits de Mer,* followed by *Sole Meunière,* had been superb. Initially, she had considered ordering pate or soup, fearing that her choice of first course would be too reminiscent of the Tako episode earlier. But a discreet word with the waitress had confirmed that the plate of seafood contained only crustaceans – seafood that carried its home on its back, unlike the unfortunate creature at lunchtime.

Hugo was savouring his rack of lamb, although that also gave Dana misgivings, because Cressida preferred to think about spring lambs frolicking in a daisy-strewn field, rather than on her father's plate. Still, it was difficult to avoid such conversationally flammable foodstuffs in a classic French restaurant. Well, all right, Hotel Du Vin. She wasn't sure how really French it was, but the food and wine certainly lived up to the description.

Cressida was happy because they served her a lovely big bowl of French onion soup, and then a magnificent roasted-chestnut risotto with pickled walnut and apple salad.

Cress had lapped it up, and Dana had to pinch herself to make sure that it was all real, both the availability of something vegan and Cressida's appetite.

The only near miss with disaster had been Alex pointing to the steak tartare again – vetoed by everyone – and his then insisting on ordering *Escargots à la Bourguignonne* instead, for his starter. This turned out to be okay as Cressida pronounced snails to be "filthy, slimy, little critters", and she would be delighted to see them boiled until they popped. The waiter didn't see the amusing side of this – being, after all, French – pointing out that they were in fact sautéed in a garlic and herb butter, and not "boiled". He said the latter word with a snub nose, and it sounded like *bouled*. It had caused a general chuckle of amusement around the table.

Unfortunately, neither Dana nor Cressida had heard Alex follow up his starter with his main course order of *Lapin au Cidre et Pates Fraiches*, which would almost certainly also have been vetoed, if it had not slipped through the net, so to speak. Otherwise, Cress with her command of French, would have known immediately.

Alex had taken great delight in explaining that it was rabbit when it arrived. Fluffy rabbits lived the same rose-tinted existence as the spring lambs as far as Cressida was concerned, and she refused to speak to Alex for a good thirty minutes afterwards. Whether or not Alex had actually enjoyed the dish was another matter entirely. Dana suspected that he ordered it to spite Cressida, since his hungry eyes had followed a waiter carrying a tall burger in a sesame-seed bun, with melted cheese and a side order of *pommes frites,* to another table.

The restaurant was pleasantly bustling with waiting

staff synchronising their moves, like dancers on a stage, across the scrubbed wooden floors. People were supping, clinking cutlery and glasses, and the conversation was muted and good humoured, rather than loud and hearty.

The lights were low, and the thickly padded leather chairs comfortable. A little soft music drifted in from the adjoining bar. It was all very agreeable. And everyone was on good form.

Hugo had wanted to order a bottle of champagne, but Dana had said a bottle of sparkling would be better, and when she had shown Hugo that the cheapest bottle of champagne was £56 for the house version, he had replied that perhaps champagne proper would be wasted on the *children*. So they had opted instead for a Pinot Meunier, and even though the other diners looked over at their table when the cork popped – people often thinking that others are having a better time than they – Dana had felt something she could not quite put her finger on. Disappointment? Regret? Irritation?

Sadness. She had felt sadness. The truth was who wouldn't want champagne? Who didn't want the real thing?

Anyway, the flickering white candles and the sparkly drink went some way to helping her relax and enjoy the occasion. And after Hugo had tipped the last of the fizz into Dana's glass and put the empty bottle, bottom-end up, into the wine bucket, he had called for the wine list again.

A brief moment of tension had ensued when Alex reached over to the wine bucket, took hold of the empty bottle of sparkling wine, and set it back into the bucket, bottom-end down.

"What did you do that for?" Hugo asked him.

"The correct way to replace the empty bottle is like that." Alex waved his hand at the bucket.

"Of course it's not. The correct way is the way I had it, upside down, otherwise how would the waiter know it's empty?" Hugo swigged the last of his fizz.

"Tristram says only peasants put it in upside down in the ice bucket," Alex replied, swigging the last of his wine too and slapping his glass down on the table.

Hugo glared at him.

Dana kicked Cressida under the table and Cressida smiled.

"So how does the waiter know it's empty then? Hey? Explain that!" Hugo's cheeks were glowing.

"Tristram says a good sommelier will know when your bottle is empty because he will have been topping up your glasses throughout the meal, and that he doesn't need any crass indication from clueless diners to tell him his job."

"Well what if you have been topping up your own glasses? How would he know then?" Hugo nodded his head, agreeing with himself.

"Tristram says that in that instance the sommelier will ignore you, and that it was well deserved since you should have waited for him to attend to your refreshments in the first place, and that if you act like a peasant then you should expect to be treated like one."

Hugo bristled.

Dana and Cressida were trying to suppress giggles. Sparkly wine tended to have that effect.

"Nonsense. I don't believe it." Hugo looked indignant.

"Well," Alex said, waving his arm in the air and calling over the waiter with his hand, "he didn't take the empty bottle when you asked for the wine list again, did he?"

Hugo opened his mouth in protest, but the waiter appeared and took the bottle, now correctly placed in the ice bucket, during which time Hugo recovered himself sufficiently to order a bottle of white burgundy.

Alex smiled and added, "Tristram said—"

"Oh bugger Tristram," Hugo cut in, "he's not paying for it, I am, and if you want another glass you'd better shut up."

Dana and Cressida erupted into laughter as Dana patted Hugo's hand, feeling just a tad sorry for him, briefly, for the second time that day.

The burgundy was drunk and the pudding course contemplated. Hugo leaned back and patted his tummy as though he wasn't sure he could fit in an elaborate dessert. Cressida wanted a plate of fruit, Dana couldn't think of anything less palatable after a meal – frigid, out of season strawberries and Kiwi's. Insipid.

Alex suggested the cheese trolley. Excellent idea, Hugo agreed. Dana, however, was irritated when they served cheese cold, straight from the fridge. Hugo thought he was the connoisseur, but in reality it was Dana who did the questioning in restaurants, and often the complaining. Hugo being a little too quick to accept things on face value.

The waitress cleared the plates and came back with the dessert menus – pointing out that there were several cheeses to choose from, and several recommended ports or Calvados to accompany them.

As Dana took the menu she looked at the waitress's hand – the latter always revealing the truth, unlike the face – and noticed that it looked very much like her own:

a little sun damage, not quite as smooth as it had once been, the suggestion of an age spot or two creeping in. Dana then turned her attention to the waitress's face. It was pretty. Her eyes were large and brown, her hair blonde with the odd grey, and a darker colour creeping in on the crown. Her cheeks were pink and flushed from the long heavy apron she wore, and the rushing around smiling, trying to please the diners. Her figure slim.

She was English, not French, and spoke with authority about the cheese when asked, agreeing that it should be served at room temperature, that she would ensure that it was.

She looked like she had cares, but was not care-worn, not yet, perhaps she would be soon.

She was too pretty, too intelligent – too smart – to be working as a waitress in a restaurant.

And as Dana looked into her eyes, she realised that she was about her own age.

Too old to be wearing a uniform and waiting tables.

Dana remembered, at that moment, that it was her birthday. And she realised that they were both too pretty, too intelligent – too smart – and too old, to be doing what they were doing.

The waitress took the order and gave Dana a terse smile, the warmth had gone out of it. Probably because she agreed with what she suspected Dana was thinking.

Hugo leaned over and gave Dana a kiss, it was so unexpected it startled her.

"Happy birthday darling," he said, raising his glass and the remnants of the white burgundy.

"Yes, happy birthday Mum," Alex and Cressida joined in.

"Only one more year to go!" Alex added helpfully.

Hugo kicked him under the table. Alex pretended to be hurt.

Glasses clinked and greetings bestowed, Hugo got up from the table.

"Just off to see a man about a dog," he announced, tapping the side of his nose.

"Shall I come Dad?" Alex asked.

"No, no that's fine, I can manage thank you."

Hugo left the table for a few minutes, and then returned with a large bin bag under his arm, and sat down again.

Dana took a deep breath. Present time. Better get my smiley face ready, and then she instantly felt guilty – it is the thought that counts. And it would be a surprise of sorts: Hugo had forgotten the birthday suggestion list so she wouldn't be getting a book, trainers, or anything else on it. So back to the scarves and blouses, certainly wouldn't be a trinket, she thought, as she unconsciously put her hand to her collarbone and felt the empty space at her neck.

Mind you, the pole dancer must have an enormous arse if it's tacky lingerie, judging by the width of the bin liner that Hugo was holding. That thought made her smile.

"Right," Hugo announced, "present time!"

He smiled at Cressida, who reached inside her handbag and withdrew a beautifully wrapped box with brightly coloured ribbon on it.

She handed it to Dana with a kiss. "Happy birthday Mum, I made the selection myself."

Dana hugged her and took the gift. She smelt the

outside of the box.

"Smells gorgeous, I can guess what this is."

Dana unwrapped it, carefully folding up the paper as she did so, and laying the ribbon, coiled neatly, to one side. She remembered, vaguely, Hugo's father commenting upon her careful unwrapping one Christmas when they had first met. Hugo's parents had made a great ceremonial-like fuss of bestowing their Christmas gift on Dana. It had been elaborately wrapped, with layers of tissue and foil paper, ribbons and bows, and Hugo's father had told a windy tale about a young girl in the olden days, in some great aristocratic house, receiving a gift from a potential suitor, and how the suitor had chosen her over all the other girls or princesses or something, because she had taken great care in unwrapping the present, and treating the wrapping more preciously than the jewel inside it.

Dana had sat in rapt attention to this tale, slightly in awe of what the wrapped gift contained. And Hugo's parents had sat smiling and looking on.

When she had got to the last layer of paper on Hugo's parent's Christmas gift, Dana felt something soft and pliable underneath, she removed the tissue paper and revealed a cotton tea towel with "Scarborough North Pier" printed on it.

Dana had never forgotten that.

And ever since had made a point of ripping the paper off any gift from them that followed, rolling it into a ball, and aiming it at the nearest bin.

This though, was different. Cressida's lovely gift contained a selection of highly perfumed Lush bath products, studded with rose buds and lavender flowers.

"Exactly what I wanted, thank you so much darling, just perfect." Dana gave her another kiss.

"For the Mater." Alex handed his mother a flat box, wrapped, curiously enough, in the Lush paper. She smiled, obviously bribed Cress to wrap it for him, but it was the thought that counted.

Dana removed the paper. "Ah Einaudi! Wonderful, thank you so much darling." Dana leaned over across the table to kiss him. "I knew you were up to something, going off to HMV."

Alex smiled.

Hugo cleared his throat, fumbled under the table and stood up with the bin liner in his hand.

Just then the waitress reappeared with their ports and Calvados, Hugo sat down again while they were put in the correct places.

Dana caught Cressida smiling at her dad and Hugo winking back at her. Alex, she noticed, took advantage of the lapse of Hugo's attention to the table and knocked back his port. He caught Dana looking at him with raised eyebrows and winked at her.

Hugo stood up again.

"And this," he said, smiling lovingly at Dana, "is from me!"

Hugo was about to hand over the bin liner when he realised his mistake, laughed and removed the black plastic, revealing a large, pink paper carrier bag with the words, Penelope's Portmanteau Vintage, printed on it. He handed the bag to Dana.

"Goodness, I wonder what is in here?" Dana said, taking the bag from him.

Hugo leaned over and kissed her.

"A very nice surprise, I hope!" he said, as he sat down and took a glug of his tawny port.

"Ooh, what's that Mum?" Cressida asked, "'Penelope's Portmanteau'? Where did you get that Dad?"

"Don't you worry about where I got it young lady," Hugo said jauntily, "I have my ways and means you know. Dad's not so clueless in the shopping department after all. I know a thing or two about you ladies. I keep my eyes open."

"It looks intriguing to say the least," Dana remarked, as she undid the ribbon on the handles, "it's certainly not a book, or a scarf." She laughed.

"You'd better believe it's not − much more desirable than that."

In his excitement, Hugo polished off the rest of his port and now sat red-cheeked and grinning. The tripartite effects of a hot bath, double dose of co-codamol and malt whisky, combined with fizz, burgundy and now the port, had dispatched all aches and pains, and with them a measure of lucidity.

Dana withdrew a pink fabric suit carrier from the bag and set the latter aside.

Cressida made *ooh* and *ahh* sounds of delight, saying, "It's clothes Mum! And it's vintage! Could be a dress!"

She smiled over at Hugo, who grinned back and nodded his head.

Alex looked bored, but give him his due, Dana thought, he's trying to show interest.

Dana unzipped the suit carrier and removed a fairly bulky item wrapped in layers of purple tissue paper.

"What can it be?" she asked in surprise.

Cressida was leaning so far over the table she was

practically on top of it.

"It's exciting. Isn't it Mum?" she said, trying to paw the tissue paper.

"It certainly is," Dana replied, "very pleasantly so."

"Go on Mum! Rip the paper!" Cressida commanded in her excitement.

Dana laughed. "Oh, okay then."

She ripped at the purple tissue paper, which fell away to reveal – a fluffy, brown and cream fur jacket.

"Oh," Dana said, shaking it and holding it up.

Hugo grinned from ear to ear.

Cressida sat, frozen, in her chair.

"Go on, go on," Hugo said, "try it on darling. Now the lady in the shop told me all about it. She said don't get it wet – or maybe it can get wet – no, that's right, it can get wet, because it is real. Dyed to look like something or other but" – Hugo took a swig of Dana's port – "it is real cat fur!"

Cressida still sat, now wild-eyed.

Alex laughed.

"It's what?" Dana asked, holding the jacket by one lapel between finger and thumb.

"He said cat!" Alex shrieked with laughter.

Hugo nodded, still grinning.

He waved an expansive arm. "Yes that's right, big cat, or cat or something – real – lovely isn't it? I knew you'd be surprised!"

Hugo wagged his finger at them. "Old Hugo's not so clueless after all, is he? Ha!"

Dana stared at the jacket and then Hugo.

Alex had his face buried in his napkin, drying his eyes from laughing so much.

"It looks," Alex said, as he raised his head, between gasps of breath, "like a tabby!" And then added for good measure, "A tabby cat!" And fell back into his napkin.

Cressida squealed, shot up from the table and ran out the door.

The waitress arrived with the cheese trolley. Dana got up carefully from her chair, threw the jacket across the table at Hugo and said, "The men will finish the meal, my daughter and I will be in the bar, where my husband is standing us two, or maybe three, champagne cocktails."

Despite what had just occurred, Dana couldn't resist a smile as she looked back over her shoulder, saw the waitress point to the fur jacket and ask Hugo, "Would you like to take home a doggy-bag for that?"

Dana knew a kindred spirit when she saw one.

The women made a big show of talking animatedly about shopping and makeup, pointedly ignoring him, Hugo noted, while they all sat in the bar – the women now on their second champagne cocktail.

Hugo's attempt at explanation had cut no ice, and his long-winded efforts to explain the Zara saga had met with firm resistance. The fur jacket – it now having been established that it was not actually a domestic cat fur product, but instead a long dead, alternative wild animal – now sat back in the bin liner, waiting to go home with them, to be disposed of. Cressida had been partly placated by confirmation that the offending birthday gift was vintage, and therefore had some modicum of partial acceptability in some circles, and partly by the champagne cocktail.

That was all very well and good, but it had left Dana

without a birthday present – Hugo being the only person not to have bestowed one, despite having made the most effort – and left Hugo feeling dazed and bewildered, for at least the third time this weekend.

It was finally agreed that they would return to Zara in the morning, Hugo with them, and put in an order for the original fur jacket, which turned out to be artificial and man-made fur, and therefore the only reason his wife and daughter had considered it in the first place.

Women! Hugo thought. There's just no pleasing them.

And, yet again, their contrariness had cost him money. The latter now bore no thinking about on any level – Hugo being quite beyond any effort at totting up the damage in the restaurant. He simply couldn't start to contemplate it: what with sparkling wine, burgundy, ports, Calvados, champagne cocktails – and now in here in the bar, not to mention the actual food, which ran to three courses apiece, the last one uneaten.

Alex and Hugo sat in silence as the women prattled on. Hugo was on another malt whisky, and Alex still had his port, although Hugo couldn't understand why they had forgotten to bring Alex one when they served the others at the table. Oh well, what's done is done.

Alex finished his drink and stood up.

"I would just like to propose a toast – now that things have calmed down a little." He looked over at Hugo. "To Mum!"

Dana smiled again and they all raised their glasses.

Hugo gave Alex a hard stare. Smart Alec, he thought.

Alex, still standing, reached into his back pocket and pulled out a small black velvet box.

"With all the, excitement, in the restaurant, I forgot to

give you this Mum." Alex handed Dana the little box.

Dana looked surprised. "Oh, what's this?"

She opened the box and looked up at Alex, beaming.

"Thank you darling." She hugged and kissed him. "So very thoughtful of you. It's beautiful."

Alex took the box from his mother's hand and slipped out a silver necklace, he undid the clasp, and stood behind her, before putting it around her neck and fastening it.

"I think it's what you really wanted, if I know my mum." He smiled.

Dana wiped her eye, there was a tear in it.

Cressida, perhaps affected a little by the cocktail, also wiped away a tear.

Alex smirked at his father and sat down.

Hugo glared at him.

Then Hugo looked around the bar – mood lighting, plush brown leather sofas, majestically stocked bar, whisky cellar, cigar humidor – knocked back his malt, took out his wallet and withdrew his credit card. He threw the plastic on the table.

"Since you are so in command of the situation Alex, could you please request the bill. When it comes, use that to settle it. I don't care to be informed of the final number thereon. I'm going to the lavatory, when I return I suggest we set off back to the hotel before the jazz bar gets too busy, and while some of us" – he looked at his wife and daughter – "are still able to walk."

His old man might have been able to walk back to the hotel – unlike Cress and maybe, just maybe, Mum, who did totter a little in her high heels – but he sure as hell couldn't dance. It was very amusing to watch his dad pull a few moves on the dance floor in the cellar bar, Alex thought, as he and Cressida sat on a velvet-covered seat in one of the alcoves, listening to the jazz band and sipping a drink each.

Actually, Alex had encouraged Hugo to take Dana's hand and lead her up onto the dance floor – suggesting that a spot of smooching to a slow song would be a good thing. He had applauded when his dad had twirled her around, in a cross between a 50s rockabilly twist and an old time tea-dance, and had egged him on further as the tempo increased and Hugo was practically jiving. Alex's attitude transcended any notions of embarrassment that some might have thought his parents would cause a teenager, unlike Cress who was permanently "mortified", as she put it, at her father's antics. Alex revelled in it all – mainly because he lived in permanent hope of an amusing catastrophe, and was ever vigilant to the myriad possibilities that his father's often misconceived actions would perpetrate.

Aside from the entertainment value that his parent's dancing afforded, Alex was taking full advantage of the cellar bar's dimly lit interior, concealed nooks and crannies, loud music, press of bodies at the bar, and the attendant distraction of the overworked staff.

In short, he had had no trouble in, one, procuring a drink containing strong liquor and, two, chalking it up to the tab he had opened on the strength of showing the bar staff his room key and card.

As a result, Alex now sat with a shot of something in front of him, and Cressida a vodka and orange. They had made judicious use of the candles, cocktail menu and flower arrangement on their little table, and had arranged it just so.

When Hugo or Dana looked over at them they saw two obedient, adoring children watching them in wide-eyed awe with hands folded in their laps.

The music played on – tributes to Duke Ellington's "Jeeps Blues", Sammy Davis Junior's "Birth of the Blues" and "Mr Bojangles" – and his parents danced on. Hugo's feet matching the speed of the song, or frequently overtaking it, at one point merging into a dancing rendition of Fred Astair, or what Alex supposed a long dead, slightly effeminate man, from a black and white Hollywood extravaganza would do in front of an audience.

Alex was pleased to see that his father had made a full recovery from his gym injuries, there was no sign of the bad back now.

Alex smirked.

As a full-blooded teenage boy, who embraced everything that life had to offer, particularly in the parentally enforced prohibition era which existed in their house, Alex was no stranger to the anaesthetic effects of alcohol.

Someone would be suffering in the morning, he concluded.

Still, his mum looked happy. Alex was pleased about that, and happy himself to sit and while away a couple of hours there watching his mum having a good time and relaxing. He knocked back his shot and just as quickly put the glass back on the table. Dana waved at him from the dance floor. Alex waved back.

"Do you want another one?" he asked Cressida,

whispering in her ear.

"Better not. I've had two champagne cocktails, wine and Calvados already. And now this!"

"Right," Alex agreed, then added, "I'll get you another one then." And he nipped back to the bar. He wasn't going to drink alone. And if the folks had had enough of strutting their stuff and came back to the table, Cressida would ostensibly be drinking an orange juice, and his shot glass could be cupped inside his hand.

Cressida giggled. He'd make sure she took it slow though.

The band played something called "Almost Blue" by some bloke called Chet Baker. The sax sounded cool enough to Alex, but he could never understand why this music always had someone sweeping with a dustpan and brush over the drums. Sounded like that to him anyway. It took the edge off it as far as he was concerned.

His parents loved it though, and danced cheek-to-cheek, with his dad making little shimmy movements backwards and then wiggling his hips forwards against his mother, like their bamboo plants in the back garden caught by a gentle breeze. This particular number was slow and romantic, well, he supposed the folks thought so anyway, since Hugo had his lips pressed to his mother's neck.

Alex shuddered at this point and held a little of the Jägermeister in his mouth, trying to get rid of the slightly gross feeling that seeing his parents paw each other tended to induce in their offspring.

The band finished the number and referred to "Almost Blue" again, and that brought another matter to Alex's mind that he had sorted out earlier. The problem with the adult channel in their room had been rectified by a call down to reception, where Alex had adopted an indignant guest approach – telling the receptionist that he could understand that the channel would be blocked to his children's room, but that for the money he was paying the hotel he did not expect to be inconvenienced again. He had fitted that errand in just after putting away the incense holder.

The bloke on reception, who took his call, assured Alex that he absolutely would not be inconvenienced again, and that by way of apology he would be given free access to the *adult* channel for the duration of his stay.

Bloody liberty, Alex thought, charging for it in the first place. The money he was spending, on Hugo's behalf, in the bars at any rate.

The place was packed now at a little after midnight. It was obviously the place to come if you had parted company with your youth but refused to acknowledge the fact. Although his dad was the most energetic person on the dance floor, there were no shortage of others giving it a go. The chatter was loud too, or at least people were insisting on shouting into each other's ears as they do at gig or disco venues: knowing full well that they cannot be heard, hurting their vocal cords with the strain of it, and saying things that could wait perfectly well until another time.

In the meantime, the folks kept strutting their stuff, and an imitation of Manhattan Transfer's "Chanson d'amour" – translating to "Love Song" as the bloke on stage told them – really got them going. Everyone was having a good time.

It was Nina Simone's "Feeling Good" that finally did it.

Probably a combination of one too many hip thrusts, a backwards skip and hop, and then a little jump to finish the sequence. Or perhaps Hugo took the title of the song literally. In any case the result was both the finale to the dancing, and Alex and Cressida's enjoyment – twofold in Alex's case because he was deprived both of the supply of Jägermeister shots and watching his dad make an arse of himself. Cressida was not too badly placed as her drink looked innocuous enough, but there was always the danger that someone would want to sip it to quench the thirst incurred on the dance floor.

She took the decision, Alex observed, to knock it back and get it out of the way.

Hugo held the small of his back as he walked back to the table, still on good form though, Dana could see, from the smile on his face, if a little over exerted, evident by the trickle of sweat down one side of his face.

"It's empty," Hugo remarked, as he picked up the glass in front of Cressida.

"Sorry Dad, it was orange anyway and you probably want a nice glass of ice water," she responded.

"Yes, that would be perfect, I've worked up quite a thirst out there!"

Dana threw her eyes upwards and smiled at Cressida.

Dana turned to Alex. "Darling would you go and fetch Dad a glass of water and I'll have one too, sparkling for me."

Alex jumped up and said, "You didn't look too bad yourself on the dance floor Mum." As he moved in the direction of the bar.

"I doubt that very much," she said, thinking that at

least she knew her limitations, unlike Hugo.

"Hang on," Hugo commanded Alex, "they'll never serve you at the bar, I'd better come with you and show my card."

He limped over to Alex.

"It's only a glass of water, not hard liquor," Alex responded.

"Yes, Hugo, let him go, I think he can handle two soft drinks," Dana said

"But how will he pay for it?" Hugo asked.

"I've got my own card and key from the hotel, they'll take that," Alex explained.

"No, they won't, not if you are under age. Only adults can run tabs." Hugo led the way to the bar with Alex following behind.

Behind Hugo's back, Alex rotated his hips, thrust them back and forth and waved his arms in the air, mimicking his father's earlier dance antics. Alex looked back at his mother and sister who were both laughing.

Despite Alex's parody of Hugo, Dana winced at the word *adult*, when would he ever learn to treat them appropriately? She worried. Treat them like children and they will behave like children – irresponsibly. She sat down beside Cressida, sighed and hugged her.

"You all right darling? Not too bored?"

"I'm okay Mum, it's not too bad, quite funny really."

"Ha! Yes, I suppose it was. I wasn't too embarrassing though, was I?"

"No, you were fine, not bad actually – for your age." Cressida nudged her mother, who laughed. "But Dad is in a league of his own."

"Mm, you can say that again. He'll pay for it tomorrow

though, only just got his back sorted out from the gym earlier."

Cressida yawned. She was tired, not surprised, Dana thought, all the excitement of the day. Still, she had eaten a belated lunch, and nibbles, and a good dinner. Which was ironic when Dana thought about it – at home Cressida was fairly laid back, with not too much to stress her, and yet food was always an issue, but here, even after the Tako restaurant incident and everything else that had happened, Cressida had eaten better than she had done in months. Maybe Hugo was right – Dana shuddered at the thought – maybe it was a phase, a test, maybe Cress would grow out of it.

Or it might equally be a typical reaction to an extreme situation: like when people cry at a happy event, or laugh at a serious catastrophe. Perhaps Cressida's eating was her own extreme reaction. Dana hoped not.

It brought to mind the death of the mother, at a very young age, of one of Dana's first boyfriends. He had been her first love, childhood sweetheart. The relationship was fizzling out, as was inevitable, but then his mother got an aggressive form of breast cancer, and within four months had gone from fit-as-a-flea to lying in bed weighing just under six stone. Dana had held bedside vigils in support of her former boyfriend. Eventually – too long to Dana's tender reflections at that age – the mother had died. It had been Dana who had been with her at the very end, the others taking their turn to sleep. It had been a little after five in the morning. The hour of darkness and desolation, the lowest ebb.

An hour after the death, everyone in the house was sitting in the living room, sunlight streaming through the windows, eating toast and laughing loudly at cartoons on the children's channel on the television.

It didn't seem disrespectful, it didn't seem inappropriate. It was in fact just right. An outlet for grief. And a reminder that life carries on.

The mother had been 50-years-old.

That thought sent a chill down Dana's back, and a firm resolution to be positive. And grateful.

Alex and Hugo trotted back from the bar, Hugo carrying two glasses of water, and Alex a half of beer.

"Here you are darling." Hugo handed Dana her sparkling water.

Dana looked up at Alex, and Hugo sighed that exaggerated, indulgent sigh of his.

"Cheeky little devil here conned me into buying him a beer." Hugo nodded at Alex. "It's just a half mind, and I told the barman it was for me."

Alex winked at Cressida, Dana smiled at Hugo. He can sometimes do the right thing, she decided.

Hugo gulped his water down and wiped his mouth with the back of his hand.

"How's the back?" Dana asked him.

"So, so. Nothing that a good night's sleep won't fix."

The band played on and the music slowed, a sure sign that the evening was drawing to a close. Cressida yawned again, much wider and louder this time, and Dana suggested that it was time for bed. Alex drained his glass and they all got up to leave, Hugo playfully resisting Alex's offer of a hand up from the table by pretending to lift Alex up off his feet. This caused a twitter of laughter. And another wince of pain from Hugo.

* * *

The hotel foyer, at just after one thirty on Sunday morning, was busier than it had been at check-in. An assortment of guests and revellers wandered about: black tie and ball gown-clad couples waiting for taxis following an event in the hotel's ballroom suite, after-dinner stragglers leaving the bar, several guests – like them – making their way up from the cellar bar to their rooms, and the more adventurous battling through the now stormy weather, up the steps to the front door, after a night out in the city.

Dana spotted the tall, dark, handsome stranger from check-in yesterday – he wore an expertly tailored Armani suit, or what looked like one, and was guiding his wife towards the lifts.

Cressida and Alex went ahead, bounding up the stairs, like puppies, leaving their parents to stand in the queue for the lifts, and be conveyed upwards after their exertions under mechanical, rather than their own, steam.

As they stood waiting, Dana looked at the back of the handsome stranger's head in front of her. His hair was closely cropped, his neck smooth. He held a guiding hand against his wife's back. He looked over his shoulder and nearly caught Dana's eye. She looked away just in time. She wasn't going to be found staring or even taking a mild interest.

Just then the lift arrived, and she felt Hugo slap her arse.

"Come on – let's try and beat the little blighters to it!" he said into her ear.

Dana hoped he was referring to the kids, and not the

couple in front, who had clearly heard her husband's comment.

The wife looked over at Hugo and then at Dana as the lift doors closed.

It wasn't a look of envy.

Cressida stood leaning against the door to their own room, while Alex sat cross-legged on the floor, tapping into his phone.

Alex looked up at his sister. "You coming out in a bit, when the folks are bedded down?"

Cressida glanced at her watch. "No, I don't think so, it's too late. I'll just Skype Emma and go to bed."

"Okay, I'll come inside to the room for a while and then I'm going to nip out for a bit with Juan. He's texted me to say he finishes work soon, said he'd wait round the back near the kitchens."

"Be careful Alex, it's late and too dark to be meeting dodgy strangers down alleyways."

Alex stood up and stretched. "It's Brighton, not Kingston Jamaica, he's not a stranger and the night is young."

"Well, it's still dark and he is still dodgy," his sister replied.

"I'll be fine, I was last night, stop fretting, you're worse than them." Alex nodded his head in the direction of his parents, who came tottering down the hallway, Hugo singing Nina Simone's "Feeling Good", very badly, and clutching the black bin liner and its ghastly, but now forgotten, contents.

"You beat us to it!" Hugo remarked, a little out of breath, "next time we'll take the stairs."

"If you're out of breath after the lift I hardly think the stairs would make any difference," Dana replied, kissing first Alex and then Cressida, "I'm off to bed, don't stay up too late watching television you two."

Dana opened their door and Hugo followed adding, "Your mother is quite correct, not too late – we have an action packed, exciting day tomorrow."

Cress rolled her eyes and Alex nodded solemnly at his father.

Dana kicked off her heels and felt a wave of relief after all that dancing. Her calves, despite their perfect shape and intimate acquaintance with strenuous exercise, would hurt tomorrow. Dancing in high heels tending to reach the parts that no amount of running could. That, combined with the narrow fitting of her shoes, had begun to cause some discomfort in the last hour or so. God knows how the Chinese put up with bound feet, or those blocky, clog, flip flop things. Or maybe that was the Japanese. Either way, they deserved a medal in the shoe endurance department.

In the suite Hugo had dimmed the lights and put on a bedside lamp.

Dana turned them up again and hit all the other lamp switches in the room.

Hugo slipped off his jacket, tie, and shoes, and threw them on top of his still-packed luggage.

Dana went into the bathroom and banged the door open.

Hugo turned on the mellow jazz channel.

Dana tugged on one of the bathrobes and knotted the belt with brutal force.

Hugo dimmed the lights again.

Dana opened the bathroom door wide to further aid the illumination of the room.

Hugo clinked some ice into a glass and splashed in a small amount of liquor.

Dana came out and glugged heavily on a two-litre bottle of water.

"Ahh," Hugo said, sitting on the edge of the bed, "this is nice." He sipped his drink.

Dana stood in the middle of the room with the water bottle.

"Does it have to be so loud?" She nodded in the direction of the music.

"It's romantic darling."

"It's loud. It'll wake the children," she said irritably.

Dana realised she was now using Hugo's phrase. And this irritated her further.

"I doubt that darling. You can be sure they will be watching some horror movie, and disregarding our instructions about having an early night."

Dana took a long pull on the water bottle.

"Come and sit here darling." Hugo patted the space beside him on the bed.

"It's late Hugo and we're all tired."

"I'm not tired." He looked at her with a lingering gaze.

"Well you should be – all that exertion on the dance floor." Dana still stood holding the water bottle.

"Not a bit of it. Just limbering up." He took another sip of his drink, and patted the bed again. "Come on, keep me company."

"I thought your back was bad. And your hamstring?"

Dana realised the futility of her excuses, Hugo had that

look on his face. It was unmistakeable.

"Right as rain now, darling. Right as rain, or as near as damn it." He slapped his leg to demonstrate.

"But you were limping in the bar."

"That was just the initial reaction after the dance, eased off now, but come to think of it, if you were minded to, well you know, give me a rub down, it could well be the final physiotherapy touch I need?" He smiled at her.

"I'm cold so I am going to put my nightwear on."

"Bravo," he said grinning.

Dana moved past Hugo to the other side of the bed and extracted her fleecy pyjamas from under the pillow. Hugo looked at them and his smile vanished.

"And I'm going to take my makeup off before my skin disintegrates."

Dana stomped into the bathroom and slammed the door.

It was always the same, she reflected, as she looked in the mirror, daubing at her eyes with cotton wool pads and makeup remover. One particularly vicious jab at her eye caused her to blink a tear away.

Hugo got suggestive and she got angry. It wasn't too often, but it was often enough.

Actually, it was more than enough. Once was more than enough. But there it was, and she could no longer remember when it had gone from never enough to more than enough.

She hated the pressure and she hated being angry, with both Hugo and herself. Her resentment spanned many levels with multiple reasons.

She heard the mellow jazz from the bedroom, Hugo clinking the ice in his glass, still sitting there no doubt, waiting for her to return to the bedroom, which she must. She couldn't spend all night in the bathroom.

She resented Hugo for the way he made her feel, and she resented her life for putting her in this situation, but most of all she resented herself for letting it get to this stage. No doubt some women accepted it as part and parcel of the longevity of married life, the natural course of things.

But not most, of that she felt sure. Most people dealt with it by separation or divorce, or found the courage to just say *no* and live on in a kind of muted companionship. But at forty-nine? Probably not.

Some women switched off. Found another way to cope with it. Her mother-in-law had been one.

Dana remembered being shocked when her mother-in-law had confided to Dana, at the age of seventy-six, that she had never enjoyed sex, not ever, didn't see the point of it, but just put up with it when it occurred. She had never initiated it, not once. Just waited for it to come round periodically, as it did, when her husband, Dana's father-in-law, required it. "I always know," her mother-in-law had told her, "when it's time. He sits on the bed and flops his *thing* out, and I know it's time for that. I always know." Dana had been horrified, for two reasons. First, that her mother-in-law had confided this intimate information and, second, that she just seemed to passively accept it without the merest hint of either resentment or pleasure. It was just a chore – like washing the dishes, scrubbing the back step, or hulling the gooseberries, neither pleasant nor unpleasant. Just another chore of married life.

But Dana found it – well. Anyway. Dana was not her

mother-in-law. And it hadn't always been like it was now, once it had been very different. She daubed at her other eye and removed all the makeup. She hurled the cotton wool pads in the bin.

There was a tentative knock on the bathroom door.

Dana froze. She looked in the mirror. She was standing in her bra and knickers, both her dress and fleecy pyjamas on the bathroom floor, the robe now hung up behind the door. Usually she would have beaten Hugo to the bedroom, and be in the pyjamas, tucked tightly up in bed, with the light out, before he had got his shoes off. But not this evening: she had hoped that his gym injuries would have taken care of it.

Before Dana could respond, the door opened a fraction.

"Can I come in darling?"

"I'm not decent."

It was not only a lame response, it was an unintended invitation.

"Good!" Hugo responded, and opened the door.

He took in the sight of Dana and smiled, walked over, stood behind her, and kissed her on the back of her neck.

Dana grimaced.

"I'm cold," she said.

Hugo pushed the door to, half closing it.

He put his arms around her waist and remained standing behind her.

"It's warm in here though," he said, kissing her again, this time further down her neck towards her back.

Dana shuddered.

"It's okay for you, you're fully dressed," she replied.

Hugo stroked the front of her thighs.

"I can easily rectify that darling," he said, between kisses which were getting lower and lower.

"No need for both of us to catch our death," Dana suggested.

She grabbed his hands, ostensibly to make a stab at showing affection, but in reality to stop them wandering.

"Then we'll keep each other warm," he said, "body heat."

Hugo let go of her hands and unbuttoned his shirt, took it off, and pressed his chest to her back.

Dana sighed, it was loud and long.

"Your skin is lovely and soft, and smells beautiful," he told her, as he resumed his kissing.

Bet he can't smell a bloody thing after all that whisky, just buttering me up. Thought all that booze was supposed to have a flaccid effect on men. Obviously not, must be the co-codamol that counteracts it, she decided.

Hugo twanged the edge of Dana's black knickers.

Oh God, why had she chosen black? She had several pairs of stout, beige, sensible running knickers with her. Not like me to slip up there.

"Come on darling, we are on holiday – romantic evening, romantic hotel—"

Dana suddenly felt belligerent. "It's my birthday, not yours. Why should I have sex on my birthday?"

Hugo looked wounded.

"Well, I just thought, you know, that with us being so close and loving and all the difficulty in arranging being here together that, well you know—"

Dana felt a twinge of guilt. Again. He had gone to a lot of trouble, and expense, not that the latter had any bearing on the matter at hand – she wasn't a prostitute –

but he probably did mean well, and was not being unreasonable in asking his wife to love him.

Dana felt herself relenting, giving in, despite having been determined that on her birthday, at least, she would have the last word.

She took his hand, patted it and half smiled.

Hugo was out of his trousers in a jiffy.

"In here?" Dana asked. "Not very comfortable, is it?"

"Rather risqué though!" he responded.

Probably doesn't want to risk me changing my mind on the way back to the bedroom, Dana decided.

Hugo whipped off his underpants. Then he fumbled with her bra clasp – why do men always fumble? The dark, handsome stranger probably being the exception.

Dana decided that she would review the new Law Society Conveyancing Protocols in her head for the next half an hour, or however long it took. She'd been meaning to make a mental note on the matter for a while.

Just before Dana began the recitation, she felt confirmation of the positive effects of the co-codamol against her bottom. She redoubled her efforts at the Protocols.

As the bra clasp resisted Hugo's best efforts, he slid the straps down over each of Dana's shoulders, as she reclined over the bathroom sink facing the mirror.

"Oh darling, you really did look most alluring tonight," Hugo whispered in her ear.

The mellow jazz played in the background.

Then a loud shout was heard from the bedroom, "Alex is gross, he's watching disgusting stuff on the TV, and I'm not sleeping in there with him tonight!" And the bathroom door was simultaneously flung open.

Revealing the floor strewn with clothes and underpants, Dana bent over the sink unit, with bra straps pushed down, and knickers around her thighs.

And Hugo from the back, stark naked except for his socks, leaning against Dana with his hands on her hips.

Dana and Hugo looked up into the mirror at the reflection of their daughter standing in the doorway, frozen in shock.

Dana screamed.

Hugo screamed.

Cressida edged backwards in silence until she was out of sight.

Then the suite's door slammed.

Dana remembered that dumbstruck look on Cressida's face. She'd seen it only once before.

And now she'd seen it again.

SEVENTEEN

Hugo was bloody furious for two reasons. One of them being Alex's unacceptable behaviour. He stood in his trousers, hastily misbuttoned shirt with the collar sticking up, no socks, and one shoe on. He was using the other shoe to bang loudly on the door next to the mini-suite.

"Alex! This is your father, if you know what's good for you, you had better open this door immediately!"

He followed it up with a savage blow to the centre of the door using his Church's handmade brogues, now scuffed and re-soled several times. He was just about to launch into another dire warning, when the door opened.

Alex stood blinking, in his pyjamas, rubbing his left eye.

"What's wrong Dad?" he asked.

Hugo wasn't buying it. Alex only called him "Dad" when he was being insincere.

"What's wrong my foot," Hugo replied.

Alex looked down at Hugo's feet, and up at the shoe he held aloft.

"Talking of your feet, why are you only wearing one

shoe? And what happened to the buttons on your shirt?"

Hugo was very red in the face and he felt very hot. It wasn't from the frisson of passion.

"I'll tell you what's bloody well wrong young man. I had to get dressed hastily all because of your antics. Your mother and I were having a very, er, civilised evening, until we were gate-crashed by Cressida, shouting and screaming about your 'disgusting' behaviour, that's what's wrong."

Hugo was even redder now.

Alex yawned. And stretched.

"Don't know what she's talking about."

"Well, I'm not buying it. Not this time. I've been taken for a fool one too many times young man. You've done something to upset her, and she came rushing into our room in the the middle of us – getting ready for bed, complaining of your carry-on, whatever it was. So what the hell is going on?"

"Dunno," Alex responded, "what did she say?"

"She said that she could not sleep in there with you under any circumstances because you were 'disgusting', and I have to warn you that it was not the first time she had brought this to my attention." Hugo still held the shoe up.

"I don't know what she's on about."

"Come on, pull the other one, it's got bells on!" Hugo laughed. "You're up to something in there."

Alex held the door open wide, and Hugo peered in.

"So? What is it? You drinking again? Got that funny incense thing going?"

Hugo looked around, sniffed the air, looked at Alex.

"Nope, none of it. I watched a bit of telly and then

went for a cra—I mean went to the toilet. Might have left the door to the bathroom open. It can leave a – lingering odour."

Alex smiled at his dad and winked.

Hugo stepped back. "Mm, right, well maybe."

He considered for a minute. What did Cress say? The television.

"So what were you watching on the television then?" Hugo asked.

"Some crime movie, a woman got attacked and then shot, might have upset Cress I suppose."

"Oh, well that's not very nice, is it Alex? She is a girl and she is young, you should know better."

Hugo thought further, considered the other possibilities.

"You weren't watching any – any other kind of film, were you, you know, the *X-rated* kind?" Hugo added euphemistically.

"Hardly Dad. Hotels of this calibre don't have those kind of films, and anyway you have to pay for that sort of film – or so Lucas's dad, Tristram says."

Hugo raised his eyebrows. Old Tristram hey? He's a dark horse. All those business trips, goodness knows what he got up to. Hugo almost felt inferior. And envious. But still annoyed.

"Right, yes, you are probably right. Well, no more television tonight. It's very late and we've all had enough excitement for one day. Now where's Cress? Hiding in the bathroom? Tell her to come out here, her mother wants to talk to her about – er, about something."

Alex looked puzzled.

"She's not in here, she stormed out when the film was

on and said she was going to your room."

Hugo shook his head. "Yes I know that, and she did, but then she saw something – I mean, she then left our room and we assumed she had, well, changed her mind and come back in here."

Hugo pushed his way into the room, looked around and opened the bathroom door. Empty.

"So where is she?" Hugo asked.

"Dunno. I made sure I saw her go into your room when she left here. She was your responsibility after that." Alex smiled.

Hugo glared at him.

Dana was fully dressed by the time Hugo got back into their suite. All the lights were on, the music extinguished.

"She can't have gone far, probably downstairs sulking in an alcove," Hugo said, rebuttoning his still-creased shirt right up to the top button.

"I'll go down and speak to her," Dana said.

"No, you stay here in case she comes back. I will go and get her and then you can have a talk and – explain things."

Dana raised her eyebrows.

Hugo pretended not to notice.

"Where's Alex?" she asked.

"In his room, I told him to stay there and go to bed. I said Cressida would sleep in our sitting room tonight."

Dana nodded and went to the wardrobe, where there was a pile of blankets. She took them out and laid them on the sofa, and then went and got a pillow from their bed and set that at one end.

"Is your phone on?" Hugo asked.

"Yes. Why?"

"Just in case Cress isn't downstairs, in case she went for a little walk or something. I'll call you if I can't find her in the lobby, okay?"

"Okay. And I'll call you if she comes back up here," Dana said.

"Right, better take my raincoat – just in case."

Hugo glanced at his watch as he left. It was just after two thirty in the morning.

If the place had been hopping earlier, it was as silent as a cemetery now. Hugo found himself practically tiptoeing down the main marble staircase to the foyer, having winced at the sound the lift-call button made, and abandoned that idea in favour of legwork, lest he wake any of the other guests up at this ungodly hour. The truth was, he was starting to feel guilty as hell, not least because, for some unaccountable reason, he was always made to feel bad when something went wrong – no need even for anyone to say anything, it was just obvious in a look or the general mood. In addition to that, he was now as "mortified" with embarrassment, as no doubt Cressida would say she was, over the incident in the bathroom. Mind you, not that he planned on any attempt at an explanation to Cressida on that matter. No way. That was firmly in the mother department. If Dana hadn't been wearing all that racy lingerie and getting all amorous on her birthday, then this latest incident would never have happened.

Christ Almighty, is there never any peace? Hugo thought, as he pirouetted down the last few steps of the stairs. And on top of it all his back, and his hamstrings, were now killing him again.

Hugo descended to the ground floor and made his way first to the corridor on his right where a number of comfortable sofas and chairs stood in alcoves, and where Cressida had last sought solace in the understanding arms of Veronique. Thoughts of the latter bucked him up a little, Veronique was very nice to him, unlike the rest of them. She had taken an interest in him and he was not a little unaffected by the attention. He realised of course that this young French lady probably had a bit of a crush on him – he being the older, experienced, English gentleman and writer. And it was flattering to have such an effect on women.

The corridor was dimly lit and completely empty. The cushions on the sofa had been plumped and squared off by the cleaner, and obviously no one had sat on them since.

He walked then towards the bar area – it too was empty and the metal grill had been pulled down over the counter. The luxurious chairs and leather chesterfields sat silent, and accusing, in their emptiness.

Hugo went back the way he had come, and ventured down another corridor towards the Spa area, it too was deserted, and there were no chairs to sit on or nooks and crannies for concealment in any event.

Trudging now, rather than tiptoeing, Hugo went back towards reception and up to the dining room and restaurant areas, he put his hand to the door of the restaurant – it was locked. He rattled it. Ditto the door to the breakfast dining area.

There wasn't a soul around. Except for one.

"Can I help you sir?" a voice enquired behind him.

Hugo turned to see a pimply youth behind the reception desk who had appeared like a rabbit from a conjuror's hat. He hadn't been there when Hugo had first come down the stairs.

The youth was wearing a uniform with brass buttons, and looked like he should also have had a fez on his head – but he didn't, just gelled-up hair, and rather large ears.

"Were you looking to order some food?" the pimply youth enquired again.

What the fuck gave him that idea? Hugo wondered. Preposterous notion at this time of night.

"Why would you think that?" Hugo said, striding over to the desk.

"It's just that you were trying the restaurant and dining room doors sir," the pimply youth replied smugly.

His face was a bizarre phosphorous green colour, almost alien-like, which, with his spots, gave him the luminous appearance of a human-lizard hybrid, like some ghastly, slightly comical 1950s horror B movie.

Hugo took a step back from the desk.

"No, I – I'm not hungry, I'm looking for someone actually."

"They won't be in there sir, the restaurant closed some time ago and the dining room doesn't open until six thirty," the Lizard explained.

"Yes I realise that, but I was just making sure."

The Lizard licked his lips, a particularly prominent spot glowed larger and greener in the light. The area behind him was pitch black. The foyer was completely silent. There wasn't even a clock ticking.

They both stood there, Hugo thinking, the Lizard smiling and glowing.

"Perhaps I can help sir?" the latter finally said.

"With what?"

"With the person you are looking for?" the Lizard replied.

"Oh, I doubt it," Hugo said. And then on further consideration explained, "I'm looking for a young girl."

The Lizard stopped smiling. Licked his lips again. The phosphorous glow grew brighter, almost pulsating.

"I can't help with that sir. I'm afraid you would have to make other – enquiries – at quite another sort of establishment," and then he added, with measured distaste, "sir."

Hugo was taken aback.

"What?" he said.

The Lizard took a deep breath and composed himself. "As I say it is not something that I can assist you with. I am given to understand that there may be *facilities* for that type of thing in the city centre, but as I say, I can't help any further."

Hugo rocked backwards. Christ Almighty! What kind of man did he think he was? How on earth would he have got that impression? The mind boggled, Hugo's certainly did at this stage.

"Good God no, I think you misunderstand me," Hugo said quickly, "I'm looking for a particular young girl."

The Lizard stood his ground, unmoving. "Indeed?"

Hugo walked right up to the desk, put his hands on the counter. "Yes! My daughter! She's gone missing!" he was practically shouting.

What Hugo didn't realise, was in fact oblivious to, was that he cut a somewhat questionable figure in his present garb and appearance – long raincoat, collar sticking up, creased shirt done up to the top button, but no tie, brown brogues, no socks, and ruffled hair – that, in addition to the lateness of the hour, not to mention his now sour-mash breath, tended to suggest a number of possibilities, not one of them even borderline decent.

"Oh," the Lizard remarked.

Hugo looked down at the reception counter and saw that a computer monitor was switched on which provided the upwards illumination, not – now that he was up close – a supernatural phosphorous glow at all, and that a game of solitaire was in progress on the computer. Obviously the pimply youth had been hunched over it and bolted up when he had seen Hugo come down. A can of Coke and a large packet of M & M's sat on the desk, and inanimately claimed responsibility for the spots.

"Who are you?" Hugo asked, now in command of the situation again.

"Laurence sir, I'm the night porter. It's my first week, I've just been promoted, I used to work in the kitchen, as a kitchen porter."

The pimply youth smiled, he was clearly proud of his achievements.

"Congratulations Laurence," Hugo said.

"Thank you sir." Laurence beamed, looking all of his fifteen years, or so he appeared.

"Now, my daughter – Cressida – got, erm, rather upset over something, you know how teenage girls can be?"

Laurence looked blank. "Er, well—"

"Yes, well never mind that, but anyway, she got upset and ran off, and her mother and I are trying to find her. So my question is, have you seen a young girl come down here a short while ago, or seen a young girl sitting perhaps over there on one of those sofas?" Hugo gestured to the dark recesses of the corridors.

Laurence considered for a few moments.

"No."

"Really? That is very odd because she is most definitely not in her room, and she hasn't come back to ours." Hugo shook his head.

Laurence shook his head.

"Now think again, very hard, this is important, she's a very young girl and she is upset, we must find her."

Laurence put his cupped hand to his chin and closed his eyes. Thinking.

Hugo peered over the top of the desk just in case. Well, one never knew. But there was nothing but the Coke and M & M's.

Laurence opened his eyes. "No, I definitely have not seen a very young girl all night."

Hugo stood back and clasped his hands together and sighed.

"Very well, I'll keep looking. She must be here somewhere. Perhaps on one of the other floors in another corridor."

Hugo moved away from the desk towards the lifts. Sod the noise, he thought.

"I have seen two women though," Laurence offered behind him.

"What?" Hugo turned around.

"I've seen two women down here a few moments ago," Laurence answered.

"Women?"

"Yes sir, they came past me and went out the front door, just a few moments ago."

"What women?" Hugo came back to the desk.

Laurence considered. "Well one of them was quite tall, slim, long blonde hair, very pretty, nice and leggy actually, I quite fancied her to be honest." Laurence smiled wistfully.

Hugo stopped in his tracks.

"What was she wearing?"

It should have stumped Laurence, but it didn't. "Well, she had on a kind of shawl thing over a cream, floaty sort of dress, very short, very leggy…"

Cressida! Excellent, Hugo thought, as he glared at Laurence for the last remark.

"That's Cressida. My daughter. Who was the other woman?"

"The other one?"

Hugo rolled his eyes, for Christ's sake!

"Yes. You said there were two women."

"Oh, yes, well the other one works here, she's a receptionist, well supervisor actually."

"Veronique?" Hugo ventured.

"Yes, the French girl. Lovely." Laurence looked wistfully again and glanced down at his game of solitaire, Coke and M & M's – obviously no substitute for either of the women.

Hugo glared at him again.

"Right. And where did they go?" he asked.

"I don't know."

Hugo looked around in desperation towards the door.

"Right, that's very helpful Laurence." Although Hugo wasn't sure whether he meant helpful for identifying Cressida, or sarcasm because Laurence didn't know where they had gone. "I'll go and look for them," he said.

Hugo walked towards the door.

"They've probably hit a club?" Laurence suggested.

A club? Hugo was aghast. Cressida was 16-years-old and it was after two thirty in the morning.

"She's only sixteen," Hugo said.

Laurence shrugged. "She looks a lot older, fooled me."

That wouldn't be difficult, Hugo decided.

"Any ideas on which club they might have *hit*?" Hugo asked, beside the door now.

He opened the side door as he spoke – the revolving door closed for the night – a howling gale met him and nearly drove him backwards.

Laurence considered again, and through the sound of the wind he said, "The Black Cat is Veronique's favourite, it's in the Lanes."

Hugo nodded. "Right, thanks, I'll try that."

He headed out into the Brighton night.

As he battled along the seafront, fighting the storm-force winds, and turned up West Street – which now manifested itself as a wind tunnel with the turbine provided by the sea at his back – Hugo called Dana's mobile phone.

"It's all okay, I've found her," he said into the phone, "well, she's been seen anyway, going out with Veronique, yes, yes, don't worry, I know where they have gone. At least she is safe, well, at least she is not on her own. They've gone to a club called The Black Hat and I'm on my way there now. I'll be back shortly." He cut the connection as he headed towards the North Laines.

EIGHTEEN

If the guests in the hotel were getting their money's worth from their memory foam, super king-size mattresses, then the clubbers were giving them a run for that money on the streets of Brighton: the place was worse than the scrum Hugo had encountered shopping at midday. Bodies everywhere, and not all of them vertical. As he turned down North Street towards the North Laines, the streets were thronged with revellers of all descriptions, the common denominator being mainly youth – and alcohol, or its effects.

It certainly was an eye-opener, he thought, as he walked briskly past some establishment painted the obligatory matt black, with a discreet brass sign bearing the name Gracie – which was essentially a hole in the wall through which a small crowd of chanting, high-octane, liquor-fuelled males were attempting to squeeze. It wasn't The Black Hat that he sought, but Hugo supposed that at least one of these chaps would be familiar with it and point him in the right direction.

He approached the man at the end of the queue, who

appeared to be aiding his friend's upright stance by means of a firm grip on his trouser waistband, belt, and prominently displayed Calvin Klein underpants.

"Excuse me, perhaps you can help?" Hugo said.

The man raised his head. He didn't look like he would be willing to help his grandmother cross the street.

"What'd you want mate?"

Hugo hesitated. "I'm looking for a nightclub?" He looked up at the outside of the present venue.

"Yeah," the man replied. It wasn't a question.

A few of the others looked around, stopped chanting.

Hugo cleared his throat. "Yes, that's right, I—"

"Course it's fucking right!" the man said, stepping closer and pulling his semi-comatose friend with him.

"I beg your pardon?" Hugo asked feebly.

"You said 'that's right', like I was a moron!"

The others in the pack also looked around.

"I didn't mean to imply you were a – a 'moron'," Hugo added quickly.

"What's that prat on about?" someone else asked, near the door of the club.

"He's looking for a club," another one of them responded.

"Good, 'cos I ain't a fucking moron, am I Si?" the man asked his semi-comatose friend, and jerked at his Calvin Klein's savagely.

The semi-comatose friend did not respond.

"So like I said, what'd you want?"

The others crowded around. Hugo felt a little weak, he looked around for a bouncer of some variety, but all he could see were the press of bodies through the narrow doorway.

"I'm looking for a particular club, it's—"

The man took an exaggerated step back, dragging the semi-comatose friend.

"A *particular* club now is it? What? This ain't good enough for ya?" The man threw his head towards Gracie.

Hugo shook his head violently.

"Oh no, it's not that, this club looks – great."

"Good, 'cos it is. Girls are mint in here. Got that sorted then." The man smiled viciously.

Then the man thought a moment, furrowed his brow, and took a real step back, leaving his semi-comatose friend to stagger blindly on his own.

"You're not queer are you? Looking for a *particular* club sounds fucking queer to me."

The man looked around at his mates for confirmation. They all shouted their agreement.

Hugo, in spite of his terror, bristled – a little.

"Certainly not, I'm happily married."

The man considered this and looked half-convinced.

"So what's wrong with this club then?" he asked.

Hugo saw an opening to escape, he had long since given up ideas of actually getting directions from this lot as to where he wanted to go.

"I'm sure this club is first rate, it's just that someone is waiting for me in the other club and I am going to meet them," Hugo managed to say all in one breath, quite a feat, given that the stress of the situation had reduced his lung capacity by about ninety-five per cent.

There were cheers and wolf whistles from the crowd. The man stepped forward and punched Hugo playfully on the shoulder. In ordinary circumstances the blow would have sent him sprawling and needing his shoulder reset under general anaesthetic. But these were not ordinary circumstances and Hugo managed somehow to stand his ground, mostly.

"He's on a promise tonight lads, ain't he?" the man said.

Hugo did his best to look smug by winking and tapping the side of his nose.

"So, what is it? Titty bar?" the man asked, having regained his grip on his semi-comatose friend's undergarments.

Hugo was about to step back aghast and utter an indignant reply, but he'd learnt his lesson. Yes indeed.

"Had my fill of that earlier. Now I'm, well, er – getting a little bit more hardcore shall we say!" Hugo nodded vigorously.

The man looked blank for a moment, and then there was a commotion in the crowd near the door as they were admitted to the dark, recessed delights of the club, one by one. The man hesitated for a moment and was then called by his mates to hurry up.

"Right," he said, a little distracted, "so what's it called then?"

"The Black Hat'?" Hugo said tentatively.

"Black hat, black hat...Tone?" the man shouted towards the door, "is The Black Hat the one on the seafront?"

A voice from inside said, "No, it's down the North Laines, that narrow road with the bike shop, it's the one with that dodgy bird with the nose-ring, the one you said you'd rather screw a hole in a barrel about."

The man nodded at Hugo by way of confirmation.

In his relief, and now overwhelming desire to get away,

Hugo said, "Have a good night."

"We will mate, they haven't got the biggest ones but they got the fittest ones." And off he went through the door, pulling his semi-comatose friend with him.

Hugo walked as far as the next corner, before resting his hands on his knees and taking a series of deep breaths to steady himself.

As Hugo resumed his walk, it dawned on him that he had, in a few short minutes, learnt an awful lot about city centre nightlife, and as a consequence of that he set himself some ground rules that he would adhere to, until his mission was complete and he was back safe and sound with Cressida.

One, he would not approach any more men – either lone or in packs, certainly not the latter, that was to be avoided at all costs. Two, it was obvious that any establishment with a crowd of men, as oppose to mixed genders, waiting outside – and especially bearing the name Gracie or similar – was likely to be a strip club and so also to be avoided, although Hugo was agog at the ready availability of this in a place like Brighton. The only strip club he had ever heard of was Stringfellows in London, and he couldn't even name the street it resided on. Mind you, bet old Tristram could give you the sat nav co-ordinates for it. Three, he needed to bear in mind that as he was not intoxicated, was slightly older than most of the other people roaming the streets at this hour, and was dressed smartly, he cut an imposing figure, and so might be mistaken for someone in authority, and therefore perhaps a threat to the young people's entertainment.

He would need to tread very carefully, he decided, as he trotted down towards Bond Street.

Despite it being practically time for morning coffee – it was nearly two forty-five – some of the pubs seemed to be doing a roaring trade still in hard liquor. Hugo passed several such establishments, with punters spilling out on the street sipping, or rather gulping, a variety of beverages as though licensing laws didn't apply here. It felt very much like the main strip in Magaluf, or perhaps Benidorm, at midnight in high summer – or probably Ibiza now – Hugo reconsidered, isn't that where the young people went these days? Benidorm was for old geezers gasping their last breath on a Senior Service cigarette, and a mild and bitter pint, before expiring quietly on a sun lounger underneath a Foster's logo sun shade.

Or so Hugo supposed, not having set foot in either place.

He walked on, avoiding eye contact with anyone who looked mildly confrontational. Past the Mash Tun, Hobgoblin, White Rabbit and the Wagon and Horses. What amazed him was that the streets were crowded even in places where no liquid refreshment seemed to be on offer. Where were they all going? Home? Somehow he doubted that. And it wasn't just in the bars that the cash registers were ringing, no end of take-aways were lining up the punters too. Although, on closer inspection these establishments appeared to be somewhat gentrified – "organic" burgers topped with chorizo and chilli jam, marinated gourmet kebabs with fresh mint – bloody hell, Hugo thought, in my day it was a bag of chips, or if you were lucky, a dodgy kebab that came out the same way it went in. Even the Chinese were in on it – Hugo's nostrils flared as he passed The Krispy Duck, which offered all manner of gourmet take-away, if he hadn't been in such a hurry he'd have had a quick look.

The wind was still howling a gale, and it carried the promise of a hard frost to come, but that didn't seem to deter the party-goers, who, to a man – and a woman – were dressed with total disregard to the elements.

The men wore jeans, mostly, and T-shirts. Those in the company of a woman opting for a shirt instead. And that was it: no jumper, jacket, certainly no overcoat. The idea of a scarf or gloves wouldn't have entered their heads. It made Hugo shudder. And as for the women – Hugo hardly knew where to look. Hadn't seen anything like it since, well – never, if he was honest, in person, at least. The closest he could liken it to was that series on television, a so-called reality programme, which followed the preparations for the wedding in certain traveller families, in *My Big Fat Gypsy Wedding*. Normally Hugo would not have countenanced such nonsense in the house, but Cressida was laughing in hysterics at it one day and Dana too couldn't suppress a chuckle. The programme followed the antics of the hen party, just before the wedding, where the women dressed in what appeared to be neon coloured lycra swimsuits or bikinis, with just the merest suggestion of a skirt, accessorised with sky-high heels, jewellery and pantomime makeup. The girls were all about sixteen but looked at least twenty-five, and what Hugo couldn't understand was how they were all so well endowed without having encountered a surgeon's knife. How the bikini dresses stayed in place as a consequence, or they were able to bend down with a modicum of modesty, entirely escaped him.

Dana had uttered one word. "Slappers".

A similar picture unfolded as Hugo strode down the street now towards his destination. Except this scenario was worse, the young ladies he encountered were – in addition to being just barely clad and in towering heels – to put it bluntly, off their faces. Which is where quite a few of them landed up, flat on. This activity tended to expose what remained intimately clad of their bodies to, not only the elements, but the general population at large.

Come to think of it, Hugo *had* seen something like it before, at least in the manner of their dress, as he and Dana had strolled along the seafront in Nice one balmy summer evening, on a wedding anniversary weekend break. It had been a popular spot for ladies-of-the-night to ply their trade, but they would not have been out of place in Fortnum and Mason's tea room by comparison with this lot.

The more Hugo saw, the more uneasy he became. Cressida, he realised with growing horror, was somewhere among this lot, or worse, in one of these dives, getting, well – off her face. God! Hugo shuddered again.

Although, hang on. Veronique is with her. He breathed a little more easily. At least Veronique is a lovely, sensible and simple French girl. She will be a good influence. Cressida was in good hands, she might be given a small glass of French wine, or perhaps even two, but otherwise there was nothing to worry about.

He trudged on, down the streets, getting narrower as he reached Kensington Gardens – the cramped width of the pavement making the crowd feel like a wave of football supporters after a match. There were whoops, high pitched laughs, jokes, screams and shouting – and in the distance police and ambulance sirens. In the main, people were well behaved, towards each other at least, if not to their livers. Hugo didn't doubt though, that in some parts of the city the emergency services had their work cut out on a Saturday night. He'd heard somewhere that it was becoming the venue of choice for stag and hen parties, and sure enough he had passed several "brides" – resplendent in pink veil, L-plates, and printed T-shirts denoting Tracy's or Sharon's Hen Do. He'd spotted one which said *Phoebe's* Hen Party, but they were the exception to the rule and he assumed they had mistaken Brighton for Belgravia. The men were harder to spot in that respect, their status not being emblazoned on their attire.

Christ, how things had changed. In Hugo's day a stag party often involved a Kiss-o-gram – he doubted if these still existed – but nowadays they all went off to a strip club, didn't they? Or perhaps they went anyway, regardless of their marital status. They certainly hadn't made a weekend of it, back in the day. Couldn't have afforded it for one thing. But money seemed to be no object for this lot. How did you get plastered, all weekend, into the early morning at that – when a pint was the best part of a fiver a shout? He had no idea. On the other hand, he hadn't made too bad a stab at spending money he didn't have himself this weekend. Hugo was marginally comforted by the fact that this particular jaunt – looking for Cressida – didn't involve haemorrhaging any more cash, or credit.

Just as he was about to make enquiries of a relatively sober and harmless group of girls as to the location of the venue he sought, he caught sight of a sign that announced The Black Hat. Bingo. He'd found it.

Hugo had expected to be confronted at the door of the club by the likes of Oddjob or Jaws from a James Bond film, or a tightly muscled man in a razor-sharp black suit, with an earpiece like a CIA agent. He'd been prepared to offer identification, threats, or even a bribe – the latter very reluctantly in view of present financial circumstances – but all he got on the door was a nod from a small blonde woman with short hair, wearing a dark trouser suit, like some relic from the long demised C & A department stores. She even opened the door for him. It all boded well, very well.

Inside, the club was not at all what he had expected – there was no fog bank of smoke from multiple cigarettes, no strobe disco lights, no Donna Summer singing "I Feel Love", no sticky floor.

At this point, Hugo realised that the last disco, or club, he had set foot in had been in 1977.

Things had moved on.

The floors were scrubbed, and waxed. An exposed brick and polished concrete bar ran for about a mile down the right hand side, offering about 500, or so it seemed, craft and micro-brewery beers. There was art on the walls that nobody had attempted to steal, old American style diner tables and red vinyl booths, candle light and West Coast surfer music. A large black hat was stencilled onto the back wall by way of concession to the establishment's name, and the centrepiece of the place seemed to be an area towards the rear, which consisted of seats inside what appeared to be a cage, but what purpose it served was not obvious. A dance-floor was opposite upon which a fair number of excited bodies gyrated to the hippy sounds.

The place was packed. And the drinks flowed. Every inch of the bar was covered in bottles, glasses – empty, full and half way to either, and elbows, resting, while the rest of the body stood or perched on stools.

Every table was taken and virtually every inch of floor space too. Hugo looked around. It was like a needle in a hay stack – how on earth he thought he would find Cressida in a dimly lit, crowded, noisy club, he never knew. Anyway, he was here now. He decided that the bar would be his best bet.

Service was, however, swift. A comely young lady – no sign of a nose-ring and looking a much better bet than a barrel, Hugo thought, much to his shame – asked him what she could get him. He said he didn't want a drink, that he was looking for someone.

"Great. But this is a club and we serve drinks. If you want anything else the Tourist Information Centre opens at ten. So what can I get you?" She didn't mince words.

Hugo wondered if the man outside Gracie hadn't been right all along.

"Oh – all right then, I'll have a malt whisky," he said reluctantly.

"House double?" But she was pouring it before he could respond.

"£8.60," she said.

Bloody hell. I won't get pissed in here, he thought, discounting the fifteen drinks he had already consumed in the course of last evening and early morning.

Hugo took his drink and tried to make his way through the crowd. The music was loud, and sounded very odd to him – a cross between the Shadows and Sergio Leone's spaghetti westerns. But the crowd were lapping it up.

Hugo moved through the club, past table after table, searching, peering, looking. He made his way towards the back near the dance floor. Cressida liked to dance, there was always a chance she could be having a boogie, as Hugo called it. He spotted one of the infamous hen parties seated in the cage area. That rather amused him as he connected the dots – hens and cages, he chuckled. Best place for them. They looked like they were well tanked-up too. Tiaras pushed to one side, veils lopsided and ripped, L-plates stuck up on the mesh of the cage wall. One of them had her T-shirt rolled up to form a sort of cut-off top, exposing rolls of most unattractive, white flesh. It was always the least attractive women who tended to expose the most, Hugo contemplated, as he shook his head. Probably by way of compensation, or perhaps as a mechanism using all avenues of opportunity to attract a male. The more Hugo looked, the more he shuddered at the sight.

He tried to pick out the girls with blonde hair, or very long dark hair, in the hopes of spotting even Veronique. Nothing. He squinted at several contenders, but it wasn't them.

He thought he heard a French accent at one point, but it turned out to be a version of Geordie, couldn't be further from Provence in every sense.

When he looked around, he spotted a flowing mane of blonde hair on a girl who sat shoulder to shoulder with a dark-haired girl, their backs to him, on the table beside the caged hens. He made his way over, uttering several "excuse me" and "pardon me" apologies, pushing past people, until he got to the table and tapped the blonde girl on the shoulder.

"Cressida?" he asked expectantly.

A woman in her forties turned around and glared — first at his offending hand, and then at his face.

"Ah, sorry, I thought you were someone else. I'm looking for some ladies and they have blonde and dark hair like yours. Sorry," he said, making it sound worse than it was.

As the music surfed on, there was a raucous scream and cacophony of cackling from the hen party. The group of ten or so women — including the one with the rolled up, cut-off, T-shirt top — screamed, waved their arms and hands in Hugo's direction and called him over. One of the party broke off and ran towards the DJ in the corner on the other side of the dance floor.

The blonde and dark-haired, mistaken-identity women in their forties looked at Hugo with further distaste at his association with the party in the cage.

Hugo looked at the hens, then over his shoulder, and then pointed a very weak finger at his own chest. He stopped short of mouthing, "Who me?"

Not that that deterred the women, two of whom jumped up, grabbed him and pulled him over to their table.

"It's us!" they all squealed in excitement.

Hugo tried to wriggle away.

"What?" He laughed.

"It's us you are looking for! We're the hen party!" a very drunk woman said in a slur of syllables.

"Quite," Hugo said in clipped tones, "but I'm looking for someone else."

He tried to break free again, but the two hen minders either side of him had more strength than the combined forces of the strip club men earlier. It was true what they said about drink – it gave you super-human strength.

"No, you're not! We're the only hen party in here," another hen with smeared red lipstick shouted, adding, "look" – as she swept her hand across the table and knocked over a large glass of something bright blue.

"I'm sorry ladies but you are mistaken," Hugo said, "now if you will just let go of my arms and belt—"

"But you said you were looking for some ladies! And that's us!" the very drunk woman said again.

Hugo laughed. He'd see the funny side of it in the morning no doubt, might as well be dignified now.

"Indeed I am, but different ones." He smiled.

They took this as a good sign.

"That's part of the act, innit Shaz? Pretending not to be him?" another, much older, woman said. She looked like someone's mother – possibly "Shaz's".

"No, no I can assure you it's no act, it's real." Hugo smiled again, trying to gently break away.

"Ere, Shaz, you'd better get out, it's your do," said the older woman, looking like mutton beside the lambs, or hens in this case. "It's her do, Shaz, she's the bride," she added.

The hen with the cut-off T-shirt and rolls of white flesh hefted herself out of the booth seat, and stood before Hugo. She looked like no bride he had ever seen, or would wish to see again.

"Where's the music," she asked, then turning and bellowing towards the dance floor, added, "oi, where's the bleedin' music!"

The hens then proceeded to slow clap, joined by the women in their forties at the next table, and eventually by the entire club, or so it seemed to Hugo.

Shaz shimmied up to Hugo – who still stood with a minder either side of him, one with a hand firmly on his coat belt – thrust her hips at his groin, pulled away to howls of laughter, whipped her T-shirt off, revealing a dirty pink, sequinned bra, and proceeded to unbutton Hugo's raincoat.

When the DJ played "The Stripper", the penny dropped.

Hugo stood rooted to the spot, too horrified to respond.

All he could think of was that nothing – not even the possibility of his encounter with the men at Gracie turning violent – could be worse than this.

What the fuck would Clint Eastwood do?

Hugo's preferred option would have been to shoot every single one of them dead with Eastwood's Magnum .44 – the most powerful handgun in the world, wasn't it? – regardless of what the man himself would have done. He did not, however, have to consider how he might acquire such a weapon, since the real stripper had shown up minutes later, complained to the manager about Hugo attempting to undercut him by performing without a licence, whereby he was forcibly ejected with the assistance of the mild-mannered blonde bouncer, who demonstrated the impressive skills that had landed her the job out front.

Hugo was now practically sprinting back to the hotel, gamely disregarding the brutal damage that a pair of leather brogues, worn without socks, will do to one's heels when one attempts to sprint in them in the rain, notwithstanding their bespoke handmade virtues and excessive cost. He had entirely given up the mission of finding Cressida on his own, and had determined to get back to the hotel as quickly as possibly, grab Dana, and resume the search with the aid of the proper authorities and in a taxi.

Nothing as appalling as his experiences tonight would have befallen him if he had been with Dana. She would have known exactly how to handle the situation and what to say.

Hugo decided that as a lone male – tall, well-dressed, distinguished looking, and not unattractive – he was simply a red rag to a bull in terms of drunken females. And just imagine if he had gone into the, well – the *wrong* type of club? God, that didn't bear thinking about. What if he had stumbled into the *particular* club that the males outside the strip club had implied? What then? Suppose he had ended up in a gay bar or something! Hugo had no doubt at all that if the females had reacted to him with such enthusiasm, then the males of Brighton, if they were so inclined, would have displayed equal fervour.

He sped on, legs pumping and brogues chaffing, straight past a man who held up a cigarette to him and said, "You got a light mate?"

En route, Hugo got his phone out – in all the excitement of The Black Hat he had forgotten to check it – and saw, to his horror, that it was stone dead. Charging the battery would have helped of course, if he had remembered to pack the charger, which he hadn't. He looked at his watch, it was now four o'clock.

Four in the morning! Christ – where had the time gone? Surely it was only minutes ago that he was sprinting down North Street, which latter he now sprinted up again. How time flies, he thought. He dared not think about what had befallen Cressida since he had set out to search for her, or worse, what Dana would have to say when he arrived back without her. The latter didn't bear thinking about. And what if something dreadful had happened? What if he was needed? He shoved the useless phone back in his pocket.

Hugo ran on, fighting the now hurricane-force winds and driving rain, turning sharply down West Street, his raincoat – still unbuttoned – flapping behind him, his heels now anaesthetised by the bitter cold, although the damage being inflicted was no less.

The streets were pretty much deserted at this hour, one or two stragglers lurking about, and a fair number of people in cardboard shelters wedged into shop doorways, but the latter were no threat: their primary objective being to sleep without encountering the icy finger of death before dawn.

The quiet on the street gave Hugo some mild comfort, as it indicated that the clubs had shut up shop for the night, and so with any luck Cressida would be heading back to the hotel. On the other hand, she might have been the subject of some ghastly lecherous attention from men – like the sort who were hanging around the strip club. Someone might have made a pass at her. Or worse. Bastard.

Hugo rounded the corner by the Odeon Cinema, trying to work out where he could get hold of that Magnum .44.

He made it through the door of the hotel assisted by a blast of cold wind, and swiftly squelched his way through the foyer, his feet swimming inside his brogues. If one of the homeless people had encountered him at this moment they would have offered him a cardboard box and a sleeping bag. He was striding towards the lifts, when he heard Laurence, the night porter, call after him.

"Sir? Excuse me sir – it's about the women," Laurence said behind him.

"Didn't find them, haven't time to chat now – it may be life and death," Hugo said, as he jumped into the lift and hit the button for the fourth floor.

As he stood in the lift willing it to go faster, his lips moved silently, composing a carefully edited version of events for Dana. And a reason why he was now returning on his own, having left his vulnerable, chaste, 16-year-old daughter to the brutal mercies of a dark metropolis.

The door to the suite was flung open and Hugo stood on the threshold – wild-eyed, dishevelled and sodden – peering open-mouthed at the scene within.

Dana frowned as she looked up at him from her seat on the edge of the sofa, where Cressida was tucked up under a blanket, half reclining, eating a large bowl of cheesy chips, and sipping a Coke. Dana herself had a plate balanced on her lap, on which lay the crusts of a sandwich from a large platter of the same in the middle of the coffee table.

"Oh," was all he managed to say from the doorway.

At the sound of bottles being clinked in the corner, Hugo looked over to see Veronique crouched down at the mini-bar. She got up and smiled at him.

"You're back then," Dana said, wiping the corners of her mouth with a napkin.

"Well – I, yes, I am. But what—" Hugo remained

standing in the doorway.

"Oh don't you worry yourself Hugo, it's all under control. Cressida is safe. Here. As you can see." Dana's tone matched the temperature outside.

"Hi Dad." Cressida gave a little wave from the sofa.

Hugo waved, rather limp-wristed, back.

"*Bonjour*!" Veronique said heartily, with an Orangina in her hand.

"But, how?" he asked

"What do you mean 'how'?" Dana replied, taking another sandwich from the platter.

"Well, I mean, how is she here? I've been all over the place looking for her."

Dana savoured her sandwich. Took a sip of her tea – she'd take her time, after all it was her birthday, well not technically, but it was not yet dawn.

"Clearly in all the wrong places though," Dana replied.

Hugo closed the door behind him. He was starting to drip on the carpet. Little dark dots were appearing on the floor beneath him.

"That's not true! I've been everywhere I – I've been subjected to unimaginable events tonight, you'd never believe it—"

Dana straightened up. "No, you're right, I wouldn't."

Hugo looked down. "I've been threatened with violence outside a strip club—"

"Indeed," Dana remarked.

Hugo looked up sharply. "What I mean is, I was asking directions, and then I went to the place where that lizard downstairs, er, I mean Laurence, said that Veronique and Cressida had headed off to and—"

"Really?" Dana said.

"Yes. And I can tell you things got even worse in there!"

"Is that so? And yet you didn't find her?" Dana asked.

"We didn't see you in the club Dad," Cressida said.

Veronique said nothing. She just smiled.

"Well I can assure you that I was indeed there. Endured an awful episode with some drunken women on some sort of nightmarish hen night—"

"Yes, well that's all very interesting but the fact remains that Cressida is here and you came back without her," Dana said, finishing off her egg and cress triangle.

"But that's preposterous!" Hugo said. "Of course I came back without her, how could I have come back with her if she was already here?"

Cressida looked puzzled, Veronique smiled.

Dana was not smiling.

"You are missing the point. The point is that she had to come back here without you because you were never in the bloody club in the first place. Therefore, you could not possibly have found her to bring her back." Dana had raised her voice.

Hugo squelched further into the room, his trousers stuck to his legs like drainpipes.

"I most certainly was. And what's more I can prove it. If you really think it necessary for me to provide evidence of my activity to save our child from the perils of the city centre. I have a receipt!"

Cressida slurped her coke. Hugo fumbled in his pocket.

"You see Dana, I took a great deal of trouble to note carefully where Laurence suggest I look, and I took even more trouble to locate the place, and spent a great deal of time in there searching for them."

Hugo continued to fumble in his pockets, then smiled, obviously locating what he was looking for, withdrew a soggy piece of paper, and handed it to his wife with the words, "Voila!"

Dana took the receipt and raised her eyebrows.

"So this is where you were for – what? An hour or more?" she asked.

Hugo shook his head. "Indeed it was and it was ghastly. Alas no sign of Cressida."

"But this receipt says: The Black Hat, Chester Street, North Laines, Brighton BN1. Is that right?"

Hugo nodded his head vigorously. "Yes, yes, that's right. One hundred per cent right."

"Well I am glad you had a nice evening Hugo, while I was here worried sick."

Dana turned to Veronique. "What was the name of the club you went to?"

Veronique said, "Le Chat Noir – in English, ze Black Cat, in ze Lanes."

Hugo looked confused, Dana almost felt sorry for him again. Almost.

"I'm sure you will agree Hugo that *cat* and *hat* are very different, as are *The Lanes* and the *North Laines,* and that, even in translation, nothing could be lost this time, except perhaps you."

Despite the events of the night, or rather early morning, Dana could not keep up the cold shoulder for long. Hugo was soaking wet, his heels bloodied from the lack of socks, and he was starting to sneeze and cough so much that she feared he had caught a cold. On top of that, he had to take two more co-codamol for his back and legs.

When Veronique had gone and Cressida lay asleep on their sofa, Dana had had to put him out of his misery, and explain how Cressida had turned up back at their room not long after Hugo had headed out. She had tried to call him, but his phone had just gone to voicemail. Veronique had brought Cress back after finding her crying downstairs in the lobby again, but had taken her on a short mission first to collect something from the club where Veronique worked on late Saturday nights. They had been gone less than forty minutes, and Veronique was all apologies for not bringing her straight back up to the room, but Cressida had been insistent that she wanted to talk to Veronique about something first.

Cressida had not referred to the incident in the bathroom, and so Dana's guess was that Veronique had explained things, in the way a big sister might, and that seemed to have soothed Cressida considerably. That, and the late night room service − which had the added bonus of abandoning the veganism − and the promise of ordering *two* fake fur jackets from Zara on the Sunday: one for Dana, and one now for Cressida.

Hugo had ventured an opinion that Veronique, being a French woman and versed in matters of the heart, would have been well placed to explain things to Cressida about the complexities and subtle nuances of the relationship between men and women, indeed she may well have had such experiences herself.

And Dana had really felt sorry for poor Hugo when she had had to explain that things were not quite what they appeared to be.

Hugo had gone to bed finally, in disgust and vowed to give up all attempt at ever understanding women again when Dana explained why Veronique had gone back to the club after finishing work.

The Black Cat was a burlesque club – Hugo's ears had actually pricked up at this. And Veronique did indeed do a show there involving a lot of tasteful, strategically placed feathers – and it was the latter that she had gone back to retrieve – her vintage ostrich-feather fans being of significant value.

But The Black Cat was not any old burlesque club. It was a lesbian venue.

And Veronique was the club's star lesbian performer.

NINETEEN

Their saving grace was that it was a Sunday, and breakfast was therefore served until the indecently late hour of eleven – which was just about manageable for some, and an impossibility for others.

Dana, having forgone her run this morning – even she didn't have the energy for anything more than a shower after the night's excitement – was seated at a large table by the window, overlooking a remarkably blue sky day: the wonders of the post-storm weather. The tide was far out and, if she squinted, the sand that had been exposed by the receding waters almost glistened in the winter sunlight. Seagulls made the most of the rich pickings that the outbound tide had unearthed, as they breakfasted on fat lug worms, and one or two unfortunate crabs who hadn't been quick enough to scuttle sideways into a hidey hole.

Dana sipped her Earl Grey tea, and nibbled with lack lustre at a croissant – she'd decided to keep an eye on the calories after her impromptu midnight snack – and watched the crowds stroll along the promenade as people took full advantage of the clement weather.

Hugo gulped his English breakfast tea like a drowning man, in between polishing off a second plate of bacon and eggs as an entree, having devoured muesli, fruit and yoghurt as an hor d'oeuvre. Dana knew a savage hangover when she saw one. Not that he'd admit it of course.

Cressida too, ate a hearty plate of fruit, pastries, toast and hash browns. She'd refused the eggs that Dana had suggested, but only because they were overcooked and rubbery. There were high hopes that the veganism remained confined to history.

Dana marvelled at how resilient youth was. Here was Cressida, who had suffered several grievous insults to her sensitive nature and beliefs, been up until five in the morning, consumed her own fair share of booze, and yet was as fresh as if she had slept ten hours straight. No ill effects at all.

Unlike Hugo, who had had to be helped downstairs, muttering about going to see his osteopath as soon as they got back, and doubting his fitness to sit in the car on the return journey, let alone do any driving.

They had got their breakfast by the skin of their teeth, it being just a shade after eleven when they had entered the dining room. The waitress had not exactly said as much, but she had glanced at her watch and given them a tight, reluctant smile, having neither the wit nor wisdom – or interest come to that – to comment on it as she led them like sheep to their table. First though, she had made sure that they were on the "bed and breakfast" list that sat on the lectern at the entrance. This first chore she had carried out with the iron-clad efficiency of a comrade in the Politbureau issuing a day pass to the decadent West.

The waitress had then indicated the breakfast buffet display and asked them whether they wanted tea or coffee. Hugo had gained some measure of approval by asking for coffee, but Dana's request for Earl Grey tea – and even worse, Cressida's for green tea – was met with the same response she would have expected had she asked for two straight shots of tequila. But still, the waitress said nothing.

She reminded Dana of someone, but she couldn't quite put her finger on it. She was short and dumpy with a dark, very severe haircut. Her best years were well behind her, although Dana doubted there had been many of those. Her air was, not exactly menacing, but one got the impression she was not to be messed with. The net result of this was that Dana had decided against ordering porridge, as it might have been a request too far. So she had stuck with a croissant from the buffet.

Anyway, whatever. It was their last day, and despite the antics of the previous twenty-four hours, Dana intended to make the most of it. There was the return journey to Zara, and Dana had also promised Cressida a mini-facial and eye-brow threading at the spa at the top of North Street, SpaZone. They did a vegetarian facial there which had impressed Cressida immensely, mind you, that was before she had given up veganism. Dana assumed she remained a vegetarian. For now. And that was fine, vegetarianism was manageable, desirable even. In fact, Dana might give it a go herself after the excesses of the weekend.

Yes, definitely, she decided as she watched Hugo spear two sausages and eat the rind of the bacon. Maybe

Cressida had a point about not eating anything she would not be prepared to kill herself. Dana couldn't see Hugo wrestling a hog to the ground, however hungry he was.

Veronique hadn't been mentioned again. Although Dana secretly hoped to encounter her before they left. Just to watch Hugo squirm. Men were so impressionable, so easily flattered.

Not everyone had made it to the breakfast table. They had left Alex to sleep on, grateful that he had not got involved in the search last night. Trotting around Brighton at that hour was the last thing she would have wanted him doing. Hugo had achieved something at least by getting Alex to go to bed early, although Dana had no doubt that he had taken full advantage of the horror movie channel and been on his phone half the night.

Hugo had his briefcase with him, and had carefully laid out his manuscript on the breakfast table, in a neat stack of papers to his right elbow. As he munched, he glanced at the top page occasionally and made a stab with his pen as some random thought came to him.

Yes, random, Dana decided.

To his other elbow he had *The Telegraph* with the crossword facing him. One or two of the lines had been completed, although it remained to be seen if they were correct. Hugo was not above keeping yesterday's *Telegraph*, filling in the solutions given in today's, and leaving the old newspaper prominently displayed on the coffee table. Dana had seen him do it once – he didn't know she had seen him, and she didn't comment on it – a couple of hours before Camilla and Tristram had called around to fetch Alex for an outing with Lucas. They hadn't stayed though, or even come into the sitting room, they never did. If there were any social interaction, it took place at school events, or at Tristram's annual Christmas drinks party or summer barbecue.

Hugo's efforts to give the impression of being a cryptic crossword genius had all been in vain.

Dana poured herself another cup of tea and observed Hugo put a thoughtfully considered full stop at the end of a sentence on his manuscript. Then he turned the crossword over and started on the polygon word puzzle. He usually managed to achieve the "average" level at that.

So all was not quite lost.

Dana heard her phone ping yet again in her bag. She was steadfastly ignoring all messages at this stage, since there was nothing to be gained by allowing herself to become distracted, or even dissatisfied, with such a short time remaining of their weekend break.

She had several missed calls on her phone too. He was persistent if nothing else. And he was, possibly, something else.

But again, no sense in listening to voicemails either, until she got back home.

"All right sweetie?" Dana asked Cressida across the table.

Cressida smiled with a mouthful of pain au raisin. She looked like a little girl again, sitting there in Dana's chunky knit jumper, a size too big – having not brought her own to their room after the hasty arrangements for the impromptu sleep over. And her hair in a French plait. Cressida had let Dana do that for her that morning. Dana sighed. It was a very rare occurrence these days, being allowed to touch Cressida's hair. She was so particular, it was either poker straight – achieved by means of straightening irons – or else *messy* as she termed it, which didn't mean not brushed after getting out of bed, but which instead took at least two hours of washing, drying, and styling with something called Salt Spray, to get the desired look.

When Cressida reached the age of thirty-five with a toddler, a baby, a mountain of ironing, a job, a mortgage and a husband, she would discover for herself that the same look could be achieved for free, with no extra effort, by simply not having even enough time to go to the toilet on her own.

In the meantime, Dana luxuriated in the sweet, fragrant and soft feeling she derived from being so close to her daughter again, to her little girl. Dana could almost smell the baby powder, so strong were the memories of happy times past that were rekindled.

"Mm," Cressida said, savouring the last of her pastry, "I'm fine Mum. How does it feel to be forty-nine?"

Dana shot her a mock look of disgust, and said, "Unless you want to give me back that sweater, it's forty from now on, thank you very much."

"Actually you don't look a day over thirty-nine. You're much better preserved than Emma's mum. She has those funny little lines running up from her mouth and those long stretchy lines down to her boobs. And her eyes are all puffy," Cressida added.

"That's not very polite Cressida," Hugo remarked over the top of his polygon.

"True though," Cressida replied.

It was true, Dana thought. Susie, Emma's mum, did look rough, and she was two years younger than Dana. It was a combination of things: Susie smoked, didn't exercise, drank far too much, and if she opened a box of Quality Street she wouldn't stop until the whole lot was gone.

It wasn't just a question of will-power though, Susie's husband was a nasty piece of work and most likely the source of driving her to all the other contributing factors that led to her premature ageing.

"Be that as it may, it is not nice to cast aspersions on others," Hugo said, adding, "*culprit*," as he jotted down the latter word on his polygon.

"Yes Daddy," Cressida said, smiling at Dana, who smiled back.

"And you can dispense with that as well. The bank of Dad is firmly closed for the weekend, pending the audit later today – aka paying the bill before we check out here. So you can return to normal and call me Dad."

Cressida scowled. "Oh. Yes Dad."

Dana smiled. "But of course, don't forget that the faux fur jackets in Zara have been pre-authorised."

Hugo looked up and muttered, "Yes, of course."

"What time are you thinking of heading off to the Amex Stadium and gym with Alex?" Dana asked.

"In the next hour or so, whenever Alex surfaces." Hugo looked at his watch. "Perhaps someone should go and get him out of bed."

Hugo shuffled his *Telegraph* and looked at Dana, who stared right back at him.

"Right then," Hugo said, throwing his newspaper down on the table, "I'll go, might take me some moments though, as I cannot walk very well with this back."

Dana ignored the comment, and said instead, "What

time do we have to check out?"

"I booked a late one – it's two or two thirty I think, I'll check on my way upstairs, apparently after that we can leave the bags with the concierge, or in the car, whatever is easier."

Hugo pushed his chair out from the table while still sitting in it, placed both hands on the table top, and leaning on it heavily, eased himself gingerly out of his seat. He then picked up his manuscript and newspaper, put it all into his briefcase, then turned his upper body in one motion, as though his neck were in a brace, and carefully put the briefcase strap over his arm.

Dana rolled her eyes but pretended not to notice him wincing with the effort. She wasn't going to help him up, or offer to carry the bag, both of which she knew he was half expecting her to do.

The comrade waitress appeared unexpectedly beside their table and started clearing plates, she looked suspiciously at Hugo, and then at his bag, as though he were smuggling Soviet secrets – or butter pats and mini jam jars at any rate – out of the breakfast buffet.

Cressida, being an oblivious teenager, asked her, "Please may I have another pot of green tea?"

The waitress stopped what she was doing and straightened up. She gave Cressida a steely glare. It was then that Dana remembered who she reminded her of – Colonel Rosa Klebb, the matronly Russian assassin from the James Bond film, *From Russia With Love*, or was she East German, Dana couldn't remember, and anyway the effect was the same: chilling.

However, before the assassin waitress could respond to the tea request – which would almost certainly have been in the negative – there was a loud, high pitched whine, growl and bark, as a fast moving ball of white and brown fur flew across the floor, up the steps towards the table and then leapt up, yelping now, into Dana's lap.

"Good God! It looks almost like—" Hugo got as far as saying.

"Oscar!" Cressida shouted, jumping up out of her seat and throwing herself at her mother's chair and its contents.

"It is Oscar!" Dana also shouted.

Oscar was engaged in frantic tail wagging and vigorous licking – his tongue lashing out at Dana's face in his anxiety to say hello.

"What the – how on earth did he get here?" Hugo had also moved over to Dana.

"Yes, yes. There's a good boy, yes, we're very pleased to see you too," Dana cooed as she kissed him back.

She wasn't yet processing the obvious – what was he doing here? Or Hugo's fairly rational – how did he get there?

Oscar couldn't have cared less. He was where he wanted to be, on Dana's lap, and having said enough hellos, was now sniffing the air in front of him as he surveyed the remnants from the breakfast table.

The assassin waitress looked ready to whip out her cyanide capsule at any moment. What wasn't clear was who she might administer it to – Dana, Hugo or Cressida.

After a lot of stroking and "good boys", Dana set Oscar down on the floor. Fortunately there were only a few late guests in the dining room: Dana feeling certain that there would be a strict no-dogs policy.

It took only a few seconds for Dana to be wracked with

worry – if Oscar was here then there must be something wrong.

Hugo, Dana knew, didn't think like her, his emotions ran straight to irritation.

"So whose incompetence has led to this latest turn of events then?" he asked, bending down – despite the bad back – to make Oscar sit in obedience.

"Yours," a voice said behind him.

They all turned as Bella marched into the breakfast room holding Oscar's lead.

"Mum?" Dana asked.

"Grandma Bella!" Cressida jumped up and ran to her grandma, hugging her passionately.

Bella carried the stick, which was now painted entirely in white, and she jabbed it in front of her as she made her way towards their table, under the icy glare of the assassin waitress.

"Mine? What do you mean and what on earth are you doing here Bella?" Hugo asked, in a slightly high pitched voice himself.

Bella got to the table and tapped in front of her with the tip of her stick.

"Glad someone is pleased to see me," she said to Cressida.

Cressida beamed and hugged her grandma again.

Dana, who was her mother's daughter, knew that there was more to come.

Hugo, being Hugo, didn't.

"Surely you didn't come all this way – just when we are ready to go home – to let Oscar say hello?" he asked.

Bella stood facing Hugo, looked pointedly at the chair to his right and back at him again. Hugo sighed and pulled the chair out for her.

"Thank you Hugo. It's nice to know that your manners are impressive," she said, "even if your DIY skills are not."

Hugo narrowed his eyes.

"Mum – what's going on?" Dana was leaning across the table.

"I'd like some tea." Bella looked around and caught the assassin's eye. "I'd like some tea please, Darjeeling, with a slice of lemon, no milk, in a proper china cup and saucer, not these silly square mugs."

There was silence, even the dog seemed to sense that a line had been crossed as he stopped sniffing under the table for a moment.

Bella might as well have asked for the launch codes to the missiles in the Cuban crisis – such was the effect of her request. The waitress said nothing.

"Er, I rather think we may have missed last orders so to speak, Bella, I think breakfast is over," Hugo said, in an effort to placate.

"I don't want breakfast. I want tea," Bella repeated.

The assassin stiffened her back, and said with as much distaste as she could muster, which was quite a lot, "*Animals* are not allowed in the dining room."

Dana looked at Hugo.

Cressida looked panicky.

Bella stiffened her own back – albeit in her chair, and responded, "I am virtually blind and therefore disabled. That *animal* is in fact my guide dog, and under the Equality Act 2010 it is illegal for you to refuse me entry with my assistance dog – as is the more proper term for him. We can argue about it here, or you can ask the hotel manager to call the police who will be more than happy to uphold my rights. Now" – Bella drew breath – "am I right in thinking that you don't want the unwanted attention to the hotel's reputation?"

Where there had been silence, there was now stunned silence. Cressida smirked proudly at her grandma, and Dana nodded her head. Even Hugo looked blindsided.

Bella was indeed her daughter's mother.

The waitress, sensing that the game was up, simply asked, "Would you like sugar with that?" and walked away.

Hugo sat down again. But Dana suspected that he knew he wasn't out of the woods yet.

"Hugo." Bella turned to him, making him jump. "As the man of the house I have a question for you."

Dana knew this was a form of facetiousness, since Bella considered Hugo to be lower than Oscar in the pecking order back home.

Hugo, however, was keen to acknowledge his promotion. "Yes indeed Bella, what is it?"

"How much do you spend, collectively, on the family's mobile phones, both the gadgets and the service charges?" Bella continued.

Hugo shook his head. "I don't know, a fair bit, the kids are always on them, stands me a fortune every month."

He glanced at Dana, who raised her eyebrows, and then he looked away.

"It's just that I'm wondering why none of you bother to actually use them for their intended purpose – making and receiving calls."

The waitress arrived back with a tray of tea and placed it before Bella, she smiled – it was half-way genuine – she had obviously practiced it in the kitchen as she considered her alternative means of employment.

"Well, I – mine's usually on all the time but I forgot – that is, I didn't bring my charger as it's playing up and I need to get a new one," Hugo said.

Dana and he both knew it was a lie.

"Quite," Bella said, "the children I understand, you know how laid back teenagers can be, but really Dana! I've been calling you every hour since six this morning!"

Bella poured her tea and savoured the therapeutic effect.

Shit. Dana felt a wave of remorse. She felt guilty and self indulgent too. She hadn't looked at her missed calls because she thought they had been from someone else.

"Sorry Mum, I really am. There's no excuse except that we had" – she looked at Hugo for help, but none was forthcoming – "a bit of a crisis last night."

Cressida stepped up to the mark. "It's all my fault Grandma, I went out with a friend, a new friend, for a couple of hours, very late and I didn't tell Mum and Dad where I was going, and they got worried and went to look for me, and we went to bed very late and just forgot about our phones."

Cressida smiled sweetly and kissed her grandma, who seemed placated with that, to a degree.

"So what's happened, it's not bad news about anyone is it?" Dana asked her mother.

Bella shook her head. "No, nothing like that."

"I sincerely hope it is nothing so trivial as Oscar pining and missing us. He's perfectly content to sit at home in his basket, in the kitchen, until we return," Hugo said, looking at his watch.

"I agree. And that is precisely where he would be now. If he could get into it."

Bella looked pointedly at Hugo.

"What do you mean, 'if he could get into it'? What's wrong with his basket?" Hugo asked tentatively.

"Nothing wrong with his basket." Bella sipped her tea.

"What's wrong with the kitchen then, or the house?"

"Nothing wrong with the kitchen or the house. The house is safe and sound and securely locked up."

Hugo held up his hands and shook his head irritably.

"Well then—" he said, laughing.

"In fact, you might say it is impenetrable..." Bella poured another cup of tea.

Dana sighed heavily.

"Impenetrable?" Hugo asked.

"Yes."

"As in – what exactly?"

"As in locked out. Can't get back in. And before you say it" – Bella closed her eyes and held up her own hand – "there hasn't been any rain, so you can't blame that for making the door stick."

"I thought you fixed it Hugo?" Dana said across the table.

"I did! Well at least I oiled it and I put WD40 on it and I unscrewed it and put it back on and—"

Dana shook her head. "In other words no." She held up a hand. "Save it. I don't want to hear any more. When we get home you can take it off and replace it. Properly."

Hugo sighed, nodded his head.

"So when did this happen Mum?" Dana put her hand over her mothers.

"This morning. I got up early, as you know I do, got

dressed, and took Oscar out around six for a little walk round the block. But when I got back to the house the door wouldn't open. I tried everything I could think of. Put the key in, took it out, put it back in, tapped the door, pushed against it. Nothing. It wouldn't budge. It was too early to wake a neighbour, especially on a Sunday. Goodness knows what they would have thought anyway."

Bella looked again at Hugo, who winced.

"And all I had was my coat, Oscar's lead, my phone – which I keep fully charged for emergencies." Bella raised her voice slightly in Hugo's direction. "And my keys."

Despite the admonishment, Hugo asked, "But why could you not go back to your place?"

Dana could see that he regretted asking the question as soon as it came out of his mouth.

Bella put the cup down in its saucer and said, "You know perfectly well that I live in a small retirement, warden-assisted, apartment. You also know perfectly well that there was all that fuss about that German Shepherd last year. Dogs are absolutely vetoed, and the warden has eyes like a hawk."

In other circumstances, Dana knew that Hugo would have retorted *just like you*, but he let it go.

"So I had absolutely no alternative but to come here," Bella continued, "and anyway, it makes a nice little day out. I always liked Brighton. When your father and I were courting" – Bella turned to Dana – "we used to get up to all sorts here!"

Bella smiled at the memory, and added, "Ha!" As she tried, surreptitiously, to feed Oscar the remains of a sausage under the table.

Cressida looked a little apprehensive at this latest

remark, and Dana could understand why, so she decided to change the subject.

And then another thought struck her, and she paused.

"Mum?" she asked.

"Yes dear?"

"Mum, how did you get here?" Dana asked with growing apprehension.

"I drove of course," Bella replied, plying Oscar with the last of the sausage.

Hugo laughed, Dana shot him a look.

"Drove? In your car?" she asked her mother.

"Well of course in my car, who else's would I be driving?"

Oh God, Dana thought. Here we go.

"Mum, you are not supposed to be driving, remember? Not until you have had your cataract operation?"

"Oh it's fine." Bella waved the question off. "I can see perfectly well."

The waitress, clearing the table beside them, looked up sharply.

Bella added, "Some of the time," and looked away.

Hugo shook his head.

"But Mum!"

"Now stop fussing, it's all instinct anyway, isn't it? Driving? Bit like swimming and riding a bike, you just know how to do it!" Bella added, draining the last of her tea from the pot.

Cressida giggled and Dana frowned at her.

"Not really Mum – you still need to see where you are going!"

"Well I'm here aren't I? In one piece and anyway" – Bella lowered her voice and leaned in confidentially to the table – "I can see quite well most of the time."

For goodness sake, Dana thought, but she was too tired to argue. Tired and it was only twelve noon.

"Well, I'm driving your car back and Hugo can take the kids," Dana said.

Hugo looked up and pulled a sulky face. "But what about my bad back? Thought I might sit in the back and stretch out?"

Dana gave him another look. Then she bent down to pat Oscar under the table.

"Right, well, what's done is done I suppose. I think we should check out and put the hotel out of its misery, take the bags to the car, and go for a nice walk with Oscar along the seafront? How about that?"

No one answered. Dana looked up and saw that they were all staring at something, or someone, behind her. She followed the direction of everyone's gaze.

Juan – Alex's gym training partner of the day before, and the restaurant's sommelier – was standing, a few paces away, facing their table.

Hugo looked at him and said, "Sorry old chap but Alex is still in bed, and he won't have time for the gym today I'm afraid because he's going up to the football stadium with me."

Juan didn't respond. He just stood there with his hands clasped in front of him. As though in prayer.

As Hugo got ready to leave the table he went on, "And it's a little too early to order any wine! Ha!"

Laughing at his own joke, he added, "Unless you have a recommendation we can't refuse or two bottles for the price of one, eh?"

Hugo chuckled again.

"I don't think he is working today Hugo," Dana said very slowly.

She immediately felt uneasy looking at Juan. She could feel the hairs on the back of her neck prickle. It wasn't just his appearance – dirty jeans, leather jacket, unkempt hair, biker boots – he looked like he'd slept in them, in fact, he looked like he hadn't slept at all.

"Juan? Isn't it?" Dana asked him.

"*Sí,*" he replied.

He stood with head down, even as he spoke that one word.

"Is everything – all right?" she asked.

"Who's he?" Bella said turning around.

"The wine waiter," Hugo replied.

"At breakfast?" Bella remarked, surveying the restaurant.

"I don't think he has come to take our order," Dana responded.

Juan continued to stare at the ground. He was wringing his hands now.

"So what does he want then?" Bella asked again.

Hugo started to move away from the table.

"No idea and I haven't got all day, I'm going upstairs to fetch Alex and then we'll be off," he said.

Juan sniffed. He appeared to be trembling as well. And then he shook his head very slowly.

"Alex," he said, very quietly.

Dana reached out a hand to Hugo to stop him leaving.

Cressida half stood up.

"What about him?" Dana asked.

Juan seemed intent on boring two holes through the floor, such was the intensity of his stare.

He shook his head again.

"*Io siento*," Juan muttered.

"What's he saying?" Bella asked.

"Speak up man," Hugo commanded.

"*Io siento mucho*," Juan said, running a sleeve across his eyes.

Dana stood up and put her hand on the table.

"Speak English if you please, we've no idea what you are saying," Hugo commanded again.

"What's he talking about Dana, have you any idea? How does he know Alex?" Bella said.

"He's sorry," Cressida said.

"He's what?" Hugo asked, turning towards her.

"He said he's sorry," Cressida repeated.

Dana's head was starting to swim.

"Sorry about what?" Hugo asked irritably.

Juan started to cry.

Dana felt sick and a little faint, she now gripped the table for support.

"Where is he?" Cressida asked him.

Juan shook his head and wiped his eyes with both fists, balling them into his eye sockets.

"I said – where is he?" Cressida said, shouting.

The waitress looked over at this latest turn of events. Oscar cowered under the table.

"Where's who?" Hugo asked, "Alex? Alex is in bed." Then turning to Dana, he said, "We already told him Alex is in bed, so what the fuck is going on?"

"Alex went out with him last night!" Cressida said, semi hysterical.

"No he didn't, he was in bed, I told him to stay there, he's still asleep," Hugo said.

"Don't be retarded Dad! Of course he didn't stay in bed! He went out with" – Cressida turned savagely on Juan – "him again!"

"Again? What do you mean again?" Hugo asked, raising his own voice.

Dana swayed slightly, still gripping the table top.

"Alex has been out two nights running with that, that – *person*. They've been to bars and clubs and all sorts. And now he's done something to him. I know he has, I told Alex not to go, but he wouldn't listen!" Cressida started to cry.

"Has he indeed? Well, young Alex is for the high jump when I get hold of him," Hugo said.

"Where is he Juan?" Dana asked very calmly.

Juan shook his head, refused to meet her eyes.

"He's in bed of course – sleeping it off. No wonder he couldn't get up," Hugo blustered.

"Do shut up Hugo and let the boy speak!" Bella now commanded from her seat.

Hugo looked surprised, but shut up nonetheless.

"Juan, please tell us," Dana asked again.

"It not my fault – I try to help him. But—" Juan said very quietly.

"Mummy! Oh Mummy!" Cressida cried.

Bella reached out a hand to quiet her.

"I go bed and then I come out again and – and, then…" Juan nodded his head slowly.

Hugo had gone a shade paler.

"Young man if you have done anything to our son – I will—"

Hugo went to move towards Juan.

"For the love of God Hugo will you shut your mouth."

Bella stood up and put her finger to her lips. "Let the boy speak."

Dana looked up at Juan.

"Juan, I am Alex's mother, now you must tell me what has happened, you won't be in any trouble, but you must tell us," Dana said.

Hugo looked like he was about to murder Juan with his bare hands, but Bella still had her finger to her lips.

"The last I see – they take him hospital." Juan's shoulders shook violently.

"What?" Dana's voice was barely a whisper now.

Juan pulled at something around his neck, he rubbed and rubbed at it. Dana was transfixed by the movement, like the pendulum of a clock – rub, rub, rub. As his fingers moved, she saw that it was a small silver crucifix.

"You've killed him!" Cressida shrieked.

Bella held onto her hand.

Juan held the crucifix tightly and said, "I no kill him, something else try…"

Dana didn't hear anything after that. Someone had hit the mute button on life. Suddenly she was underwater, holding her breath, she knew there were noises above the surface – exclamations, screams, growls, a plate falling to the floor and breaking – but she was holding her breath as she fell further and further into the black depths of the water, which felt cold, but oddly comforting, as they closed around her.

She remembered only two occasions in her life that were so stressful that she wanted to retreat somewhere dark and silent, crawl under the bed or into a closet and just hide. One was when she was told her father had died, the other one was too stressful to recount even years later.

And now this was a third. She knew it was bad, instinctively knew the moment she had turned around and seen Juan. Like you just know when two police officers turn up on your doorstep. You just know – two of them give the game away, and you just need to look at their body language. They haven't come to give you home security advice. And Juan hadn't come to ask if Alex could come out to play in the gym.

It wasn't meant to be like this, not now, not here. He wasn't even eighteen. He had to finish school, go to university, get a job, laugh with his friends, burn dinners he tried to cook, fall in love, buy a house, get married, have children, sit up all night as he nursed their fevers, worry about whether to put his parents into a care home. Your children out live you. No one should have to bury their children. It wasn't meant to be like this. Who had decided that it would be? Why?

Alex had never been ill, not seriously – the worst he had ever been was with flu. He'd never hurt himself – other than chipping a tooth at cricket – never broke a bone, never sprained an ankle, never had a deep cut. He'd taken knocks and given them in equal measure. But he'd always rebounded. Always. He was Alex. His mother's son.

Dana felt someone pulling her, pulling her up out of the blackness, she was still holding her breath, but now she could sense hands on her body, gripping her and pulling her back up to the surface. She opened her eyes and saw Hugo standing in front of her with a hand on either shoulder, shaking her.

"Dana." She heard faintly.

He shook her again, more firmly.

"Dana," Hugo said.

This time she heard him and looked into his eyes.

"Dana we have to go, to the hospital, okay?" he asked more gently.

Dana looked around her, everything was exactly the same, everyone in the same position, she felt herself nod her head.

"Okay," she said, "where?"

"Didn't you hear him?" Hugo asked.

Dana shook her head, she could feel the trickle of tears down her cheeks.

"Royal Sussex County Hospital, Juan says that is where the paramedics took him when they couldn't, well, that is after they were treating him, he thinks. I can't really make out what he's saying. Anyway they won't give him any information at the hospital because he is not next-of-kin, so we have to go Dana, now."

"Right." Dana shook herself. "Of course." She looked around for Oscar. "What about the dog?"

"I don't know, we'll leave him in the car or something, but let's go now, okay?" Hugo picked up her bag and handed it to her.

Dana took it and shoved it over her arm. She saw the others pick up their things. Saw Juan rooted to the spot, eyes downcast.

Bella was on her feet. "Give me your room key," she said to Hugo.

"What for?" he asked.

"I'll take the dog and put him in there for a bit. It's fine, they allow pets, there's a charge of £20 or something, but it will be fine. I'll also get a coat for Dana, she looks cold."

Dana looked over at her mother. She didn't feel cold

but she was shivering or shaking, she couldn't decide which.

Hugo handed Bella the key, and after securing Oscar to the lead again, she marched off with her stick tapping the way before her, out of the dining room.

Even though she knew he wasn't there, Dana kept thinking that they needed to go and get Alex out of bed. She knew he was not in the bed, and that it lay cold and empty, but for some reason she kept thinking that they needed to wake him up, bring him with them. It was irrational, and Dana supposed it was what happened to people in shock. Like a new widow thinking she had to have tea on the table for her husband when he comes home from work.

Dana felt like they were leaving him behind, just going off like this. It didn't feel right. He'll wake up and we will all be gone, and he will be alone. She didn't even try to blink away the tears now, or to get a tissue out of her bag, or even to wipe her eyes with her sleeve. She heard Hugo speak again.

"Let's all go and wait in reception for Bella," Hugo said, adding, "including you young man," as he grabbed Juan's arm and led him out.

Dana stumbled blindly behind them, Cressida holding onto the edge of Dana's blouse, which had now – for both of them – become apron strings.

The foyer was, as yesterday, busy and noisy. Guests checking out, bags everywhere, the concierge run off his feet – answering questions, giving directions, barking orders to the porters, answering his phone, calling taxis, opening doors, directing traffic.

As they waited – Dana on a chair with Cressida practically on her lap – Hugo tried desperately not to think of anything, nothing at all. In order to remain useful and practical, he had decided not to dwell on matters until they reached the hospital, not to speculate or wonder, just to deal with the practicalities of getting them all there.

And so he looked around him – albeit with a very firm grip on Juan's arm – and observed, without thinking, his surroundings. He allowed himself to call to mind a John Wyndham novel – he was rather fond of his books – *The Midwich Cuckoos*. He remembered that it had also been made into a film, although for some reason they had called it *Village of the Damned*, probably in homage to the Hollywood money that had facilitated it. Anyway, he recalled reading the bit where the protagonist is confronted by the children, who could read minds, and challenged about his thoughts, which he was trying to conceal, mainly because he planned later to blow them all to smithereens. But because he was suppressing his thoughts, all the children could "read" was that he was thinking about a brick wall – because that was all the protagonist would allow himself to think.

It wasn't Clint Eastwood, but it was a jolly good substitute, Hugo decided, as he stood there with Juan under house arrest. All he would allow himself to think about until they got to the hospital was – *a brick wall*.

Bella seemed to be taking an age, he speculated, as he looked towards the lifts. And fancy driving down with her eyesight! Lucky they weren't having to deal with a hospital visit there too. But stop, he told himself. The brick wall.

People were coming and going at a rate of knots today, no doubt the pleasant weather helped: nothing like a brisk stroll along the seafront to blow away the cobwebs. Hugo almost envied them their carefree Sunday. Christ. How different his was turning out to be from the one he had planned.

Juan squirmed under Hugo's hold on his arm, and so Hugo tightened his grip, didn't want the little bugger slipping away. A tall, dark man, in a spiffy suit, walked past with a guiding hand on his wife's back, he glanced at Hugo and Juan, and then at the arm that Hugo had extended around Juan, and just very faintly, nodded his head, as though in confirmation of something. He looked Hugo in the eye.

Hugo then remembered that he was in Brighton and immediately dropped Juan's arm. But it was too late, the tall, dark man in the spiffy suit – probably Savile Row, Hugo decided – smirked.

"Ponce," Hugo said under his breath.

Juan, unexpectedly released, made a movement, but Hugo was quicker – a surge of testosterone most likely being responsible, in protest to the Ponce's insinuation – and he had Juan in a vice-like hold once again.

Hugo, like most men, was probably unconscious of the role that Juan was in fact playing in this crisis. Juan – unlike the immediate life or death situation that confronted them, unlike his wife's and daughter's emotions – was a tangible thing to grab hold of and deal with. Dealing with Juan was a practicality, a problem that he could solve, it was a way of controlling the situation.

More significantly though, and Hugo was blissfully unaware of this, was that dealing with Juan meant that

Hugo did not have to confront his own emotions.

"Grandma!" Cressida said, waving to Bella who was now making her way back towards them, prodding her stick as she went, reminding Hugo of Charlton Heston in *Moses*, albeit without the beard, parting the waves of the red sea. Actually, if he was honest, there was just a hint of a beard.

Dana and Cressida stood up as Bella advanced towards them, giving Dana her coat.

"Oscar is absolutely fine, I've given him a little biscuit and left a saucer of water, and put the telly on for him," Bella said, as they moved towards the front door.

"The television?" Hugo asked.

"Yes, just in case he – well, makes any noise," Bella replied.

Waste of electricity, Hugo thought, still, at least he wasn't paying that bill.

"Fine. Darling have you got your car keys?" he asked Dana, once they were outside.

Dana rummaged in her handbag, Hugo glanced at his watch. Come on, it's at least twenty minutes since Juan had first appeared, anything could have happened in that time.

Stop it. Brick wall. He tried to relax.

"Will we all fit?" Bella asked.

"Of course," Hugo answered.

"There are five of us," she said again.

"The car has five seat belts Bella, plenty of room."

Juan muttered something about getting the bus and meeting them there.

Hugo pulled him back by the collar, if his back hadn't been playing up, he'd have given him a boot in the backside to go with it.

Dana found the keys and handed them over. "Have you got the ticket to get out of the car park?" she asked him.

Hugo patted his jacket pocket. "Yes, just checked that. Let's go."

They descended the steps of the hotel, and turned right towards the NCP, walking first briskly, and then breaking into a jog, Bella bringing up the rear with Cressida at her side.

Thankfully the car park was deserted. Hugo located the ticket machine, inserted the ticket, and then – despite the gravity of the situation – winced slightly at the price displayed.

Fuck, no wonder it was deserted, who could afford to park at these prices? He inserted his plastic and continued to think of the brick wall, might just adopt it as his new motto.

The machine spat out the ticket and a receipt, and they all hurried towards Dana's car, which sat in bay number 105, with windows frosted by condensation.

"I'll drive," Hugo announced, opening the driver's door.

The others had to stand and wait, as the central locking had long since stopped working properly.

Once opened, Dana got in the front beside Hugo, and Juan – now prisoner-like – sat in the middle of the back seat, flanked by the guards Bella and Cressida.

Hugo shivered – the car was cold, it would be, he supposed, having sat there since Friday night – and proceeded to clear the windows by wiping them vigorously with a large yellow micro-fibre cloth.

"Start the engine Hugo, it's freezing," Dana said.

"Yes, yes but it's no good if I can't see where I am going." He continued to wipe.

Dana got out some tissues and tried wiping her side of the window.

Finally Hugo turned the key in the ignition.

Nothing.

Hugo smiled nervously and turned the key again.

There was a little gasp from the engine, as though someone had cranked a ratchet one or two notches.

Hugo concentrated hard and turned the key again.

Nothing.

"Pull the choke out!" Bella commanded from the back.

Hugo turned around in his seat, forgetting his back.

"Cars haven't had chokes since the 90s Bella, modern cars don' have them," Hugo told her irritably.

"I know but this isn't a modern car, is it?" she replied.

Hugo let out a very long breath and turned back around in his seat.

"It just needs to warm up, that's all," he said.

He turned the key in the ignition again.

Nothing. Not even a gasp this time.

"What's wrong with the car Daddy?" Cressida asked.

"I'm not sure sweetheart."

Hugo was very sure what was wrong, knew without a shadow of a doubt what the problem was.

"The jumps," a little voice said from the back seat.

They all looked at Juan. "Jumping wires," he added.

Hugo glared at him.

"And what exactly do you suggest we connect the 'jumping wires' to?" Hugo asked him.

Juan sat back even smaller in his seat.

"The place isn't exactly chock-a-block with other cars, is it?" Hugo added.

He turned the key again, although he now knew it was futile.

"Stop doing that!" Dana said, shouting.

Everyone froze.

Hugo withdrew the key from the ignition very slowly.

"You didn't do it, did you?" she said.

Hugo knew better than to reply. He sunk a little in his own seat.

Brick wall.

"You didn't charge the battery, did you?"

No sense in saying anything, he decided.

"Like I asked you on Friday. You didn't charge it, did you Hugo?"

Dana turned to face him.

Hugo looked down at the steering wheel and shook his head very slowly. He wasn't an idiot. Several thoughts came into his head. He had intended to charge the battery but it had slipped his mind, what with fixing the lock and everything. Random words and phrases passed through his consciousness, among them – "last straw". But no sense in dwelling on the negatives.

Brick wall, he decided.

"Well it's no good sitting here arguing," Bella said from the back, "we'll have to go in my car."

She got out, and was swiftly followed by Cressida and Juan – the latter, judging by the look on his face, eager for any opportunity to escape such confined quarters.

Dana sat for a few seconds staring at Hugo.

"When all this is resolved we need to have a talk," she said, as she undid her seat belt and got out.

Hugo followed her and locked the car. He still held the parking ticket in his hand, and wondered, briefly, if he would have to make the payment all over again when they eventually got the car going.

"Where's your car Mum?" Dana asked.

"Outside the hotel, in front of the entrance."

They were all walking towards the car park exit. Hugo stopped.

"So we passed by it on our way here?" Hugo asked her.

"Yes," Bella replied, "I have a disabled badge, so I can park it anywhere."

Hugo spread his hands in exasperation and laughed.

"But why didn't you say so?" He asked.

"Because you insisted that Dana's car had five seat belts, and therefore plenty of room. My car is a mini and it has four seat belts, remember?"

Hugo just shook his head, he daren't glare at Bella.

Juan, Hugo observed, listened to this latest exchange with a glimmer of hope, but Hugo grabbed his arm again.

"And don't you even bloody well think about the bus again – Bella's car also has a trunk, if need be," he told him.

Juan looked wild-eyed – almost as if he could attest to the confines of such a space from previous experience.

They hurried on back towards the hotel, and would have provided a casual observer with more than a moment's pause, such was the spectacle they presented: Hugo marching arm in arm with Juan, Cressida still hanging onto her mother's blouse, and Bella now hobbling behind with her white stick.

After some minutes, they reached Bella's brown Mini, parked up directly outside the hotel entrance, her blue badge prominently displayed. Hugo wouldn't have been surprised to have seen it wheel-clamped, in fact would been secretly delighted, if the circumstances demanding its use were not so grave.

But the mini was unencumbered, and Hugo knew that it would start perfectly first time. Bella maintained her car meticulously and had it serviced regularly. Hugo had offered once to undertake the maintenance for her, but Bella had declined for some reason, saying that her man at the garage was reliable – whatever that was supposed to infer. Anyway it was up to her if she wanted to fritter away her money, he could have done a perfectly capable job of changing the oil, topping up the anti-freeze and putting air in the tyres. It was her loss. And then he remembered Dana's car. But that had just been a slip-up, and no sense dwelling on it now.

Brick wall.

"Let Hugo drive Mum," Dana said, when they got to the car.

"I'm perfectly capable," Bella protested.

"Yes, but the traffic is heavy and you don't know the way," Dana said.

Bella sighed and tossed Hugo the keys, saying, "Neither does he."

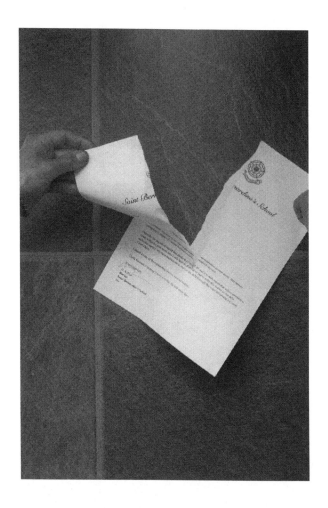

TWENTY

They ran through the automatic doors marked Emergency. Then a second set stood in their path. Hugo grabbed the handle and pushed, even though a sign cautioned Automatic Door – Do Not Push.

It slowed their opening. It slowed them down.

They forced their way through in a rush. And then stopped suddenly when confronted by a queue of people, pressing against a glass-fronted reception desk. A small crowd waited as a lone receptionist took infinitesimal details. Pointless, innocuous, tedious, time-consuming details.

Dana walked forward.

"Excuse me!" said a raucous, overweight woman in tight leggings, "we're all waiting."

Dana stood there pale, shaking, trying to gear up for a confrontation. Failing in every way, as her grief overwhelmed her.

The other people in the queue stood. Watching, but they held their ground firmly. Wouldn't budge.

Hugo stepped in front of Dana, and looked at the

raucous woman, her greasy hair scraped back in a tight, untidy knot on her head. Her face contorted with indignation, even the spots on her bad skin burning an angry red.

"Terribly sorry to barge in like this, but the doctor said that if her Ebola symptoms came back to go straight to the hospital without delay." Hugo pointed to Dana as he spoke.

The floor cleared immediately. Those in the queue scattered like rabbits. Muttering that they would take a seat in the waiting room.

The raucous woman edged backwards without taking her eyes off Dana, and said that she'd take some paracetamol after all, and maybe come back tomorrow.

Hugo gently, but firmly, moved Dana to one side, and explained to the receptionist why they were there. The woman behind the glass took his name and told him to take a seat in the waiting area while she got the doctor to come and see them.

Dana still stood. Stricken. Speechless.

Hugo led her away.

The pervading air was not one of misery or despair. No one was dying. No one lay on life support. There wasn't even any blood. An old woman in a wheelchair, with a leg in bandages and three teeth, cackled at a joke cracked by a nurse at her feet. A man with a little boy shook his head and smiled when someone asked how the child had trapped his finger inside the tin money-box.

A middle-aged woman laughed as she knitted beside her young pregnant daughter, who stretched the half finished, little blue wool jacket across her substantial belly. A man in white painting overalls lay propped up on a trolley, sipping steaming tea from a styrofoam cup.

The grey rubber floor squeaked when people walked across it. The drinks machine in the corner hummed. A small black TV screen, mounted high on the wall, played a series of infomercials about flu and hygiene. A paramedics radio squeaked, "A new call Dave, time to go." The sound of the hot-air dryers came on intermittently as the lavatory door nearby was opened and closed.

It wasn't right. It didn't feel right.

Alex was in here dead, or dying, somewhere.

How could people be laughing?

How could they carry on as normal? It was all wrong. Everything was all wrong.

One by one they all sat down on red, glossy, metal chairs. Welded to the floor. In a row. Dana. Hugo. Bella. Cressida. Juan. Lined up like nine pins against the wall.

Waiting for the wrecking ball.

Hugo asked if Dana wanted a coffee?

A coffee? Was he mad? He might just as well have asked her if she wanted to go paragliding.

She wanted her Alex.

She'd written a poem once, when he was very small – *My Boy*. It was a bit silly really, and she couldn't remember why she had done it. When she read it back to herself she felt embarrassed. She'd never shown it to anyone except Alex. She'd read it out to him when he was six. He had said he didn't really understand it, but it was lovely Mummy, just like you. Dana tried to recall it now:

A month late
he'd turn out never to be one to keep to a date

Dirty Weekend in Brighton

Such fun to be with on family days out
always seeking a thrill
From the helter and skelter to a giant tidal wave
which often made Mum lose a little more will

Summer days by the salty sea
with bucket and spade and then fish and chips
always wanting to stay longer - please Mummy can we?

Fully awake, at rest, or in slumber
he rarely resisted a mother's embrace

Gentle goodnight kisses always soft and warm
Fragrant with powder and then after shave
Whatever Mum wanted he gave it with grace

And when he fell over with tumbling wet tears
his mother was there to soothe and care

Then he grew more, with shoulders big and wide
making his own choices, some of them wise

Soon he became the one to soothe and embrace
when his mother's trembling lip doubted the news of his leaving

No lateness this time for two separate journeys
one filled with hope
and one long remembered
with cheers for the cup, birthday bright candles, wet salty tears
and a mother's grieving
please son – can we stay a little longer?'

Time went by. How much Dana couldn't tell. A trolley with wonky wheels screeched by. Names were called. People with bandaged fingers, sprained ankles, arms in slings, stepped forward.

A child prattled looking at a book.

Curtains round a cubicle were opened and closed, the metal rings scraping along the overhead rail.

A stethoscope was dropped.

There was the sound of a soft knock at a closed door.

A snapping on of latex gloves.

An unanswered phone ringing in the distance.

Dana closed her eyes and tried to listen to the silence underneath it all.

"Mr and Mrs Robinson?" a gentle voice enquired.

Dana heard words, but didn't take them in. She felt Hugo shake her arm. She opened her eyes.

"Alexander Robinson's parents?" a slim, older woman in a light blue uniform asked.

Dana jumped up out of her chair, her coat and bag falling onto the floor, her left heel crushing the Gucci logo underfoot.

Cressida held a hand over her mouth, her face tear-stained.

Bella pulled herself to her feet leaning on her stick, her dependence on it no longer feigned.

Juan remained seated, his head in his hands.

Dana opened her mouth to say, "Yes – is he? is he—" but it was a whisper, barely audible. She wanted to hear what the nurse had to say, and yet she didn't want to listen to a word of it.

Hugo stood up, and putting his hand into Dana's answered, "Yes we are, is there any news?"

Not one of them, at that moment, wouldn't have sold their soul to the devil to have been anywhere else than where they were now.

The nurse pursed her lips – it wasn't a smile and it wasn't a grimace – it was, her job. She put her hand on Dana's arm, very gently. Dana's knees weakened a little. Cressida let out a little cry, and immediately stifled it by clamping her other hand over the one already on her mouth.

"He's in a recovery room and the doctor will see you shortly with more information."

"Recovery?" Dana managed to ask.

He was alive then. He was alive.

"So what happened? How is he? Will he be okay? Can we see him?" Hugo's relief was palpable, as his words tumbled out.

The nurse was about to respond, when the old lady with the three teeth tipped out of her wheelchair onto the floor. The nurse rushed over to help, and said over her shoulder, "I've just come on duty so I don't have all the details yet, but the doctor will be with you soon."

Then, with the aid of another nurse, she got the old lady onto a trolley and whisked her off down the corridor.

"But – can't we, can't we see him?" Hugo asked no one in particular.

"Oh goodness," Bella said, "what does all that mean?"

Cressida had rallied slightly and added, "It means he's okay, doesn't it? Alex is going to be okay, isn't he Daddy?"

Hugo looked confused for a moment or two, but then he patted Cressida on the shoulder and agreed. "Yes darling he will be fine."

Juan raised his head, straightened up in his chair. Cut his eyes from Cressida to Hugo and back again.

"That's not what she said though, is it?" Dana's voice was tinged with annoyance. "Why can't she give us more information? I don't understand it."

Hugo spread his hands. "The doctor will be here in a moment and we'll know what's happening then."

"They can't just leave us waiting here." Dana looked around at the others.

No one had an answer, or at least one that was helpful.

"They're very busy," Hugo said.

"But surely we can have more information than that?" Bella asked.

"All in good time, Bella, you know what these hospitals are like, probably some emergency they have to deal with first. The nurse said the doctor would come and see us, so we will just have to wait," Hugo told her.

Dana didn't care how busy they were, at this moment – God forgive her – she didn't care about anyone else in the world. Just her Alex. Everyone in the entire hospital could be critical for all she cared. Only one person mattered. Only one person warranted the busy staff's attention.

Dana gave Hugo a look. It was one she rarely used, mostly because it tended to shatter the peace. But some occasions called for it. And this was one of them. She didn't need to say anything because this look said it all: I won't be placated, I won't be patronised, I won't be contradicted, I will brook no argument, I will listen to no other point of view, in this instance I am right and my word shall be final.

As Dana stared at him she saw recognition in his eyes.

Hugo knew the look. He'd been on the business end of it on precisely three occasions in his married life – the first when the house had nearly been repossessed because he hadn't paid the mortgage for five months without telling Dana, the second when he suggested that his mother should come and live with them, and the third when he suggested that Dana pursue a full-time partner's career in her law firm and he stay at home and be the "homemaker".

And now there was a fourth time.

He visibly blanched at the look, and said, "But of course not too busy to inform us about what is going on."

Everyone remained standing.

"I'll see what I can find out," Hugo said, moving towards the reception desk.

They all watched him walk over and wait while a teenager, with a bloodied tea towel held to his scalp and a skateboard under his arm, was dealt with by the receptionist. Then Hugo stepped forward, spoke, nodded and came back over to them.

"The receptionist says all the information she has is that Alex was admitted at five this morning and is in no immediate danger." Hugo looked a little pale.

"Five o'clock? What on earth was he doing at that time?" Bella asked in a loud voice.

All eyes turned on Juan, who put his head back into his hands.

"No immediate danger! What the hell is that supposed to mean? That he was in immediate danger but is no longer? What kind of danger?" Dana's voice was shrill.

Hugo stood impotent. "I don't know, that's all she said," he responded softly.

"Well I'm not having that!" Dana said.

She went to stride over to reception, when both Hugo and Cressida put an arm on her.

"Mum wait, please don't make a scene, it'll only make things worse. The doctor will be out in a minute, please Mum." Cressida turned appealing eyes to Dana.

At that moment Dana almost hated them all. Their weakness. Their acceptance. Their trust in the system. Dana didn't trust anything. Neither did her Alex. He questioned things, took nothing on face value.

If Alex were here he would back his mum up, he would demand answers, he would get them.

If Alex were here.

"It might be better to wait dear," Bella said, "I come to these places every month for my clinics, and if the receptionist says that is all she knows then it probably is. They have their procedures, their routines. If it was anything life-threatening they would have you in a room now talking to you." Bella put her hand on her daughter's arm and smiled.

Dana faltered, nodded her head slowly.

"Okay, but I'm only giving them twenty minutes at the most, then I want to see my son."

Bella sat back into her chair heavily. Cressida gave Juan a look of pure revulsion, and sat beside her grandmother.

"Anyone want a coffee?" Hugo asked, searching his pockets for some change, "I think I saw a Costa Coffee machine sign up there." He pointed down the corridor.

There were muttered negatives from everyone.

Dana raised her eyebrows and looked at him.

"No, you're right. Probably best to just wait here."

Hugo sat down, deflated.

Dana remained standing.

A name was called out. The heavily pregnant woman stood up with her mother, the latter looking around, smiling at Dana. Expectant, not in the maternity sense, but expectant of a congratulatory smile, an indulgent look, the way pregnant woman and their relatives always looked – thinking that the whole world was as overjoyed as they were at the happy event to come. One was supposed to *coo* and grin, and give up seats on the train, and hold doors open, or help with heavy shopping bags, or give up a place in a queue, or let them use the toilet first in public lavatories. Complete strangers were expected to act like blood relatives, and share in the joy and the practicalities.

And that wasn't the end of it. When the baby was born one was expected to *coo* again, and say *ahh*, and to give up seats on trains, hold doors open, carry one end of the buggy up or down stairs, petition Parliament for breast feeding zones in public places – well maybe not the latter, but it felt like it.

Dana didn't smile this time and she didn't *coo* or think *ahh*. She gave the pregnant woman's mother a cold stare. The earth would still be spinning whether the baby was born or not. It didn't make any difference to her. The pregnant woman was so engrossed by her condition, so self-indulgent of her swollen belly, and her birth plan no doubt, that she didn't even notice Dana and her family waiting with dread behind her. If the pregnant woman didn't care about Alex, then Dana didn't care about her. They had nothing else to worry about except bean bags for the labour, sonic whale music for the birth, knitted booties and baby powder. Sod them Dana thought. Sod them.

Dana stared harder at the mother, the latter looked away, confused and surprised by the ferocity of Dana's look.

They bustled off into a cubicle, the knitting being hastily stuffed into a bag as they walked away.

Oh my God, Dana thought, when did I become so cynical? It's almost nasty. She tried to remember when she had been pregnant, how she had felt. It seemed such a long time ago. Had she felt special? Had she expected people to treat her like she was special, to be excited about her condition? She couldn't remember. Probably. Yes, she probably had felt special. She remembered when she had been carrying Alex. At first she had felt in awe, and then later mostly tired. But when she really thought about it, she hadn't needed to expect anyone else to treat her like she was special, because that is what people did automatically, naturally.

Dana remembered shopping in Waitrose one day when she had been heavily pregnant, and an older lady had come around the corner with a shopping basket and banged into her "bump". It was just a gentle knock but the lady had been so upset, so genuinely upset at what she called her own stupidity, the lady had gently stroked Dana's bump and insisted on taking her for a nice cup of tea, to make sure she was all right. In fact Dana wasn't worried at all, she didn't really know anything about being pregnant, and supposed that the baby was well protected, which in reality it was.

The lady was lovely. They had Earl Grey tea and walnut cake, and the lady told Dana all about her little dog who was like a child to her, she hoped Dana didn't think her silly. She had always wanted a real child, but it never happened she said.

People could be nice, they could be more than nice. Strangers often were the kindest. Those closest to us, sometimes just useless. Dana looked across at Hugo, who had got his manuscript out of his briefcase and was making corrections and notes. Probably trying to please me, she thought, and take his mind off things. Hugo looked up at Dana and half smiled. Like a schoolboy, seeking praise, or at least not punishment.

Dana sighed. Three children. She had three children, two she had given birth to, and one she had married.

Birth. They had been events. Alex's the worst. He had been a month late and Dana had been belligerent even then. Wouldn't hear of being induced. Until it had gone over the month and become very necessary. Alex had taken a long time to arrive. Dana had refused any pain relief, there was almost an intervention – a surgeon hovering outside the door with a forceps kit – but in the end Dana had done it herself.

Hugo, Dana remembered, had spent most of his time in the delivery room doing his VAT return. Another business that didn't last the course. Still, he hadn't been much use during the labour anyway, so completing his VAT return was as good an activity as any other. It had meant that Dana could concentrate on the task at hand, without having to worry about him too.

But when Alex had finally arrived she had been overwhelmed. She remembered holding him minutes later, wrapped in a white sheet, both of them. She had looked into his eyes, and he had stared right back at her and she remembered thinking that this boy would be no one's fool, he would be smart, the way he looked at her even then. Dana didn't know if new babies all looked at their mothers like that for the first time, but she could have sworn that Alex was thinking even then, like her looking at him, both of them weighing up the situation, working out what was to come.

And Hugo had been clueless, loving and caring, but clueless. When Alex was three weeks old, Dana remembered sitting downstairs in the sitting room with a cup of tea, resting, while Hugo took care of bath time and changing. She was just looking out at the garden thinking about planting a new tree before autumn, when Hugo came rushing down the stairs, holding Alex at arm's length with both hands, and giving him to Dana. Alex was screaming and Hugo was breathless. "He just rolled off the bed while I was getting a nappy," Hugo said.

Tiny baby Alex had a cut on his lip and was bleeding. Dana had gone numb. But in the end it was just a nick, no serious damage.

Dana knew that new born babies don't roll, Hugo had dropped him, or more likely put him so close to the edge of the bed, that when Hugo sat down on it Alex just plopped off the side. Hugo was distraught and never changed a nappy again.

And now they were here. Not sure why, only that it couldn't be good. Things happen to teenagers – on the football field, in cars, on dangerous streets, on rugby fields. Bad things that change everything. A friend of a friend had a son who played rugby, and then one day at the age of eighteen he couldn't play any more. He couldn't do anything any more. His parents, or more likely his mother, returned to changing nappies fifteen years later.

What the fuck were they doing back there? Dana looked over to the emergency treatment area – a row of doors and a narrow opening in the wall, with a sign that stated No Admission, she could see doctors and nurses rushing about in all directions. Alex was back there somewhere.

"What the fuck are they doing?" Dana asked.

"Dana dear, language," Bella said, looking over anxiously at Cressida.

"She's heard worse than that Mum, says worse than that," Dana replied, "but what are they doing?"

"It's only been like four minutes Mum," Cressida said, "and actually I never use the F-word." She looked offended.

"It can't be four minutes, must be longer," Dana challenged.

"It is four minutes, I'm timing it," Hugo added, without looking up from his manuscript.

"*Por favour Señora* but it is four minutes and thirty-five *secondo*."

Everyone looked up. Juan had spoken. He still sat, head in hands.

Everyone glared at him.

And what the fuck is he doing here? Dana asked herself.

"Why are you still here?" Dana asked in Juan's direction.

There was silence.

Juan looked up.

"I said" – Dana moved towards him – "what are you

still doing here?"

Juan opened his mouth, no words came out.

"It's all your bloody fault anyway," Dana continued.

"Dana please! Swearing won't help anyone," Bella admonished again.

"It will bloody well help me," Dana replied.

Juan spread his hands, then brought them together and wrung them. His eyes a little wider now.

"Isn't it?" Dana asked him.

Juan opened his mouth again, and again nothing came out.

"How would your mother feel, hey? Sitting here, with you in there." Dana nodded her head towards the emergency area.

Juan shook his head.

"And don't bloody well pretend you don't understand me," she added.

He said nothing.

"So, how would she feel, your mother, thinking that you were dead? How would she feel?"

Dana was standing over him now with tears in her eyes, her voice cracking.

Juan nodded his head, wouldn't meet her eyes.

"Shall I tell you how it feels, do you want to know? How a mother feels?" Dana had tears running down her cheeks.

"*Señora*, I—" Juan said.

Dana kicked his foot with hers.

"Dana! Please, I know you are upset but—" Bella heaved herself up, leaning on her stick.

"I'm speaking to you," Dana raised her voice a little.

Juan looked ready to bolt.

Dana kicked his foot again, harder this time.

"Mum!" Cressida stood up now.

"I'll tell you, shall I? So that you can call your mother and tell her how it feels to think she has lost a son." Dana was crouching down, leaning over him.

"It hurts here!" Dana tapped Juan's head.

Juan recoiled.

"And it hurts here!" She poked the lid of his eye.

"But most of all, it hurts here!" Dana stabbed at his chest.

If there had been a hole in the ground Juan looked like he would have jumped into it.

Dana put her hands over her eyes and turned away. Bella went to take her arm, but Dana resisted it. She turned around with her back to them all, and her shoulders shook.

Not a word was uttered for several minutes.

Everyone stood, everyone waited. Dana composed herself. She wiped her eyes and sniffed, ran the back of her sleeve over her nose, something she only did when out running. She didn't care now. She turned around.

"Anyway, blame won't change anything. What's done is done. But I do want to know why you are still here?" Dana asked in an icy cold voice, all hot emotion now gone. Juan jumped up, obviously sensing an opportunity to escape.

"*Sí, Señora*, I understand, Juan go now and leave the family in privates," he said.

Hugo sprung forward, and in a flash he had hold of Juan by the scruff of the neck, bad back notwithstanding.

"You'll do no such thing, my man. You will stay exactly where you are. And face the consequences, whatever they may be," he said.

And with that, Hugo moved his hand to Juan's shoulder and pushed him back down into the chair.

Things might be rough in Colombia if you were in the wrong company, but it was as nothing compared to events unfolding now.

Juan resumed his previous position, head in hands, only now he was shaking a little too.

In his burst of action, Hugo had sent his briefcase and manuscript crashing to the floor, and now his research pages, post-it notes and chapter headings were strewn at their feet.

It broke the tension, and with a certain measure of relief everyone, except Juan, bent down to help pick them up, with Bella stabbing at the odd page with the tip of her stick, being unable to get on her hands and knees to assist.

Cressida assembled a neat pile of pages, attempting to put them in numbered order, Dana took handfuls of pages – some with only a few words scrawled on them, some photocopied articles, and some in French with the odd word translated in biro at the top – Hugo was stuffing it all back into his briefcase. Cressida handed him her neat pile and smiled at him. Dana shoved a sheaf of what she had gathered into his hand, and bent down to grab a few stray, bright pink post-its near the chair, ripping one that was lodged under the metal edge of the chair leg. She slapped that on top of what Hugo was already holding.

He seems to have a lot of paperwork anyway, remains to be seen what he will make of it. Mincemeat probably, Dana decided.

Why can't he just get a real job? Might manage to get a night's sleep then, rather than worrying constantly. What does a writer of athletics textbooks make anyway? Dana wondered, more than a writer of athletic textbook research notes. And more than nothing wouldn't be difficult.

Cressida sat back down. Juan was now massaging his temples. Hugo sat down and hung the strap of his briefcase across the back of his chair. Dana sat down.

Bella remained standing. She wasn't leaning on her stick, she was leaning on the back of her chair.

"Sit down Mum, you'll get too tired standing up," Dana said.

"Do you want to sit on my coat Grandma?" Cressida asked, "the metal is quite cold and uncomfortable."

"You missed one," Bella said.

"What?" Cressida asked.

"You missed one," Bella repeated.

Dana looked up.

"One what?" Dana asked.

Bella was looking down at the floor, tapping her stick.

"One of Hugo's papers."

Hugo looked up.

Bella prodded her stick up and down.

"Doesn't look like a page for a book though," Bella continued.

Everyone looked down at Bella's feet.

"What is it?" Dana asked.

"Looks like a letter," Bella said.

Hugo sprung to his feet.

"From the school," Bella continued.

Dana stood up.

Hugo lunged forward to grab the letter.

Bella drove the white stick down savagely, its tip

skewering the letter.

Dana bent down beside it. She looked at it on the floor under the stick. She locked eyes with Hugo who was bent down on the other side of the stick.

Dana put her hand on the top of the letter, Hugo put his hand on the bottom, they both pulled. The letter tore in half.

Dana stood up with one half, Hugo with the other.

Cressida said, "Well it can't be about me, I haven't done anything wrong. I haven't had detention for two years."

"From the looks of it, I don't think that is the only thing that hasn't happened for two years," Bella said, sitting down again.

Dana stood reading her half of the letter, and then grabbed the other half from Hugo and read that. She nodded her head, very slowly, up and down, several times. She turned to face Hugo. He swallowed hard. For the fifth time in his married life, he was staring down the barrel of The Look.

"Dana, I, look – I got the letter, it was delivered, I mean it arrived just, it just arrived. I was going to tell you, I didn't want to spoil your birthday, look, I—"

"The letter is dated seven days ago," Dana said.

"Yes but—"

"Ten thousand pounds," she replied, in a whisper.

Hugo looked down at the floor.

"Ten thousand," she repeated, a little louder.

Cressida looked up.

"Ten – ten – ten thousand pounds!" Dana shouted.

Cressida jumped. Juan looked up, cut his eyes from Hugo to Dana.

Hugo looked around the waiting room, made a tiny motion with his hand to silence her.

"How could you," Dana shouted again. It wasn't a question.

Hugo looked stricken. Juan looked confused: it was clearly nothing to do with him, but it was trouble nonetheless.

"Dana I—"

Dana cut him off, "It was all you had to do. The only thing you had to worry about. Top up the fees, I do everything else: the mortgage, the council tax, the fuel bills, the cars, the food, the insurance, the phones, the school trips, all of it. All you have to do is pay some money every month, that's all."

"I just got a little behind, I—" Hugo mumbled.

"A little behind? £10,000, Hugo, is not 'a little behind'! It's a national debt where he comes from," Dana said, kicking Juan's chair.

Juan jerked.

"I'll soon catch up, once the book is finished..." Hugo said, his voice trailing off.

"Ha!" Dana laughed, but without any mirth. "Oh yes, the book. The fucking book. That'll do it, Jesus, I'd forgotten about the book, well of course, stupid me, why was I worrying? The book, that'll sort it! Solve all our problems!

"Only problem is you are not actually writing it, are you? There's a lot of talk, and a whole lot of research, and by God a whole lot of notes, but no actual, honest-to-goodness fucking writing going on, is there? But hang on – don't panic, 'it's early days yet.'" Dana mimicked a hearty laugh and drew breath. "Early days – these things can't be rushed, can they, all in good time, hey Hugo? Like the lock on the sodding front door, like your sodding parents' ashes – that was another financial catastrophe, wasn't it? Couldn't even bury the fuckers without a debt collector's letter, all in good time. Like the battery on my car, like the, like" – Dana looked wildly around the room – "the sodding hole, in the sodding fence, that killed the sodding cat!

"But all in the fullness of time, no rush, in due sodding course, manyana – in fact you'd be more at home with him" – Dana kicked Juan's chair again – "where manyana is a way of life!"

Hugo took a step back, shoulders slumped.

"I only meant that when it's finished I can concentrate on getting more – lucrative – employment," he said.

"*More* lucrative? What? As opposed to the only marginally lucrative employment you currently have? Is that what you mean?"

"I acknowledge that my present coaching job is not highly paid and—"

"Not highly paid? Are you joking? It's not a fucking job Hugo, it's" – Dana paused for breath and shouted – "a fucking hobby!"

Cressida sat terror stricken in the chair, clutching Juan's arm. Juan looked like he would have taken the option of a firing squad, rather than sit listening to this.

Bella said not one word nor betrayed one emotion.

"I do my best," Hugo said, but the mistake of uttering these words was evidenced by the rapidly desaturating colour of his face.

"Your best? Oh well, if you want to talk about doing your best." Dana threw her arms up in the air and back down again. "Then let's please talk about that."

"I only meant I do my best for the family," he said.

"Really. And doing your best for your family includes putting them into incalculable debt, having your children thrown out of school, and jeopardising the roof over their heads, does it? Is that *doing your best*? Oh no wait – I forgot, you have plans, of course. Apart from the book, there's the French olive oil importation business, isn't there? Hugo The Importer, importing French olive oil based upon sound market research. The result of that research being – import it because – no one else is doing it! Bingo. Why didn't anyone one else come up with that money-spinning idea? Hugo must be a genius!"

Dana drew breath. Everyone else held theirs.

"Oh, and let's not forget the soap. Yes of course, the French olive oil soap – you are going to make a fortune importing that too. Because, and there it is again, that market research – no one else is doing it! Sound business reasoning – I bet they don't teach that on the MBA at Harvard. There are no flies on you, are there Hugo?"

Hugo was leaning against the toilet wall opposite.

"Yes, yes, I can see the success now that it will all bring, riches beyond our wildest dreams – best selling author, importation entrepreneur, all our worries will be over. Dana needn't worry, silly Dana, leave it all to Hugo. He'll sort it out, just like the paint brush design patent, only that didn't work out so well, did it? Shame we had to spend £12,000 on patents before we realised the Chinese were already doing it. Oh yes, and let's not forget the organic produce delivery business, wasn't your fault you bought the sign-written van before noticing that Tesco and Sainsbury's did it for half the price."

Dana's hands were balled by her sides and her face was crimson.

"In fact, I think I can just give up work now. No more early a.m. starts in the office or late p.m. finishes for me. No. My future looks rosy. No, I don't need to worry, do I? The school are just bluffing, aren't they? They're not really going to issue a County Court Summons in the next seven days, are they?"

Hugo was pale against the dark wall.

"I don't need to worry, because," Dana screamed, "Hugo, my husband, will take care of everything. *There are no fucking flies on him!*"

The waiting room, previously as loud as a bar on a wild Saturday night, was now silent.

Someone coughed quietly, trying to stifle it. A few people had walked away. The teenager with the skateboard smirked. A skinny, worn looking woman in a cleaner's uniform looked daggers at Hugo. Cressida sat wild-eyed, and Juan was now holding her hand and whispering into her ear.

Hugo slumped down onto his haunches.

No one said anything. Enough had been said. If it was too much then time would tell.

Dana's phone pinged in her pocket.

Then a cheery, Scottish voice said from behind, "Alexander's family?"

Everyone turned to look at a young, rosy-cheeked doctor in rolled-up shirt sleeves, with a stethoscope round his neck.

Everyone got to their feet to face him.

"He's up to visitors now, so if you want to follow me, you can see him." The Scottish doctor turned on his heel and they all followed.

They walked behind the doctor, single file, through the gap in the wall with the sign that read – No Admission, past a nursing station, monitors on wheels, drips, cubicles, doctors, nurses, computers, blood-pressure monitors, trolleys, boxes of medical instruments, gloves, hand sanitiser. Monitors beeped, phones rang, people called out. The nerve centre of the hospital. Organised chaos.

The doctor led them to a door, half solid, half obscured glass.

"He's just in here, having a wee rest," he said.

He opened the door. Dana, Hugo, Cressida, Bella and Juan looked in.

Alex lay on a couch, in a pale-blue hospital gown, a canula inserted in his hand to which a drip of something was connected, the index finger of his right hand clamped to a pulse monitor. When he had been born, he had had a little jaundice and had looked suntanned, Dana remembered. Now he was as white as the sheet he lay against. His eyes were blood shot when he opened them.

Dana fell upon him. Her heart hurt. She had a pain in it. She couldn't cry, she could only hold him.

Hugo did cry but then coughed to conceal it. Patted Alex on the shoulder, very gently.

Cressida burst into floods of tears and was consoled by Juan.

Bella shook her head.

"Hi," Alex said, very weakly to everyone.

"What's wrong with him?" Dana asked, still buried in Alex's arms.

"Well, a wee spot of alcohol poisoning," the cheery Scottish doctor said from the door – there not being

391

enough room for him, the patient, and the five visitors.

"Ahh," Hugo said.

"Aye," the doctor confirmed.

"Alex," Dana muttered.

"And will he be okay?" Hugo asked, "is there any, um, long-term damage?"

"Ach, noh, he's had gastric lavage − a stomach pump − and IV fluids to rehydrate him as you can see there, but no long-term damage. We've seen much worse, I can tell you. Not to be repeated though, is it fella?"

"No," Alex responded limply.

"Thank you God," Dana muttered again.

"And if his mate there hadn't acted so quickly and done what he did, well as I say, not to be repeated," the doctor added.

Everyone turned to look at Juan who cracked a smile. Dana grudgingly looked up at him, but wouldn't have been surprised if she had seen a gold tooth glinting in the bright light of the room. There wasn't, only very white, straight teeth. Someone had taken care to look after his orthodontic health as a child.

"How long will he have to stay in hospital doctor?" Dana asked, turning towards the door.

"He'll be good to go later today, we just need to monitor him for a wee bit, he'll need to rest, so straight to bed young man, I'll leave you folks for a few minutes."

The doctor turned to go and Alex said, "Thanks doc."

The doctor came back into the room, squeezed past the others, and high-fived Alex.

"No problem mate," he said, adding to Dana, "you've got a good lad there, despite the teenage stunts, most lads would have been more worried about a telling-off from their parents, rather than how their mum would worry."

Alex was left to rest, and the others traipsed off to get another, or rather a proper, breakfast in the cafeteria. Dana said she would catch them up. She wanted to get some air outside, clear her head.

Outside, the pregnant woman and her mother stood waiting for a taxi. Dana stood near them. She looked over at the pregnant woman's mother. Dana smiled. The woman smiled back. Dana hesitated, and then walked over to the soon-to-be grandmother.

"I'm sorry if I wasn't very friendly earlier, it's just that, it was my son, we didn't know what had happened, or how serious it was and, well, I just didn't want you to think I was being rude."

The mother smiled warmly and shook her head. "No need to apologise, really, I did wonder if there was something serious wrong, you all looked so terribly worried. Of course you wouldn't be smiling, so don't be silly. Is everything okay?"

"Yes," Dana replied, "he'll be fine, a bit of a teenage thing and very stupid of him, but boys will be boys, they go out late at night and drink and well, end up here." Dana waved her hand at the door.

"Ah, yes, boys can be a handful." The woman smiled again.

"When is your daughter's baby due?" Dana asked, looking towards the young woman.

"Any time now, it'll be all go soon!" the woman replied.

"Oh that's good, as long as everything is all right. I used to worry at the slightest thing when I was expecting, it's a worry until the baby is born safe and sound." Dana immediately regretted saying this.

The taxi arrived and the daughter called her mother over. The woman smiled at Dana and said, "Yes, safe and sound it will be. And a little bit of a challenge, but we'll cope." The woman held up one of the leaflets she was clutching.

Down's Syndrome – New Parents Guide.

As she walked down the hospital corridor, Dana thought about two things: life and death. How close we are to both – one minute living, thriving, relishing life – and the next minute it's over, shut down, switched off. And you couldn't always see it coming, in fact you never saw it coming, not necessarily the death part, because obviously if you were terminally ill that was inevitable and you could prepare – but the thing that caused it, you didn't see that coming. One minute you were living and then something hit you, or shot you, or fell on you, or stabbed you, or sometimes you ingested something that did it. And if you managed to sidestep all that, then some menacing disease was waiting in the wings to achieve the same effect.

But it was all worse, she decided, for those you left behind, because once you were dead you didn't have to worry about it, but those you left behind lived life with the death and it never ended. It got a little easier, she supposed, but the pain could never go away, certainly not the loss of a child. And it didn't matter what that child had done, what terrible things, or great things, or petty slights, or neglects of its parents – you would always mourn in the same way. Because love, parental love – a mother's love – was the only love that was truly unbiased, non-judgmental and totally forgiving.

Dana would remember that, try and remember that always now, when Alex was being demanding or difficult or there were issues at home, she would always remember this day, and how close it had been, or how close she had thought it had been.

We always say things like this, she thought, when some crisis occurs or we hear that someone has had a brush with death, we say, "We should live life to the full and appreciate every moment after this," but then life gets back to normal, and we forget in time how it felt to have been so close to losing what is precious to us. Dana vowed to remember and not forget.

Every child is precious to its mother and every child gives their parents hope – eternal optimism, even when things don't go to plan. We live our lives, to a certain extent, vicariously through our children, from the moment they are born.

And as long as they are alive, there is hope. This, Dana decided, explained in no small part the smile on the soon-to-be grandmother's face as she knitted the little blue jacket.

Dana found them all crowded around a small table in the Friends of Brighton Hospital cafeteria: the table littered with plates, muffin wrappers, teas, coffees and a half-finished glass of milk. Bella was doing a crossword puzzle from her book. Hugo and Cressida were repeating a series of words in Spanish, as Juan instructed them over an impromptu language lesson. Hugo's attempts brought laughter from Cressida, who sat very close to Juan.

"*Dante, eska, erm, gym, per favour?*" Hugo laboured over

the words, sounding like Mr Bean if he could talk.

Cressida wailed in laughter.

Juan shook his head. "No, no, no, like this – *donde es que el gimnasio favor*? *Donde*, no Dante, Dante is poet, no?"

Hugo had another go, botched it again. Everyone laughed.

Dana approached the table.

"Hi," she said, feeling like she was gate-crashing a party.

Everyone looked up, apprehensive. On tenterhooks. Hugo gave her a weak smile.

"Are you all right dear? Have you been back in to see Alex?" Bella asked.

"I'm fine. No, I was just outside getting some air, clearing my head. It's a lovely day now, bright and sunny."

"Mum, Juan has been teaching us Spanish, he says" – Cressida looked over at her dad – "some of us have more promise than others." She giggled.

Juan didn't giggle. He smiled at Cressida, and then looked up into Dana's eyes.

Hugo cleared his throat.

"Actually, I nipped back in to see Alex," Hugo said, holding his palms up to Dana to reassure her, "it's okay, he's fine. I just wanted a word with him. Juan says it is all his fault and he accepts full blame and responsibility."

Dana nodded slowly, looking at Juan.

"Except that isn't true," Hugo continued, "yes, Juan did go out to a couple of bars with Alex, and yes Juan is a bit older – only by a couple of years as it happens, not a decade. But Alex is nearly eighteen and knows right from wrong on his own. Apparently, Juan had given Alex a bottle of Aguardiente, Colombia's national drink, gift-boxed and wrapped, to give to us as a present – sort of hospitality gesture I gather.

"Anyway after the last bar, Juan said he needed to go to bed as he had work the next day and he left Alex at the door of the hotel, saying goodnight. He'd had a bit to drink fair enough, but was still coherent. Alex says he then got a notion to go and sit on the seafront and look at the sea."

Dana shuddered at the potential consequences of that action. Didn't they do something called "tombstoning" – jumping off the end of the pier?

Hugo went on, "And while he sat there on a bench, he opened the box, found the bottle and decided to have a taste. And the rest, as they say, is history. Suffice to say, Alex found the liquor to be to his liking and polished off the lot."

Dana felt sick.

Hugo cleared his throat again and continued, "But Juan felt something wasn't quite right, so when he got up to his room in the staff accommodation, he decided to nip down and make sure that Alex had got back to his room okay. He knocked and knocked, but there was no reply, so he went back outside, and for some reason – intuition if you will – he wandered across the road and found Alex slumped on a bench, on the upper promenade opposite the hotel, called an ambulance and, well here we are."

Hugo clapped Juan on the back and said, "Alex was admitted about five this morning, and Juan wanted to wait until he had some news to bring us, but I gather they wouldn't give him any as he isn't next-of-kin, so eventually he decided the best thing was to come and get us."

Juan kept his eyes glued to Dana.

Dana nodded her head very slowly.

Cressida beamed at Juan.

Dana looked away. "Right what I suggest is the following: Mum, you and Cressida get a taxi back to the hotel – God only knows what havoc Oscar is causing in the room, and Hugo and I will see you back there later, hopefully with Alex."

"I can drive back to the hotel dear and then come and fetch you later," Bella said.

"No Mum," Dana said firmly, "we've had enough excitement for one day, get a taxi and we'll call to let you know when we are leaving."

Bella got up and put her puzzle book away, muttering about how she was perfectly fine to drive. She kissed Dana goodbye and put her hand briefly on Hugo's arm, he smiled just as briefly.

Cressida hugged and kissed Hugo, saying, "Give my love to Alex, see you later."

She turned to her mother and Dana hugged her hard.

Cressida said softly in her ear, "Grandma Bella told me not to worry about school. She said as Easter was next month there might not be any eggs, but the Easter Bunny would bring something else instead. But not to tell Dad."

Then she walked after Bella, pointing out where the taxi sign was.

Juan got up and shook Hugo's hand. Dana looked up at him again. She loved him and loathed him in equal measure. Loved, only because he had saved her son's life. Loathed, because he had, well, not caused its near loss, but because he had been part of it. But she knew that wasn't a reason to hate him. And she knew she wouldn't, not for ever. She would never see him again after today, but she knew – in a part of her that she didn't yet acknowledge – that she would come to blame herself, and only herself, for what had happened. It was evidence, surely, of her failure as a mother?

Juan walked past Dana, stopped and said in a very small voice, "Sorry. *Mi culpa.* In my country we give gift to new friend – so, ahh, Aguardiente – the drink, was gift" – he shook his head – "and Alex say, your birthday" – he shook his head again – "*pero*, but – *mi culpa*, my blame."

Dana was still angry, but regretted what she had said to him earlier in the waiting room.

"It's okay," she said, "I won't tell your mother." She smiled, terse, but a smile.

Juan looked up at her. "*Mi madre está muerta.*"

Dana's Latin was better than her Spanish, but she knew what he had just said. Juan's mother would never know what it was like to lose a son, but the son knew what it was like to lose a mother. The feeling was the same.

She took his hand, squeezed it very hard and whispered to him, "Thank you. *Gracias.*"

TWENTY-ONE

Sunday nights were not the busiest in the hotel's calendar, and so securing the rooms for a third night had not been difficult, albeit not without cost either.

Bella's lack of luggage had not proved a hindrance: she hadn't lived through the war as an adult, but she was no stranger to making do and adapting, and, truth to tell, once the anxiety of the crisis had passed, she was able to enjoy being in a luxury hotel with her family safe and sound around her. At her age she had learned the true values of life.

Alex was eventually released from hospital with dire warnings of the consequences of repeating the escapade. He'd worked up an appetite during his sojourn at the Sussex County, and was looking forward to some slap-up room service. And lots of Coca Cola.

Juan had slunk off somewhere in the melee of Alex's release and he wasn't seen again, not by them at any rate. Alex had been warned by his father to ignore any and all messages from him.

Cressida kept quiet about having his phone number

and Facebook profile. What they didn't know couldn't worry them.

They had glimpsed Veronique behind reception as they had helped Alex upstairs on their return, but Bella had gone up to reception for them, while the Scottish lady with the short blonde hair had dealt with their Sunday night extension booking.

Veronique had given them a little wave, and Hugo had given a half smile in return, but by then Veronique was already dealing with a new family checking in, and didn't see it.

Oscar was very excited to see them, and Hugo had been dispatched to walk him briskly along the promenade before bed, although it was, at this stage, too late to prevent what had already been deposited on the carpet.

After a room service dinner in the mini-suite, it was decided that a good night's sleep had been earned by all, before an early start on Monday morning.

Bella took the *children's* room. After finishing a packet of shortcake biscuits and her new travelling jigsaw, she turned off a film on the adult channel, knocked back her third, mini-bar Scotch, and fell asleep.

In the mini-suite, the sofa was dragged through to the bedroom. Alex lay on it with a cold compress held to his temple. He was out cold in five minutes flat and dreamt of a raucous party held by his newly founded Riot Club, in the dining halls of his hallowed college in Oxford. With liberal quantities of champagne. Certainly no Aguardiente.

Cressida squeezed into the gap at the bottom of her parent's super king-size bed. Her hot little body wriggling, as she skipped from sleep induced H & M changing room to changing room in her new clothes.

Hugo tossed and turned into the small hours, wrestling with the numbers on the hotel bill, which grew larger with every minute – enhanced further by Oscar's attempt to rearrange the mini-suite while they were at the hospital, which included a bout of gastroenteritis, courtesy of the illicit sausage at breakfast. Eventually, Hugo was snoring until the dog, itself sleeping and nestled between him and Dana, bit him savagely, three times, when he turned over and disturbed it.

In the stillness of the night, the porter did his rounds, delivering the morning's newspapers and slipping the final accounts for those checking out under their doors. When he got to room 422, he had to apply no small amount of pressure to the envelope, to compress it sufficiently so that it would fit through the fairly wide gap underneath the door.

Dana lay very still in bed, allowing a wave of relief – if not quite happiness – to ease her into the long night. At some point she fell asleep, as the *pitter-patter* rhythm of rain in the dirty Brighton night marked the end of the weekend, and lulled her into a dream of happy families.

And a red silk dress.

After all, tomorrow is another day.

Fiona H Joyce

Acknowledgements

Grateful thanks to my editors, particularly Dr Rosemary Joyce for editorial assistance and encouragement.

Thanks to Alex Voice for design help, camera work, helpful contributions and general support.

Many thanks also to G. A. Reichenbach for photography, editing of the same and cover design.

And when thou art spoiled, what wilt thou do?
Though thou clothest thyself with crimson,
though thou deckest thee with ornaments of gold,
though thou rentest thy face with painting,
in vain shalt thou make thyself fair;
thy lovers will despise thee,
they will seek thy life.

Jeremiah 4:30

3 Point 4 Grams

ONE

White lead and crushed red rocks. But that was in 3500 BC and she had been a Sumerian queen.

This is 2000 odd AD and there aren't so many queens now. Not in Lower Bridgedicker at any rate.

Nowadays it was more a dispersion of pigment in oil. But that didn't mean the danger was entirely absent. Many crimes had been committed over an indiscretion with its use, or as the result of leaving its trace on a face or a garment. The lead might be gone now, but the potency of the effects of its use were no less powerful.

For most people it was the colour. That was what drew them. The rods and cones of their retina receptors processed the light into nerve impulses which shot into the brain cortex through the optic nerve. And they saw pink, or orange, or purple, or coral or – Lydia shuddered at the thought – nude, the modern answer to not wanting to commit.

And red. Now that was a colour.

But it was the smell that really counted. That heady, soft but pungent, gentle but brutal, rose-scented-pear-drop-lavender-forget-me-not-love-heart-violet-flavour-sherbet-childhood-memories-grandma's-moth-ball-oak-wardrobe-fresh-mown-dew-covered-early-morning-grass: savage but beautiful fragrance.

With a little bit of – something extra. Something special. Something that didn't have a name or a description. Another ingredient. Something hidden.

Lydia's earliest memory had been of her mother in the chemist's shop. Buying glycerine and castor oil. And being shown a small box of the latest colours – just in from London, and invited to take a look. And her mother had silently taken one out of the box. Removed the lid. And gently – like a fine lady, applying smelling salts to the delicate air in front of her – she had moved it back and forth, just under her small but perfectly formed nose, drawing in the current that the movement left in its wake. And her mother had quietly replaced the lid and shaken her head once.

'No. It won't work. It smells…' her mother had said to the Chemist's assistant who stood behind the waxed, brown wood counter, '…of nothing.'

And so Lydia had learnt, from that time, all those long years ago, that it was the smell that really mattered. Even though it only accounted for one per cent of it. It was the smallest but most important element.

She looked out the window. The sun was bright, the

ground dry.

Lydia took a cool-bag out of the fridge and carefully put them all inside it.

You see, the melting point is generally between fifty-five to seventy-five degrees centigrade.

And today it was hot.

The new novel by Fiona H. Joyce coming soon.

Made in the USA
Charleston, SC
13 August 2016